INSTRUCTOR'S MANUAL

to accompany

THE LONGMAN READER
Eighth Edition

Judith Nadell

John Langan
Atlantic Cape Community College

Eliza A. Comodromos

PEARSON
Longman

New York Boston San Francisco
London Toronto Sydney Tokyo Singapore Madrid
Mexico City Munich Paris Cape Town Hong Kong Montreal

Instructor's Manual to accompany Nadell/Langan/Comodromos, *The Longman Reader, Eighth Edition*

Copyright ©2007 Pearson Education, Inc.

ISBN: 0-205-52136-3

1 2 3 4 5 6 7 8 9 10–OPM–09 08 07 06

CONTENTS

EXEMPLIFICATION　43

DIVISION-CLASSIFICATION　57

PROCESS ANALYSIS　71

COMPARISON-CONTRAST　85

COMBINING THE PATTERNS   155

TEACHING COMPOSITION WITH
THE LONGMAN READER

Teaching offers many pleasures. Among the foremost, for us, is the chance to get together with colleagues for some shoptalk. Trading ideas, airing problems, sharing light moments, speculating about why some assignments set off fireworks and some fizzle—all this helps us in our day-to-day teaching.

In this *Instructor's Manual*, we would like to share with you some thoughts about teaching freshman composition and about using *THE LONGMAN READER*. We'll explain our approach for introducing each pattern of development and indicate what we emphasize when discussing the professional essays in each section. Also, we'll offer possible answers to the "Questions for Close Reading" and "Questions About the Writer's Craft" that follow each professional essay. These responses aren't meant to be definitive. Although we purposely avoided open-ended, anything-goes questions, we understand that the responses represent *our* view only. You may not agree with all our interpretations. That's fine. If nothing else, our answers may suggest another way of viewing an essay.

AT THE START OF THE COURSE

Frankly, many students dread freshman composition—a bitter pill to swallow for those of us who have made the teaching of writing our life's work. But it's important to understand that many students' past experiences with writing have not been positive. Rather than trying to pretend that all our students are pleased about being in a writing class, we work to get out into the open any unhappiness they may have about writing and writing teachers.

Here's how we go about airing any negative feelings that may exist. On the first day of class, we acknowledge students' feelings by saying something like this: "I guess some of you wish you didn't have to take this course. In fact, you may feel that the only thing worse would be having to take a course in public speaking." Our remark elicits smiles of self-recognition from many students, and the whole class seems to relax a bit. Then we ask students to explain why they approach the writing course with such uneasy feelings. Many have sad tales to tell about writing courses and writing teachers. Here are summaries of some of the comments we've heard over the years:

- In the past, my papers were returned so covered with red ink that I could barely make out my own writing. I felt discouraged to see how much I had done wrong and angry to see my work covered over with comments.
- I could never figure out what my teachers wanted. Different teachers seemed to look for different things. Since there were no clear standards, I've never understood the qualities that make up good writing.
- Writing papers always took me too much time and felt like an endless chore. Getting the first draft done was hard enough, but revising was even worse. And the payoff for writing several drafts didn't seem worth the effort.
- I knew in my head what I wanted to say but didn't know how to get my thoughts down on paper. My ideas never came out quite right. I had writer's block

whenever I sat down to put pen to paper. I stared at the desk, daydreamed, fidgeted, and had real trouble getting started. Finally, just before an assignment was due, I dashed off something to hand in, just to get it over with.

As such sentiments are aired, students discover that their experiences have not been unique; they learn that others in class have had similarly frustrating experiences. We also confirm students' impressions by telling them that each semester many students recount comparable sagas of woe. We reassure the class that we understand the obstacles, both inner and outer, they have to face when writing. And we tell them that we will work to make the freshman writing course as positive an experience as possible. But we also say that we'd be dishonest if we led them to believe that writing is easy. It isn't. We have no magic formula for turning them into A-plus writers. On the other hand, because we are writers and because we work with writers, we know that the composing process can be satisfying and rewarding. We tell the students that we hope they'll come to share our feelings as the semester progresses.

From here, we move to an activity that continues to break the ice while familiarizing the class with the workshop format we use at various points in the semester. Students form groups of two and then four, chatting with each other for about five minutes each time. To get them moving, we put some questions on the board: what is your name? where are you from? where are you living while attending college? what other courses are you taking? what is your intended major? and so on. After a few seconds of nervous silence, the class begins to buzz with friendly energy.

When ten minutes or so have passed, we stop the activity and explain why we "wasted" precious class time just socializing. During the semester, we explain, they will learn a good deal about writing from other classmates as they meet in small groups and respond to each other's work. So it makes sense for them to get to know each other a bit right at the outset. Also, we tell students that we hope they will find sharing their writing as interesting and enjoyable as chatting together has been. As a final step in building a spirit of community, we circulate a piece of paper on which each student writes his or her name and e-mail address. Before the next class, we have the sheet typed and reproduced so that everyone can have a copy of the class directory, or we post the directory on our class website or message board.

ASSIGNING THE FIRST TWO CHAPTERS IN THE BOOK

During the first or second class, we emphasize to students that the course should help them become sharper readers as well as stronger writers. With that in mind, we assign Chapter 1, "The Reading Process," as well as Chapter 2, "The Writing Process," up to the section titled "Organize the Evidence" (p. 39). While the writing chapter may be assigned all at once, we've found that it works more effectively when broken into two assignments. Since the writing process *is* at the heart of the course, we want to make sure students read the chapter carefully enough to understand the process fully.

When students return to class having read the reading chapter and the first part of the writing chapter, we answer any questions they may have and go over the answers for the activities in the writing chapter (see page 12 of this manual). Then we move into a discussion of prewriting. We tell the class that prewriting loosens a writer up. Exploratory and tentative, prewriting helps reduce the anxiety many people feel when facing the blank page. With prewriting, a writer doesn't have to worry, "This had better be good." After all, no one except the writer is going to read the prewritten material.

The best way for students to discover what prewriting is like is for them to try it for themselves. So we say, "Let's suppose you had to write an essay on why students dislike English classes or what instructors could do to make English courses more interesting." Then we ask them to select one prewriting technique discussed in the book (questioning the subject, brainstorming, freewriting, or mapping) to generate the raw material for such an essay. Often, we distribute scrap paper or yellow lined paper for them to use, reinforcing the message that prewriting is tentative and vastly different from finished work.

At the end of the class, we ask students to use the prewriting just prepared in class as the basis for the first draft of an essay. And we assign the rest of the writing chapter, telling students to pay special attention to the guidelines in the chapter, especially those in the sections "Organize the Evidence" and "Write the First Draft."

At the start of the next class, we review the rest of the writing chapter and discuss the answers to the chapter's activities. We've found that many students do not understand that writing is a process. Having them go through the sequence described in the chapter introduces them to the concept of a writing process and shows them what one such process might be like. Now that they have had a taste of the writing process, it is time to explain (as *THE LONGMAN READER* does on page 13) that each writer customizes the steps in the sequence to suit his or her needs and style. Not everyone writes the same way, we emphasize, and we urge students to choose the approach that works best for them.

Students then take out the first draft of their papers. But we do not have them hand in the essays. Instead, we have them get back into the same groups of two they were in during the previous class and spend about ten minutes giving each other feedback on the effectiveness of the drafts. They are asked to use the checklist on the book's inside front cover to focus their observations. After hearing their partner's response to their work, students get busy revising their essay right there in class. We then collect the papers, promising only to read—not grade—them. Reviewing the papers, we explain, will give us a good sense of what each writer does well and what needs to be worked on. Finally, we end the class by telling students that we don't expect them to have mastered all the material in the book's first two chapters. But now that they have read the chapters carefully and have worked through the reading and writing processes, they should have a clear sense of how to proceed during the rest of the semester. We assure them that throughout the course we will refer to the opening two chapters as need arises.

WAYS TO USE THE BOOK

THE LONGMAN READER is arranged according to these nine patterns of development: description, narration, exemplification, division-classification, process analysis, comparison-contrast, cause-effect, definition, and argumentation-persuasion. Introductions to the patterns are designed to help students understand the distinctive features of specific rhetorical strategies. The more accessible experiential patterns are presented first, before the text moves on to the more demanding analytic patterns.

If you adopt a rhetorical approach in the course, you need not feel confined by the order of patterns in the book; each chapter is self-contained, which makes it possible for you to sequence the modes however you wish. And, of course, there's no need to cover all the essays in a chapter or even all the rhetorical patterns. It is more realistic to assign two or three selections per pattern, perhaps concentrating on one of the selections for class discussion. A word of warning: If you tell a class which of several assigned selections will be discussed, some students will skip the other selections. You'll probably want to explain to students that there are many ways to use a rhetorical pattern and that reading *all* the assigned essays will give them an understanding of the options available.

For rhetorically organized courses, we suggest that you emphasize early in the semester that professional writers don't set out to write an essay in a particular mode. The patterns emerge as the writers prewrite and organize their ideas; writers come to see that their points can best be made through a particular rhetorical strategy or combination of strategies.

It's helpful, we've learned, to assign selections before *and* after students write an essay. For example, if students are going to write a causal analysis, you might have them read Buzz Bissinger's "Innocents Afield." Then, after reviewing their drafts and seeing the problems they have had with, let's say, causal chains, you might have them examine the way Darley and Latané trace complex causal relationships in "Why People Don't Help in a Crisis."

Some instructors using a rhetorical approach in their courses place a special emphasis on exposition. If this is your orientation, you might want to begin with the exemplification chapter. That section stresses the importance of establishing a clear thesis and providing solid support for the essay's central point. Then you might move to the description and narration chapters; these underscore the importance of, respectively, a dominant impression and a narrative point, both developed through specific supporting details.

If you prefer to design the course around themes rather than rhetorical patterns, the thematic table of contents (at the front of the textbook) will help you select essays on timely issues. For such a course, we recommend that you have students read a number of essays on a given theme. The fact that several essays on the same theme use different rhetorical strategies helps students see that the patterns are not ends in themselves, but techniques that writers use to make their points.

CREATING A PROCESS-ORIENTED
CLASS ENVIRONMENT

We've found that creating a workshop atmosphere in the classroom helps students view writing as a process. When a new paper is assigned, we try to give students several minutes to start their prewriting in class. In other classes, time may be set aside for students to rework parts of their first draft. We may, for instance, ask them to sharpen their introduction, conclusion, sentence structure, or transitions.

In our experience, it's been especially productive to use class time for peer evaluations of first drafts. For these peer review sessions, students may be paired with one other classmate or they may meet with three or four other classmates. (We've found groups of more than five unwieldy.) Feedback from someone other than the course instructor motivates students to put in more time on a draft. Otherwise, some students will skip the revision stage altogether; as soon as they've got a draft down on paper, they'll want to hand it in. Hearing from other classmates that a point is not clear or that a paragraph is weakly developed encourages students to see that revision involves more than mechanical tinkering. They start to understand that revision often requires wholesale rethinking and reworking of parts of the essay. And, after a few feedback sessions, students begin to identify for themselves the problem areas in their writing.

You'll find that many students squirm at the thought of reacting to their classmates' work. So it's not surprising that they tend to respond to each other's papers with either indiscriminate praise or unhelpful neutrality. To guide students, we prepare a brief checklist of points to consider when responding to each other's work. (You might, for example, adapt the checklist on the inside front cover or those in each of the pattern chapters to fit a particular assignment.) With such a checklist in front of them, students are able to focus their impressions and provide constructive feedback.

There are a number of ways to set up peer review sessions. Here are a few possibilities:

- After pairing students or placing them in small groups, have each essay read aloud by someone other than the author. Students tell us that hearing another person read what they've written is invaluable. Awkward or unclear passages in a paper become more obvious when someone who has never before seen the essay reads it aloud.
- Place students in small groups and ask them to circulate their papers (in hard-copy or via e-mail) so that everyone has a chance to read all the essays. Then have each group select one especially effective paper to read aloud to the rest of the class. Alternatively, you may ask each group to select a strong essay that needs work in a few spots. These essays are then read aloud to the rest of the class. Everyone discusses each paper's strengths and what might be done to sharpen the sections that miss the mark.
- Ask one or two students to photocopy their drafts of an assignment, making copies so that everyone can look at the papers. In class, the other students—either as a whole or in groups—react to the papers up for scrutiny that day.

A quick aside: At the start of the course, students are reluctant to "offer their papers up for sacrifice"—as one student put it. But once they're accustomed to the process, they are not at all skittish and even volunteer to be "put on the chopping block"—another student's words. They know that the feedback received will be invaluable when the time comes to revise.

As you no doubt can tell, we have a special liking for group work. Since it gives students the chance to see how others approach the same assignment, they come to appreciate the personal dimension of writing and develop an awareness of rhetorical options. The peer process also multiplies the feedback students get for their work, letting them see that their instructor is just one among many readers. Group activities thus help students gain a clearer sense of purpose and audience. Finally, we have found that peer review encourages students to be more active in the classroom. When students assume some of the tasks traditionally associated with the instructor, the whole class becomes more animated.

SOME CAUTIONS ABOUT GROUP WORK

If you are new to group work, you may have the uneasy feeling that the group process can deteriorate into enjoyable but unproductive rap sessions. That *can* happen if the instructor does not guide the process carefully.

Here are several suggestions to steer you clear of some traps that can ensnare group activities. First, we recommend you give very clear instructions about how students are to proceed. Providing a checklist, for example, directs students to specific issues you want them to address. Second, we believe in establishing a clear time schedule for each group activity. We might say, "Take five minutes to read to yourself the paper written by the person on your left" or "Now that all the papers in your group have been read, you should vote to determine which is the strongest paper; then take five minutes to identify one section of the essay that needs additional attention." Third, although we try to be as inconspicuous as possible during group work, we let students know that we are available for help when needed. Sometimes we circulate among the groups, listening to comments, asking a question or two. But more often we stay at the desk and encourage students to consult with us when they think our reaction would be helpful.

RESPONDING TO STUDENT WORK

Beyond the informal, in-class consultations just described, we also meet during the course with each student for several one-on-one conferences of fifteen to thirty minutes each. Depending on our purpose, student needs, class size, and availability of time, a number of things may occur during the individual conferences. We may review a paper that has already been graded and commented on, highlighting the paper's strengths and underscoring what needs to be done to sharpen the essay. Or we may use the conference to return and discuss a recent essay that has or has not been graded. In the last few years, we have tended not to grade or write comments on papers we're going to review in conference. Instead, we take informal notes about the papers and refer to them when meeting with students. We've found that this approach encourages students to interact with us more freely since their attention isn't riveted to the comments and grade already recorded on the paper. Finally, we end each conference by jotting down a brief list of what the student needs to concentrate on when revising or writing the next assignment. Students tell us this individualized checklist lets them know exactly what they should pay attention to in their work.

When students hand in the final draft of a paper, we ask them to include their individualized checklist. Having a checklist for each student enables us to focus on the elements that typically give the student trouble. And, candidly, having the checklist in front of us tames our not-so-noble impulse to pounce on every problem in an essay.

In our oral and written comments, we try to emphasize what's strong in the essay and limit discussion of problems to the most critical points. Like everyone else, students are apt to overlook what they've done well and latch on to things that haven't been so successful. If every error a student makes is singled out for criticism, the student—again, like everyone else—often feels overwhelmed and defeated. So unless a student is obviously lackadaisical and would profit from some hard-hitting, teacherly rebukes, we try to make our comments as positive and encouraging as possible. And rather than filling the paper with reworked versions of, let's say, specific sentences and paragraphs, we make liberal use of such remarks as these: "Read these last three sentences aloud. Do you hear the awkwardness? How could you streamline these sentences?" or "Doesn't this paragraph contradict what you say at the beginning of the preceding paragraph? What could you do to eliminate the confusion?"

When responding to a paper, we often suggest that the student review or reread a professional essay, the introduction to a rhetorical pattern, or sections of the writing chapter. And we always end our comments with a brief list of points to be added to the student's personalized checklist.

USING PORTFOLIOS TO ASSESS
STUDENT PROGRESS

You may wish to have your students present a portfolio of their work for grading at the conclusion of the course, instead of giving grades for each paper in succession. Using such a portfolio system alters somewhat the way you respond to individual student papers as they are submitted, because you assign no grades to them. The written and oral feedback on a paper is geared solely to making the essay a more effective piece of communication rather than to justifying a particular low or high grade. This forces all concerned—instructors and students—to stay focused on how to improve writing rather than on what might pull a paper down or on what score a paper should get. If students balk at "floating free" of grades for the whole course, you might occasionally supply a tentative grade or give students grades on one or two essays so they get a feel for the standards. As the course progresses, however, the issue of what constitutes a strong paper should be resolved. The students will be reading the successful papers in the text, examining and commenting on the essays of other students, and hearing a plenitude of helpful comments about writing.

You should indicate clearly at the start of the course that students must complete each essay as well as all other practices, journal entries, and so forth that you assign, but that the writing component of their final grade will be based upon a portfolio of polished work. Clearly establish the minimum number of essays to be included in a completed portfolio. Typically, a course might be represented by four final-draft essays, plus some late-in-the-term in-class writing. In addition, you may wish to examine the successive drafts for one of the revised papers. In order to receive a grade, each student meets with the instructor for a conference about the writing progress demonstrated in the portfolio. After discussing the writing's strengths and areas needing improvement, the instructor and student agree on a grade.

Such a portfolio system has several advantages. It stresses to students that writing well is an ongoing process and encourages them to make subsequent revisions of their essays as they acquire new insights into writing. It forces them to take responsibility for their progress beyond the achievement they reach in the first submitted version of an essay. It instills the notion of a writing community, for once they have gotten beyond the initial series of structured feedback sessions that you have built into the course, students must initiate feedback from their peers and from the instructor on any revisions they do. Finally, such a system dramatizes the reality that writers write for other people, and that reaching the audience, not jumping hurdles to get a grade, is the goal of writing.

AT THE END OF THE COURSE

Even if you don't use formal portfolios for grading, we suggest you ask students to present their best revised work to you at the end of the semester. Our students keep all their papers in a folder, and so have no trouble retrieving essays written weeks or months earlier. Near the end of the course, we ask students to select—for one more round of revision—three or four essays, with each paper illustrating a different rhetorical pattern. We use these reworked versions of the essays to assign a final grade to each student. If you structure your course around themes and issues, you'll probably want to require that each paper deal with a different theme.

As the semester draws to a close, we also ask students to complete the questionnaire at the back of the book. Their responses let us know which selections worked well and which did not, helping us make adjustments in future semesters. So that you too can find out how the class reacted to the assigned selections, you might ask students to give the completed forms to you rather than having students mail their questionnaires to the publisher. If you do collect the forms, we hope that you'll forward them to us at Longman after you've had a chance to look them over. This kind of student feedback will be crucial when we revise the book.

An especially rewarding way to end the semester is to have the class publish a booklet of student writing. Students revise and then submit two of their strongest papers to a class-elected editorial board. This board selects one essay from each student in the class, making an effort to choose essays that represent a mix of styles and rhetorical approaches. After a table of contents and a cover have been prepared, the essays are gathered, duplicated, and stapled into booklet form. Depending on the equipment and funds available, the booklet may be photocopied or designed on a computer.

Students respond enthusiastically to this project. After all, who can resist the prospect of being published? And knowing that their writing is going public encourages students to revise in earnest. The booklets yield significant benefits for us, too. They help build a bank of student writing to draw on in subsequent semesters. As a bonus, the booklets allow us to reconnect with the experiences, thoughts, and feelings of the students passing through our classes year after year. Such booklets have been an ongoing source of pleasure.

A SUGGESTED SYLLABUS

On the following pages we present a syllabus that will give you some further ideas on how to use **THE LONGMAN READER** (LR). Note that the syllabus assumes the course meets once a week, for three hours, over a fifteen-week period. The syllabus can, of course, be easily adjusted to fit a variety of course formats.

Week 1

- Provide an introduction to the course, and handle necessary business matters.
- Direct a "getting to know each other" activity (see page 2 of this manual).
- Have students prepare an in-class writing sample to get an initial sense of their writing needs.
- Assignments—ask students to:
  a. Read "The Reading Process" in the LR.
  b. Read "The Writing Process" in the LR through page 39.

Week 2

- Discuss assignments, including the writing process activities.
- Return the in-class papers. Review common sentence skills problems.
- Read and work through the rest of the writing process chapter.
- Introduce students to "Description," covering selected material on pages 71–83.
- Assignments—ask students to:
  a. Read the introduction to "Description" in the LR (pp. 71–83).
  b. Do the assignment based on the photograph that opens the chapter (p. 73).
  c. Read two (instructor-designated) description selections. (We suggest that the first selection be Parks's "Flavio's Home.") Before doing so, complete the Pre-Reading Journal Entry for each.
  d. Answer the close reading and writer's craft questions following the selections.

Week 3

- Answer questions about the description chapter, and discuss the two assigned description selections.
- Have students do prewriting (brainstorming, freewriting, group work, etc.) for one of the writing assignments at the end of the assigned description selections. (If they select the "Writing Assignment Using a Journal Entry as a Starting Point," they should have already done prewriting—through the journal entry—before reading.)

- Assignments—ask students to:
  a. Complete the description essay.
  b. Review grammar, punctuation, and usage as needed.

Week 4

- Initiate peer review of students' description essays (see pages 4–6 of this manual). Give students the option of handing in their papers in present form or revising them by the next class.
- Introduce students to "Narration," covering selected material on pages 123–36 of the LR.
- Read and discuss in class a narrative selection: Gholson's "Charity Display?" or Hughes's "Salvation."
- Assignments—ask students to:
  a. Read the introduction to "Narration" (pp. 123–36) in the LR.
  b. Do the assignment based on the photograph that opens the chapter (p. 124).
  c. Read two more (instructor-designated) narrative selections, first completing each Pre-Reading Journal Entry.
  d. Answer the close reading and writer's craft questions following the selections.

Week 5

- Pass back and discuss students' description essays.
- Answer questions about the narration chapter, and discuss the two assigned narrative selections.
- Have students do prewriting (brainstorming, freewriting, group work, etc.) for one of the writing assignments at the end of the two assigned narrative selections.
- Assignments—ask students to:
  a. Complete the narrative essay.
  b. Review grammar, punctuation, and usage as needed.

Week 6

- Initiate peer review of students' narrative essays (see pages 4–6 of this manual). Give students the option of handing in their papers in present form or revising them by the next class.
- Introduce students to "Exemplification," covering selected material on pages 169–83 of the LR.
- Read and discuss in class an exemplification selection: Sykes's "The 'Values' Wasteland" or Savan's "Black Talk and Pop Culture."
- Assignments—ask students to:
  a. Read the introduction to "Exemplification" (pp. 169–83) in the LR.
  b. Do the assignment based on the photograph that opens the chapter (p. 172).
  c. Read two more (instructor-designated) exemplification selections, first completing each Pre-Reading Journal Entry.
  d. Answer the close reading and writer's craft questions following the selections.

Week 7

- Pass back and discuss students' narrative essays. Answer questions about the exemplification chapter, and discuss the two assigned exemplification essays.
- Have students do prewriting (brainstorming, freewriting, group work, etc.) for one of the writing assignments at the end of the two assigned exemplification selections.
- Assignments—ask students to:
  a. Complete the exemplification essay.
  b. Review grammar, punctuation, and usage as needed.

Week 8

- Initiate peer review of students' exemplification essays (see pages 4–6 of this manual). Give students the option of handing in their papers in present form or revising them by the next class.
- Introduce students to "Division-Classification" or "Process Analysis," covering selected material on pages 223–39 or 280–95 of the LR.
- Read and discuss in class a division-classification selection, Ericsson's "The Ways We Lie," or a process selection, Shipley's "Talk About Editing."
- Assignments—ask students to:
  a. Read the introduction to "Division-Classification" (pp. 223–39) or "Process Analysis" (pp. 280–95) in the LR.
  b. Do the assignment based on the photograph that opens the chapter (pp. 227 or 282).
  c. Read two more (instructor-designated) division-classification or process analysis selections, first completing each Pre-Reading Journal Entry.
  d. Answer the close reading and writer's craft questions following the selections.

Week 9

- Pass back students' exemplification essays. Answer questions about the division-classification or process analysis chapter, and discuss the two assigned selections.
- Provide prewriting (brainstorming, freewriting, group work, etc.) for one of the writing assignments at the end of the two assigned selections.
- Assignments—ask students to:
  a. Complete the division-classification or process analysis essay.
  b. Review grammar, punctuation, and usage as needed.

Week 10

- Initiate peer review of students' division-classification or process analysis essays (see pages 4–6 of this manual). Give students the option of handing in their papers in present form or revising them by the next class.
- Introduce students to "Comparison-Contrast," covering selected material on pages 335–49 of the LR.
- Read and discuss in class a comparison-contrast selection: Carson's "A Fable for Tomorrow" or Suina's "And Then I Went to School."
- Assignments—ask students to:
  a. Read the introduction to "Comparison-Contrast" (pp. 335–49) in the LR.

b. Do the assignment based on the photograph that opens the chapter (p.337).
c. Read two more (instructor-designated) comparison-contrast selections, first completing each Pre-Reading Journal Entry.
d. Answer the close reading and writer's craft questions following the selections.
e. Write a comparison-contrast essay.
f. Review grammar, punctuation, and usage as needed.

Week 11

- Pass back and discuss students' division-classification or process analysis essays.
- Answer questions about the comparison-contrast chapter, and discuss the two assigned selections.
- Initiate peer review of students' comparison-contrast essays (see pages 4–6 of this manual). Give students the option of handing in their papers in present form or revising them by the next class.
- Introduce students to "Cause-Effect" or "Definition," covering selected material on pages 381–96 or 432–44 of the LR. If appropriate, introduce cause-effect activity described on page 102 of this manual.
- Read and discuss in class a cause-effect or definition selection: King's "Why We Crave Horror Movies" or Cole's "Entropy."
- Assignments—ask students to:
  a. Read the introduction to "Cause-Effect" (pp. 381–96) or "Definition" (pp. 432–44) in the LR.
  b. Do the assignment based on the photograph that opens the chapter (pp.383 or 434).
  c. Read two more (instructor-designated) cause-effect or definition selections, first completing each Pre-Reading Journal Entry.
  d. Answer the close reading and craft questions following the selections.
  e. Write a cause-effect or definition essay.
  f. Review grammar, punctuation, and usage as needed.

Week 12

- Pass back and discuss students' comparison-contrast essays.
- Answer questions on the cause-effect or definition chapter, and discuss the two assigned selections.
- Initiate peer review of students' cause-effect or definition essays (see pages 4–6 of this manual). Give students the option of handing in their papers in present form or revising them by the next class.
- Introduce students to "Argumentation-Persuasion," covering selected material on pages 476–509 of the LR.
- Read and discuss, in class, one pro-con set of essays: Alter's "Time to Think About Torture" and Porter's "Now the Talk Is About Bringing Back Torture."
- Assignments—ask students to:
  a. Read the introduction to "Argumentation-Persuasion" (pp. 477–511) in the LR.
  b. Do the assignment based on the photograph that opens the chapter (p. 482).
  c. Read three more (instructor-designated) argumentation-persuasion selections, first completing each Pre-Reading Journal Entry. (At least one of these selections should focus on a controversial social issue—see pages 127–128 of this manual.)
  d. Answer the close reading and writer's craft questions following the selections.

Week 13

- Pass back and discuss students' cause-effect or definition essays.
- Answer questions about the argumentation-persuasion chapter, and discuss the three assigned argumentation-persuasion selections.
- Initiate prewriting (brainstorming, freewriting, group work, etc.) for one of the writing assignments at the end of the three assigned argumentation-persuasion selections. The writing assignment should require the student to focus on a controversial social issue.
- Assignments—ask students to:
  a. Complete the argumentation-persuasion essay.
  b. Review grammar, punctuation, and usage as needed.

Week 14

- Answer questions about the argumentation-persuasion chapter, and discuss the three assigned argumentation-persuasion selections.
- Initiate peer review of students' argumentation-persuasion essays (see pages 4–6 of this manual). Give students the option of handing in their papers in present form or revising them by the next class.
- Ask students to revise several essays written earlier in the course. These essays should be submitted in the final class (see pages 7–8 of this manual).
- If appropriate, have students organize a forum on controversial issues. (See page 128 of this manual for our comments on the activity.)
- Assignment—ask students to prepare their oral presentations for delivery during the in-class forum on controversial social issues.

Week 15

- Have students submit their folder of revised work.
- Have students deliver their oral presentations on controversial social issues.
- Provide group feedback on the forum.
- Conclude the course.

ANSWERS FOR CHAPTER 2, "THE WRITING PROCESS"

Activities: Prewrite (pp. 26–27)

1. **Set A**
    3 Abortion
    2 Controversial social issues
    5 Cutting off state abortion funds
    4 Federal funding for abortions
    1 Social issues

    Set B
    4 Business majors
    3 Students divided by major
    1 College students

2 Kinds of students on campus

5 Why many students major in business

2. "Day-care," "male and female relationships," and "international terrorism" are clearly too broad to be used as topics for a two- to five-page essay.

Activities: Identify the Thesis (pp. 30–31)

1. **Limited Subject**: The ethics of treating severely handicapped infants

   FS Some babies born with severe handicaps have been allowed to die.

   TB There are many serious issues involved in the treatment of handicapped newborns.

   OK The government should pass legislation requiring medical treatment for handicapped newborns.

   A This essay will analyze the controversy surrounding the treatment of severely handicapped babies who would die without medical care.

   Limited Subject: Privacy and computerized records

   TB Computers raise some significant and crucial questions for all of us.

   FS Computerized records keep track of consumer spending habits, credit records, travel patterns, and other personal information.

   OK Computerized records have turned our private lives into public property.

   A In this paper, the relationship between computerized records and the right to privacy will be discussed.

2. Below are possible thesis statements for each set of points.

   Set A
   Possible Thesis: Students in college today are showing signs of increasing conservatism.

   Set B
   Possible Thesis: If not closely monitored, experiments in genetic engineering could yield disastrous results.

3. Below are possible thesis statements for each set of general and limited subjects.

General Subject	Limited Subject	Possible Thesis
Psychology	The power struggles in a classroom	The classroom is often a battlefield, with struggles for power going on among students and between students and teacher.
Health	Doctors' attitudes toward patients	In hospitals, doctors often treat patients like robots rather than human beings.
American politics	Television's coverage of presidential campaigns	Television coverage of political campaigns emphasizes the visual at the expense of issues.

13

| Work | Minimum-wage jobs for young people | The minimum wage is too low to inspire young people to work hard and advance themselves. |

Activities: Support the Thesis with Evidence (pp. 38–39)

1. In each set below, the irrelevant point is preceded by an "X."

Set A
Thesis: Colleges should put less emphasis on sports.
Encourages grade fixing
X Creates a strong following among former graduates
Distracts from real goals of education
Causes extensive and expensive injuries

Set B
Thesis: America is becoming a homogenized country.
Regional accents vanishing
Chain stores blanket country
X Americans proud of their ethnic heritage
Metropolitan areas almost indistinguishable from one another

2. Below are possible points of support for each thesis statement.

Thesis: The trend toward disposable, throw-away products has gone too far.
1. Fast-food chains generate huge amounts of non-biodegradable refuse.
2. Parks and recreational areas are strewn with non-recyclable beer cans.
3. Roadways are littered with non-returnable soda bottles.

Thesis: The local library fails to meet the needs of those it is supposed to serve.
1. The hours are limited and inconvenient.
2. The part-time, inexperienced staff provide insufficient assistance.
3. The collection is outdated and incomplete.

Thesis: Television portrays men as incompetent creatures.
1. College male washing colors and whites together, to horror of older women in laundromat.
2. Father caring for child but unable to cope with emergency.
3. Husbands concerned only with taste of product, while wives are knowledgeable about healthfulness.

Activities: Organize the Evidence (pp. 45–46)

1. **Thesis:** Our schools, now in crisis, could be improved in several ways.
   I.   Teachers
        A. Certification requirements for teachers
        B. Merit pay for outstanding teachers
   II. Schedules
        A. Longer school days
        B. Longer school year

III. Curriculum
    A. Better textbooks for classroom use
    B. More challenging content in courses

2. **Thesis:** Friends of the opposite sex fall into one of several categories: the pal, the confidante, or the pest.

   Overall Pattern of Development: *Division-Classification*

   - Frequently, an opposite-sex friend is simply a "pal."—develop with *definition*
   - Sometimes, though, a pal turns, step by step, into a confidante.—develop with *process analysis*
   - If a confidante begins to have romantic thoughts, he or she may become a pest, thus disrupting the friendship.—develop with *cause-effect*

DESCRIPTION

OPENING COMMENTS

Some colleagues tell us they prefer to omit description when they teach freshman writing. Emphasizing the analytic side of exposition, they consider descriptive writing a digression, a luxury that they don't have time for in an already crowded syllabus. To them, descriptive writing belongs in a creative writing course, not in freshman composition. On the other hand, some instructors *do* include description, but they discuss it after narration.

We feel that descriptive writing should be included in freshman composition. And we've found that description can be covered before narration with excellent results. In other words, we recommend that description be the first pattern studied in the course.

Why do we feel this way? For one thing, when students begin by writing descriptive essays, they learn the importance of specific details, and they start to develop the habit of observation. (The sensory chart described on page 75 of the text is one way to encourage such attention to detail.) Also, since descriptive writing depends on creating a dominant impression, description helps students understand the concept of focus early in the semester.

Descriptive writing also teaches students to select details that enhance an essay's central point. Finally—and most importantly—students can discover real pleasure in writing descriptive pieces. They are challenged by the possibility they can make readers feel as they do about a subject. They enjoy using words to share a place, person, or object that has personal significance to them. Every semester, we have several students who admit that descriptive writing changed their attitude toward composition. For the first time, they see that writing, though difficult, can be rewarding and fun.

The selections in this chapter represent the wide range of techniques found in descriptive writing. We suggest you start with Parks's essay because its imagistic power dramatizes the way vivid sensory details support a dominant impression. Similarly, Angelou's essay "Sister Flowers" captures the way our sensory perceptions affect our emotional responses. This piece is particularly useful in showing students how to use metaphor and simile to convey abstract concepts and shape concrete images. We think that students will find David Helvarg's "The Storm This Time," about the effects of Hurricane Katrina on the Gulf Coast, to be compelling, dealing, as it does, with a recent event of such magnitude. That essay also gives students the chance to compare photographs with written descriptions. And White's justly celebrated "Once More to the Lake" serves as a poignant rendering of personal experience. To create his effect, White uses flashbacks, a technique usually associated with narration. Finally, using a restrained tone and carefully chosen details, Judith Ortiz Cofer evokes the mood of precious childhood memories.

ANSWERS FOR PREWRITING ACTIVITIES

Below we provide suggested responses to selected prewriting activities at the end of Chapter 3 (p. 82). Of course, other approaches are possible.

1. There are many ways to use description in these two essays; below we've listed some of the possibilities. In classroom use of this activity, we suggest you have students share their responses. They'll be surprised and often delighted to discover their neighbors have devised quite different uses for description in the essays. Sharing and comparing such prewriting conveys the invaluable point that writers are individual and their writing is unique.

    Topic: How students get burned out
    Describe ineffective studying methods: cramming, skimming
    Describe student with six courses struggling with homework
    Draw portrait of aloof professor assigning too-difficult work
    Describe student working and carrying full load

    Topic: Being a spendthrift is better than being frugal
    Describe allure of some purchase: dress, sneakers, etc.
    Describe appeal of shopping center or mall
    Describe gourmet meal at expensive restaurant

    Topic: Being a spendthrift is worse than being frugal
    Describe shocked clerk ringing up your large purchase
    Describe empty pockets and meager lunches after a spree
    Describe sleepless night after charging a lot

ANSWERS FOR REVISING ACTIVITIES

Below we provide suggested responses to selected revising activities at the end of Chapter 3 (p. 83). Of course, other approaches are possible.

3. Here are some possible ways to revise the sentences to create distinct, contrasting moods. Other versions are, of course, possible.

    a. Around the filthy, lopsided table slouched four grubby, droopy-eyed old men.

    Alert and eagle-eyed, the four natty old poker players sat tensely around the felt-topped table.

    b. Enticed by media attention to the movie's special effects, hordes of boisterous teenagers thronged the street outside the theater showing *Race to Doom*.

    Snaking down the alley beside the theater, a line of silent, slouch-hatted customers waited to see the notorious film.

    c. The skinny twelve-year-old girl teetered, wobbled, and finally tripped as she walked into church in her first pair of high heels.

    With head held high, hips swaying, and her eyes roving to see if anyone noticed, Mary Beth strolled down Main Street in her first pair of high heels.

4. We suggest that you offer your students the chance to read each other's revisions of this paragraph. Such exposure to the versions of others helps them see a variety of possibilities in improving a piece of writing.

17

Here are the main problems in the paragraph:

- — Details about driving on Route 334 are irrelevant and should be eliminated.
- — Statement that car has been "washed and waxed" detracts attention from arrival at farm.
- — Short, choppy sentences could be combined with others nearby: "Its paint must have worn off decades ago"; "They were dented and windowless." For example, such combined sentences might read: "Then I headed for the dirt-colored barn, its roof full of huge, rotted holes"; "As I rounded the bushes, I saw the dirt-colored house, its paint worn off decades ago"; "A couple of dented, windowless, dead-looking old cars were sprawled in front of the barn."
- — Spatial order is broken by placing description of house in between details about what is near the barn.

FLAVIO'S HOME

Gordon Parks

Questions for Close Reading (p. 90)

1. The dominant impression is implied. While Parks is explicit about his overall attitude to poverty in paragraph 1, this material is not the thesis. Rather, the dominant impression pertains more specifically to Flavio. It might be stated as "Even in the midst of the worst afflictions of poverty, the human spirit survives in certain optimistic, energetic, caring individuals such as the twelve-year-old boy Flavio."
2. In Flavio's family, there's no sense of understanding or emotional nurturing of children; rather, all the family's focus is on survival. At twelve, Flavio is the oldest child of eight, ranging down to infancy. His parents work, leaving him with the care of the household and the other children. His mother is a laundress who washes clothes in the river, and the father sells bleach and kerosene at a small stand. The parents seem too fatigued to be interested in their children; the father relates to them primarily by giving commands and demanding instant obedience.
3. The neighborhood is on a steep, difficult-to-climb mountainside. Paragraphs 2–3, 14, and 21 describe the sights and sounds Parks encounters on this arduous climb. He reports encountering "mud trails, jutting rock, slime-filled holes and shack after shack propped against the slopes on shaky pilings." The trail is also crowded with people going up and down; "bare feet and legs with open sores climbed above us," Parks writes (21). While the mountainside is "a maze of shacks," from it one can see the beaches with the "gleaming white homes of the rich" (2). Flavio's home is described in paragraph 6. It is a one-room shack, six by ten feet, constructed of miscellaneous boards with numerous gaps in the walls. The wooden floor is rotten and spotted with light leaking in through the holes in the roof. One corner has a hole dug for a toilet; it lets out onto the side of the mountain.
4. Flavio seems well aware that hosts should not eat in front of guests, but he is probably afraid that his domineering and skeptical father would be angered by an offer to join them. He may also be reluctant to be a good host because there isn't enough food to go around; his family lives on the brink of starvation, and he knows the guests do not need the food as much as his family. Parks and Gallo understand that Flavio really can't or shouldn't offer food, and so they refuse.

5. *barrios* (1): Latin-American term for districts
   jacaranda (2): tropical tree having clusters of pale purple flowers
   jaundiced (3): yellow-toned, ill with a disorder of the bile (liver)
   spigot (14): faucet

Questions About the Writer's Craft (p. 90)

1. The dominant impression we receive of Flavio is of a child ravaged by poverty yet who possesses an open and persevering soul. Throughout the essay, Parks reveals Flavio's character by describing what Flavio says and does rather than what the boy is like as a person. He gives us numerous details of Flavio's physical appearance (3, 11, 23), pointing out the boy's thinness, stick-like limbs, sunken eyes, jaundiced coloring, wrenching coughs, and filthy, skimpy clothing. Parks also notices one other thing—the brilliant smile that instantly crosses Flavio's face as he sees the strangers. Parks details each time the smile reoccurs—when the boy opens the door (4), offers food (10), carries Parks's camera (22), recovers from a coughing spell (23), and enters the doctor's office (29). The nobility of the boy's spirit also comes through in other details: his competence in household tasks and care of his siblings (5, 7, 9, 23–26) and his refusal to let Parks carry wood for him (22).

2. Parks describes how household tasks are made difficult by the need to conserve water. In paragraph 7, we see the process by which Flavio gets the rice washed, the children bathed, and the floor scrubbed, with only one pan of water. In paragraph 10, the boy serves dinner, a task complicated by the existence of only three plates and two spoons. He prepares breakfast in paragraph 23, making a fire and reheating the dinner. These processes add to the dominant impression of Flavio by showing us his discipline, ingenuity, and steadiness.

3. Parks conveys strong sensory images in such phrases as "a rusted, bent top of an old gas range," "a piece of tin," "grimy walls," "a patchwork of misshapen boards," "other shacks below stilted against the slopes," "rotting," "layers of grease and dirt," "shafts of light slanting down," "spaces in the roof," and "large hole." We are able to flow from image to image because Parks uses numerous transitions of spatial organization: "beneath it," "between them," "under layers," slanting down through," "in the far corner," and "beneath that hole." Parks also uses a clear organizational pattern in the description; he begins describing the room with one important object, the stove. Then he moves from the walls to the floor; he ingeniously indicates the roof's condition by pointing out the sunlight dappling the floor from the holes above. He concludes by describing a hole in the "far corner" that serves as a toilet and that empties out onto the slope of the mountain. This detail, that the latrine empties essentially into thin air, conveys the precariousness and primitiveness of the home.

4. The effect of this scene is to dramatize the huge disparity between the rich and poor in Rio, between not only their dress, but their emotional lives, the one basic and elemental, the other extravagant and romantic. The hotel lobby is filled with people dressed up for the evening in formal attire; Parks finds himself hoping the elevator will be empty since he has just been in the slums and is not very presentable. But a couple in evening clothes enter the elevator and embrace romantically, totally ignoring him. This action symbolizes the way in which the moneyed classes so easily ignore the "stink of the favela," even when it is right in the elevator with them.

THE STORM THIS TIME

David Helvarg

Questions for Close Reading (p. 97)

1. Helvarg does not explicitly state his thesis until the end of the essay. In paragraphs 26 and 27, he says that the hurricanes of 2005 caused a massive coastal environmental disaster for which people were unprepared and from which they must recover in a more environmentally sound way than in the past.
2. The subject of the section "Urban Floodplain" is the damage done in the city of New Orleans itself. Helvarg drives to New Orleans from Baton Rouge, and tours the Lakeview section, which had been flooded, and the central business district, which had not. He describes Lakeview as a disaster area, and the central business district as a staging area for emergency personnel. In the last paragraph, he explains the purpose of his trip—to travel around the "new urban landscape" of the region to view the effects of Katrina. The remainder of the essay describes his trip throughout the Gulf region.
3. The activity that shows life going on as usual appears in paragraph 24, where Helvarg describes how people attending a football game in Baton Rouge will be allowed to return home after curfew as long as they show their ticket stubs at the roadblocks. This is the last description in the essay, before Helvarg turns to the statement of his thesis and conclusion. Its purpose is to provide a hopeful contrast to all the accumulated details of destruction that preceded it, and to symbolically point to the future, in which people will again take up their normal activities.
4. According to one dictionary, *eco-* means "habitat" or "environment," and *geek* means "a person of an intellectual bent who is disapproved of." In this paragraph, Helvarg is characterizing himself as a person too caught up in environmental issues, worrying about the threats to birds and swamps rather than the threats to people's livelihoods caused by the destruction of the casinos. An *ecogeek*, therefore, is a person who focuses on environmental issues at the expense of (more important) people issues. A related neologism is *treehugger*.
5. *consortium* (1): a group formed to perform a task beyond the capacity of any one member
    infiltrating (4): gradually entering an area through small gaps or by filtering through
    Woodstock (5): a 1969 rock festival attended by thousands who camped out together
    salvage (8): to save, especially from ruin
    ruptured (10): burst
    antebellum (11): pre–Civil War
    festooned (13): hung
    storm surge (16): sea water pushed on shore by the force of high winds
    adjuster (18): a representative of an insurance company who determines the amount the company must pay on a claim
    mercenary (23): one who works only for money, especially a hired soldier

Questions About the Writer's Craft (p. 98)

1. Helvarg uses a spatial organization in this essay, traveling from place to place and describing what he sees. Helvarg keeps the reader oriented as to his movements by describing how he travels from one place to another. For example, at the beginning

of the essay he arrives in Baton Rouge by plane; then he drives south toward New Orleans, where he begins to see destruction when he is near the New Orleans airport. In paragraph 4, he tells the reader he is driving into Lakeview. He describes Lakeview and then drives to downtown New Orleans, the site of the next descriptive section. In paragraph 7, he has crossed the Mississippi west of New Orleans into Algiers; in paragraph 8 he is back in Lakeview. In the next section, paragraph 10, he drives through Plaquemines Parish; in paragraph 12, he is "approaching the Empire Bridge." Helvarg provides similar transitional information about his travels as he describes each place he visits. It's possible to trace his trip on a map from these transitional cues, which provide the reader with a sense of being on the ground with him.

2. Helvarg describes smells and tastes as well as sights. For example, in paragraph 4, Helvarg describes both the smell he expected (the smell of death as in a war zone) and the smell he actually smelled—"the smell of a dead city, like dried cow pies and mold with a stinging chemical aftertaste." In that description, he includes the sense of taste as well as the sense of smell. Another description that focuses on the sense of smell is in paragraph 9, in which Helvarg describes Bob Chick's house as "reeking of mold and rotted cat food." He says, "I try not to breathe too deeply." These descriptions are particularly vivid because they engage a sense other than the sense of sight, giving the description more than one dimension.

3. Helvarg compares the post-Katrina Gulf Coast to a war zone in paragraphs 4 and 24, helping the reader understand the scale and randomness of the destruction. Since a war zone is full of damaged or destroyed buildings and other property, as well as dead or wounded people, the images this comparison conveys contribute to the dominant impression of the essay, which is that property and environmental damage was widespread, serious, and random. Helvarg points out, in paragraph 24, that the analogy fails if you consider the death toll, which was less for Katrina than in a typical war zone.

4. The photograph of the marked doorway (p. 94) provides more information than the author gives in paragraph 6. In paragraph 6, Helvarg describes in general how rescue workers indicate a house has been searched, but he does not describe a particular door. The photo specifically illustrates the general procedure that the workers were following, so its impact goes beyond the impact of the rather vague verbal description. In the case of the photo of Bob Chick (p. 95), an argument can be made that it is superfluous because Helvarg has captured Chick's situation vividly in paragraphs 8 and 9. Furthermore, his description of the photo in paragraph 9 ("He's wearing a mask, rubber boots and gloves, but still manages to give an expressive shrug of resignation when I take his picture") is so accurate and complete that the photo simply confirms it. (On the other hand, one can argue that the photo of Bob makes him a symbol of all the people struggling to recover from Katrina, and that is enough to warrant the photo's inclusion. Note that this argument has nothing to do with the author's powers of description, which are considerable.)

If students were writing this essay, they might or might not include the photos that accompany it, although it's likely that most would include them since photos provide visual breaks from the text and show actual scenes of destruction and real people, both of which help to bring the subject to life. Students might indicate they would use the photos to refresh their memories of what they saw as they were writing the essay. Or they might cut the verbal description of a photo's particular scene from the text and convey those particular details via the photo and caption, rather than in the main part of the essay. If there were more photos, some students might even turn this piece into a photo essay, in which the photos dominate and the text supports them.

SISTER FLOWERS

Maya Angelou

Questions for Close Reading (p. 104)

1. The dominant impression is implied and can be stated as, "The care and attention of a loving mentor is crucial to a child's healthy development, particularly in times of crisis." In addition, Angelou seeks to draw a portrait of beloved Mrs. Flowers, the essence of whom Angelou expresses when she writes, "[Mrs. Flowers] was one of the few gentlewomen I have ever known, and has remained throughout my life the measure of what a human being can be" (5).

2. Mrs. Flowers represents for Angelou the gentility and sophistication as well as the benevolence that she has read about in novels and seen in films, but has never encountered first-hand, especially not among her fellow townspeople. She says, "She appealed to me because she was like people I had never met personally" (11) and calls her "the aristocrat of Black Stamps" (2). Flowers's stunning beauty and impeccable grooming (2–4) powerfully impress Angelou, who lives in a community of relatively poor and minimally educated people. Still more fascinating is Flowers's refined grace (12), dazzling intellect, and stirring eloquence (22), all of which inspire Angelou to strive for a standard she previously thought accessible only to privileged whites. Angelou reflects, "She made me proud to be Negro, just by being herself" (11). Most of all, Angelou is profoundly honored and grateful that Flowers would not only spend time with her but also impart to her the "lessons for living" that would form the foundation of Angelou's subsequent existence.

3. Angelou humorously describes her frustration and embarrassment when witnessing her unrefined Momma speaking to the highly educated and proper Mrs. Flowers. In particular, Angelou is ashamed of Momma's calling Mrs. Flowers "*Sister* Flowers." To the young Angelou, such an informal appellation is inconsistent with what she considers the obvious superiority of her elegant neighbor. In Angelou's opinion, "Mrs. Flowers deserved better than to be called Sister" (7). Worse still is Momma's flawed grammar as she speaks to Flowers; Angelou agonizes over Momma's incorrect and missing verbs and says that she "hated [Momma] for showing her ignorance to Mrs. Flowers" (7). Despite Angelou's intense embarrassment over Momma, Momma and Mrs. Flowers share an amicable and mutually respectful friendship—a fact which perplexes Angelou, who calls their relationship "strange" (6). Mrs. Flowers does not object to Momma's calling her "Sister" and in fact might be pleased to be included in the community of women; similarly, Momma feels enough kinship with Mrs. Flowers to call her "Sister." The two women often engage in "intimate conversation" with each other (10), and it is implied that Momma has asked Mrs. Flowers's assistance in mentoring the withdrawn young Angelou. Years later, Angelou finally realizes that Momma and Mrs. Flowers were indeed "as alike as sisters, separated only by formal education" (7), a notion reinforced by Mrs. Flowers's insistence that Angelou appreciate the wisdom of "mother wit," such as that of Momma (35).

4. The first significant lesson Mrs. Flowers teaches Angelou is about the beauty and power of language. In the process of convincing young Angelou that she needs to participate verbally in class, Flowers explains that "it is language alone which separates [man] from the lower animals," a notion that was "a totally new idea" to Angelou (23). Soon after, in a statement that Angelou remembers as "valid and

poetic," Mrs. Flowers says, "It takes the human voice to infuse [words] with the shades of deeper meaning" (24). Mrs. Flowers's melodic, invigorating reading of *A Tale of Two Cities* convincingly illustrates to Angelou the vast power of words. (Clearly, this lesson had a tremendous impact on Angelou, presently a renowned writer not only of novels but also of poetry.) The next important lesson concerns the nature of wisdom and intelligence. Probably perceiving Angelou's embarrassment at Momma's lack of refinement, Mrs. Flowers informs her that many unschooled people are more knowledgeable and intelligent than some highly educated scholars. "Mother wit," she asserts, is every bit as valuable (if not more so) as book knowledge, for it contains "the collective wisdom of generations" (35). Mrs. Flowers's lesson on knowledge is summed up when she advises Angelou to "always be intolerant of ignorance but understanding of illiteracy" (35). Following this advice, it seems likely that young Angelou would think twice before judging Momma harshly again. Beyond these explicitly stated lessons, Angelou also receives the invaluable understanding that she is a unique and likable individual worthy of the attention of an exemplary woman, a realization that will help rebuild her wounded self-confidence.

5. *taut* (2): tightly pulled or strained
voile (2): a light, sheer fabric
benign (4): kind and gentle
unceremonious (8): informal
gait (8): particular way of walking
moors (11): broad area of open land, often containing patches of wetness
incessantly (11): continuing without interruption
scones (11): small, biscuit-like pastries
crumpets (11): small, round, cake-like breads
heath (11): large area of land containing low-growing shrubs
chifforobe (17): tall piece of furniture containing drawers and space for hanging clothes
sacrilegious (17): disrespectful of something held sacred
infuse (24): to introduce into as if by pouring
couched (35): expressed
aura (42): an invisible atmosphere seeming to surround something or someone

Questions About the Writer's Craft (p. 105)

1. Angelou relies primarily on visual and occasionally on both tactile and auditory impressions to convey Mrs. Flowers's "aristocratic" appearance. In paragraph 2, Angelou describes her graceful bearing that never evidences extremes of weather and her thin frame, which lacks the "taut look of wiry people." Mrs. Flowers's attire is the next object of Angelou's attention, as she observes the elegant woman's airy "printed voile dresses," "flowered hats," and gloves (2). Angelou then describes Mrs. Flowers's "rich black" complexion, comparing it to the visual and tactile image of an easily peeled plum (3). Angelou also details Mrs. Flowers's "slow dragging" smile (15), thin black lips, "even, small white teeth" (4) and "soft yet carrying voice" (6). Later, she mentions Mrs. Flowers's "easy gait" (8). In general, Angelou organizes these details of Mrs. Flowers's appearance spatially, moving from her physical carriage and attire up to her face and zeroing in on her smile (although she returns to Mrs. Flowers's "easy gait" later in the essay).

   To describe her reaction when she first arrived at Mrs. Flowers's home, Angelou invokes the sense of smell when, for example, she cites the "sweet scent of vanilla" (29). She then draws upon the visual sense to describe what she observes: "browned

23

photographs" and "white, freshly done curtains" (32). The next part of the visit calls upon the visual as well as the taste faculty, as Angelou describes eating Mrs. Flowers's delectable cookies ("flat round wafers, slightly browned on the edges and butter-yellow in the center") and drinking the refreshing, cold lemonade (34). The tactile sense is appealed to when she mentions the "rough crumbs" of the cookies scratching against her jaw (34). And the sense of sound is evoked as Angelou remembers Mrs. Flowers's reading voice, "cascading" and "nearly singing" (37). Overall, Angelou organizes this last set of richly textured sensory impressions spatially as well as chronologically; that is, she presents the details as she moves through the house and as the afternoon progresses.

2. The first figure of speech is the simile Angelou uses in comparing herself to an old biscuit (1). This image establishes young Angelou's shame and withdrawal following the rape; indeed, her depression is what prompts Mrs. Flowers to find time to talk with the child. Angelou then employs a series of striking figures of speech to describe Mrs. Flowers's character and demeanor. The most powerful appear in paragraph 11. There Angelou provides a series of similes using *like* to compare Flowers with the gentle, elegant "women in English novels who walked the moors...with their loyal dogs racing at a respectful distance" and "the women who sat in front of roaring fireplaces, drinking tea incessantly from silver trays full of scones and crumpets." The final simile of the paragraph is an implied one; although it lacks *like*, it deliberately mirrors the structure of the previous two similes: "Women who walked over the 'heath' and read morocco-bound books and had two last names divided by a hyphen." The function of these similes comparing Mrs. Flowers to female British gentility is to reinforce the notion of her as "the aristocrat of Black Stamps" (2). The basis of Mrs. Flowers's allure for Angelou is her otherworldly elegance and sophistication, particularly when juxtaposed with the ordinary citizens of Black Stamps. That this elegant and gracious woman actually seeks out the young Angelou is enough to transform the child from an "old biscuit" into one who excitedly runs down the road, flush with the pleasure of being liked.

3. The technique of imagined conversation injects humor into Angelou's portrait of herself as a child, while also allowing readers greater insight into her character by giving them access to her mental processes. The young Angelou's imagined scoldings of Momma resoundingly illustrate her embarrassment with "uncouth" Momma. Here, Angelou seems caught between two worlds: that of "backwards" Momma and Black Stamps and that of education and opportunity seemingly offered by the outside world. As Mrs. Flowers instructs, however, much wisdom resides in "mother wit" like Momma's, and given this lesson, young Angelou would probably be led to reevaluate her embarrassed attitude toward Momma.

4. From Angelou's very first statement about Mrs. Flowers, it is apparent that race is a significant facet of life in Angelou's town. Mrs. Flowers is said to be "the aristocrat of Black Stamps," a statement that draws its power from the notion that aristocrats have traditionally been white. This depiction of Mrs. Flowers as uniquely regal is heightened by Angelou's comparing her to English female gentry (11) and by her observation that Mrs. Flowers behaves differently from the average "Negro woman" (14) in town. Most significantly, Angelou states that Mrs. Flowers made her "proud to be a Negro, just by being herself" (11), a difficult feat given the racist climate of the day. The town's appellation, "Black Stamps" (12), implies the existence of a "White Stamps," a fact later confirmed when Angelou mentions "powhitefolks" (13). Angelou indicates that no Negro, not even the elegant Mrs. Flowers, is immune to the disrespect of the town's self-aggrandizing poor whites. Indeed, even Angelou's reverence for Mrs. Flowers "would have been shattered like the unmendable Humpty-Dumpty" (13) if the "powhitefolks" had called this revered idol by her first

name, Bertha. Angelou lives in a world that would sanction such racially inspired disrespect and insult. In paragraph 42, Angelou refers to "Southern bitter wormwood," a subtle reference to racism. In such a world, it is difficult for a Black child—especially one so traumatized and wounded—to develop a strong sense of self. But that is just what the encounter with Mrs. Flowers achieves; it makes young Angelou "feel proud" to be a Negro, and with that comes the loosening of trauma's hold on her.

ONCE MORE TO THE LAKE

E. B. White

Questions for Close Reading (p. 112)

1. White's thesis is implied. One way of stating it is as follows: "In taking his son to revisit the lake where he experienced so many significant childhood events, White learns that he can only partly recapture the feelings and atmosphere of days long past. Instead, he gets in touch with a premonition of his own death."
2. White suggests that his return to the lake was rather casual and impulsive (1). While he normally preferred the ocean, he says, sometimes the turbulence of the sea made him long for the calm of a placid lake in the woods. In addition, he could take his son along and introduce him to fresh water fishing. On a deeper level, he seems to have longed to revisit a place of significance from his youth and to share its pleasures with a son.
3. In paragraph 4, the author lies in his bed, hearing his son sneak out in the dawn light to take a motorboat out on the lake, just as White had himself done as a boy. His son's behavior is so similar to his own as a youth that he suddenly feels as if "he was I, and therefore . . . that I was my own father." Another significant transposition occurs when they are fishing (5). A dragonfly, an unchanging element of nature, alights on his rod and gives him the dizzying feeling that he has moved back in time, until he "didn't know which rod [he] was at the end of." Finally, in paragraph 10, he identifies deeply with his son's attempts to gain mastery over the motorboat; he feels again all the same feelings he had in his youth as he grew to have a "spiritual" relationship with the motor.
4. The visit shows that things have remained much the same through the years. Nature has not changed much, nor has the town or the accommodations. In fact, White feels that the visit reveals the "pattern of life indelible" (8). Some details have changed, however, in keeping with the times. For example, the road has only two tracks, from the tires of automobiles, not three, from horse-drawn carriages (7); also, the boat is a modern outboard, not the one- and two-cylinder inboard motors of his youth. The waitresses are still country girls, but they have been impressed by the actresses in the movies and keep their hair cleaner than the waitresses of the past (7). Finally, the store serves Coke rather than old-fashioned sodas like Moxie and sarsaparilla (11).
5. *incessant* (1): continuous, not stopping
   placidity (1): peacefulness, calmness
   primeval (3): primitive
   transposition (4): a reversal or switching of place

undulating (6): rippling, moving in wave-like fashion
indelible (8): permanent, unerasable
petulant (10): irritable, grouchy
languidly (13): lifelessly, spiritlessly, without energy

Questions About the Writer's Craft (p. 112)

1. White presents the descriptions of the present-day lake very objectively. "There was a choice of pie for dessert, and one was blueberry and one was apple, and the waitresses were the same country girls . . . the waitresses were still fifteen; their hair had been washed, that was the only difference—they had been to the movies and seen the pretty girls with clean hair." But White's descriptions of the past are sensuous and evocative, full of imagery that suggests they are more powerful than the present images. The memories of the past overtake and dominate the present experiences.

2. In paragraph 2, White calls the lake a "holy spot" and recalls a memory of the lake at dawn, when the woods along the shore seemed to form a "cathedral." Later, in paragraph 10, he describes the experience of learning to operate a motorboat as getting "really close to it spiritually." His description of the summer at the lake in paragraph 8 uses prayer-like language: "pattern of life indelible," "summer without end." These images convey White's almost religious reverence for nature: its beauty, peace, and permanence.

3. This passage uses the metaphor of a melodrama for the storm. This comparison points out that the storm is full of noise and turbulence but, in reality, is not dangerous. The storm's "audience," the children, in particular, get all excited about it, but to White, an old hand at the lake, the storm's "drama of electrical disturbance" is familiar. The storm is a joyfully scary event; the "gods grinning" suggests a pagan image of nature gods playing with the elements just for fun. The campers celebrate by running about and swimming in the rain. There is a serious undercurrent to the storm, however. While a harmless imitation of danger, it nevertheless sets the stage for White's premonition of death in the next paragraph.

4. The feeling grows out of a complex of events. The mock-danger of the storm has intensified everyone's reactions. White has enjoyed the storm as a piece of theater; he remains on the sidelines wittily analyzing the scene. But the storm arouses the vitality of his son, who joins the frolicking campers. This action is the final example of how the son is growing up and away from his parent. (The boy takes the boat out by himself, for example.) When White feels a "sympathetic" iciness in his groin as his son dons his cold wet swimsuit, he is on one level identifying sensuously (again) with the boy's experience. In "biblical" terms, a child is the fruit of its father's "groin," and so the iciness also represents White's sudden awareness that his vitality is decreasing; to use the image of the melodrama, his scene is ending, while his son is center-stage. The many transpositions of identity between father and son have hinted at this final thought; White feels more and more like his own father, who, we can assume, has died.

A PARTIAL REMEMBRANCE OF A PUERTO RICAN CHILDHOOD

Judith Ortiz Cofer

Questions for Close Reading (p. 119)

1. Cofer states her thesis in the second paragraph, partly in the first sentence and partly in the last: "It was on these rockers that my mother, her sisters, and my grandmother sat on these afternoons of my childhood to tell their stories, teaching each other, and my cousin and me, what it was like to be a woman, more specifically, a Puerto Rican woman. . . . And they told *cuentos*, the morality and cautionary tales told by the women in our family for generations: stories that became a part of my subconscious as I grew up in two worlds, the tropical island and the cold city, and that would later surface in my dreams and in my poetry." The rest of the essay describes one of these story-telling sessions, and includes a recounting of one of the family *cuentos*.

2. The participating women include her grandmother, her mother. and her aunts, all members of older generations. At the time of the essay, the author is aged eleven or twelve, no longer a child who can be told to leave the room or "go and play." Yet, she is not a woman who can freely participate in the sessions. Rather, she sits quietly, occupied in some childish pursuit such as reading a comic book, and is allowed to "overhear" the stories. As she writes, she sat "pretending to be in another world, while absorbing it all in a sort of unspoken agreement of my status as silent auditor" (3). These sessions occur in the late afternoon, when the men are still at work, and the boys of the family have gone off to a park to play baseball.

3. The story about Maria La Loca is designed to warn women against trusting men too much. Being left at the altar is equated with going crazy, becoming ugly and ridiculous (3, 6, 8, 11), and of course, with never having another chance to marry. It is a tale that suggests that women's fates are tied up with how they are treated by men, and that therefore, they should be extremely sensible and careful so that they too are not victimized. Mama's views are based on the treachery of men in Mama's time. She described how, when she was young, a man could leave a girl at the altar and never be found, never be held accountable. Married men, she says, sometimes had several families all over the island of Puerto Rico. "Hombres with the devil in their flesh, . . . [would] take a job at one of the haciendas, only to have a good time and to seduce the women" (4). As Cofer puts it, "in Mama's eyes, a man set free without a legal contract was a man lost" (5). She believes that men marry because that is the only way they can have legitimate children and also obtain sex, which Mama euphemistically explains as "what no decent (synonymous with 'smart') woman would give away for free" (5). Her negative opinion of men is also conveyed in her "little swipe at men," the use of the word *macho* to describe the man who abandoned Maria, at a time when *macho* meant "stud" in the reproductive sense, rather than a dominating, womanizing male (8).

4. Throughout the telling of the *cuento*, Cofer shines a spotlight on Mama's daughters, in each instance describing the woman's relationship to men and her reaction to the story. In this way, the personalities and personal histories of the women become like refractions of the story, each woman's life measured to the standard of her husband's treatment of her.

   In paragraph 5, the youngest and yet-unmarried aunt, Aunt Laura, is pictured. She is embarrassed by the story because she is the same age as Maria had been—seventeen—and she is also engaged to be married. Her fiancé has gone to New York

27

to "make his fortune" and will return in a year for the marriage. According to Cofer, Mama was doubtful about the marriage occurring, because to her, "a man set free without a legal contract was a man lost" (5). Cofer returns to Laura in paragraph 11, where she describes her as "on the verge of tears" and nervously rocking in her chair.

Aunt Nena, the oldest daughter, is described in paragraph 9. She is married, but not happily. Her husband had lost his first wife, and so she cared for two stepchildren in addition to her own three, while her husband lived on the mainland in order to earn money. His "main interest in life was accumulating wealth." Cofer notes that the future held sorrow for this aunt, as she later leaves her children with Mama to "slave" in a factory to help her husband with his dream. She apparently suffered greatly from the separation from her family. Finally, she was different from the other women in the family, in that she read all the time, but she "came alive to Mama's words, rocking gently" in her chair (9).

Also in paragraph 9, Cofer describes her mother, a daughter happily married who could view the La Loca story peacefully and "conspiratorially." She had married young, "an unspotted lamb," into a well-respected although not wealthy family. Her husband, we learn in paragraph 7, is in the U.S. Navy, and the family shuttles between Paterson, New Jersey, and Puerto Rico. Like Aunt Nena, she endures separations having to do with her husband's military position, during which she is terrified. However, she can relax when her husband returns, suggesting that their marriage is strong and that he is a protective man. Overall, she does not seem to be as sad as Aunt Nena.

5. *intricately* (1): using many interrelated parts or facets
    embellishing (2): enhancing (a tale) with fictitious additions
    cautionary (2): giving warning
    histrionic (3): affected in behavior or speech
    conclave (3): a private or secret meeting
    auditor (3): listener; person who overhears
    impassively (3): without showing any sign of emotion or feeling
    ministrations (3): attentions
    matriarchal (3): like a woman who runs a family or tribe
    quest (7): search in order to find something
    chameleons (7): lizards with the ability to change the color of their skin
    surveillance (7): watch kept over a person, group, etc.
    conspiratorially (9): acting secretly together toward the same goal
    aberration (9): deviation from what is common, normal, or right
    mesmerizing (10): fascinating, hypnotizing
    denouement (11): the final resolution of a plot
    ravished (11): raped
    impromptu (13): without previous preparation

Questions About the Writer's Craft (p. 119)

1. Cofer provides numerous details about Maria. First, she describes her physically (6). She is "a town character," who combines the body and face of a fat old woman with the movements of a young girl. "She would swing her hips in an exaggerated, clownish way, and sometimes even hop and skip up to someone's house" (6). She avoids speaking, but grins an ugly smile when questioned, much as a shy or awkward child might do. People taunted her, but she seemed not to notice. She was also reputed to hum to herself all the time. Later in the essay, we are given a description of her as the abandoned young bride-to-be: "a princess in her lace as she waited at the altar" (11). In between, we are provided the details of her tragedy; she

"was once a beautiful girl. . . . 'but this *macho* made a fool out of her and ruined her life'" (8). Her illness is called a "honeymoon with death" that left her "ravished, no longer young or sane" (11). At the end, we are told the final detail, that the song Maria hums incessantly is the wedding march (13). Maria's decline after her abandonment represents, according to Mama, the fate of any woman who fails to be vigilant and careful in her choice of a man. The focus on her physical appearance makes Maria a visible, ever-present reminder of how low a woman can fall if she makes a poor choice. She is an object of mockery whose degradation is visible to all.

2. The details about the young Cofer reflect off the haunting power of the story of Maria La Loca. During her childhood, Cofer felt that she was an "odd-ball," like Maria, because she led a dual existence. Part of her time was spent in New Jersey, where she was treated like an immigrant, and part was spent in Puerto Rico, where her English-accented Spanish made her seem American. In neither place did she truly fit in. She and her brother became "cultural chameleons," who could "blend into a crowd," quietly adjust to apartment life during stormy weeks in New Jersey, or fly free during summers in Puerto Rico. She was, she says in paragraph 7, on a "serious quest for a definition of normal." The cautionary tale of the weird Maria echoes all the more strongly in the mind of a child ill at ease everywhere.

3. Cofer "braids" the story with descriptive material about the listeners, her aunts and mother because she wishes to show the effects of the story on the women. She also wants to convey the power of storytelling and the values it embodies in the culture of Puerto Rico. Mama's narrative is essentially a story within a story. The encasing story is a simple one, just the tale of how the women gathered, Cofer had her hair braided, and the grandmother danced Cofer around to the wedding march at the end of her story.

    The grandmother's narrative is told in paragraphs 4, 6, 8, and 11–13 and is handled as direct quotations from Mama. The reader can recognize when the story resumes because it comes as dialogue. After each of these narrative paragraphs, Cofer clearly signals the reader that she is switching topics. At the start of paragraph 5, the phrase "The whole time she was speaking" helps the reader switch out of the narrative into the storytelling scene. In paragraph 6, the second sentence of the paragraph indicates that Cofer is leaving the story to provide her own description of Maria La Loca (6) and of her (Cofer's) position as an outsider to the pueblo (7). In paragraph 9, Cofer moves from providing a bit of linguistic background to Mama's story to a description of her mother. She handles this by describing her own action of peeking at her mother. After this long interlude, Cofer returns to the story of Maria by using a transition indicating the time: "That day, Mama told . . ." (11). In paragraph 13, the two stories merge, as Mama indicates that the tune Maria always hums is "The Wedding March," and pulls Cofer into "an impromptu waltz."

4. The braiding serves two purposes; it displays the grandmother's values and also parallels her storytelling. Mama begins to braid the author's hair near the start of the story without being asked, with the goal of taming Cofer's messy mop. She is clearly a person with a great deal of personal strength, who likes things disciplined and clear rather than all in a mess. That the braiding displays the grandmother's character comes through in Cofer's first description of the braiding in paragraph 3: "Mama had taken my long, tangled mane of hair into her ever-busy hands. Without looking down and with no interruption of her flow of words, she began braiding my hair, working at it with the quickness and determination that characterized all her actions." Cofer returns to the braiding several times in the essay, each time providing more clues about the grandmother. In paragraph 5, Cofer reports that the braiding was painful: "Mama would be weaving my hair into a flat plait that required pulling apart the two

29

sections of hair with little jerks that made my eyes water; but knowing how grandmother detested whining and *boba* (sissy) tears, as she called them, I just sat up . . . straight and stiff. . . ." We learn here that a kind of stoicism and bravery is admired in this family. Later, in paragraph 11, the author mentions that the story was making her Aunt Laura very uncomfortable, but that Mama "ignored Laura's obvious discomfort, digging out a ribbon from the sewing basket she kept by her rocker while describing Maria's long illness." She demands of Laura the same bravery in response to pain that she expects of the young girl whose hair she is braiding.

Also throughout the essay, Cofer suggests the parallel between the braiding and the grandmother's story. In paragraph 8, Cofer comments that Mama was "knitting my hair with the same intensity she was putting into her story. . . ." In a sentence that is itself a marvel of braided images, Cofer explicitly discusses this parallel in paragraph 10: "The aroma of coffee perking in the kitchen, the mesmerizing creaks and groans of the rockers, and the women telling their lives in *cuentos* are forever woven into the fabric of my imagination, braided like my hair that day I felt my grandmother's hands teaching me about strength, her voice convincing me of the power of storytelling." Finally, Cofer notes the story ends just as the grandmother finishes the braid: "Mama lamented while tying the ribbon to the ends of my hair, pulling it back with such force that I just knew I would never be able to close my eyes completely again" (11).

NARRATION

OPENING COMMENTS

In our classes, we introduce narrative writing *after* description because we have found that descriptive writing helps students acquire many of the skills needed to write engaging narratives. For example, through descriptive writing, students discover the need to generate evocative details, use varied sentence structure, and establish a clear point of view.

Also, we often encounter students who are reluctant to write a narrative at the very start of the course. Schooled in the belief that a lightning bolt will strike them if they use "I" in an essay, they are more comfortable starting with description because it lends itself more easily to the objective third person point of view. (Even though both narration and description can be written in either the first or third person, beginning writers tend to associate narration with the first and description with the third person.)

Even if it is not the first pattern covered, we suggest that narration be introduced near the beginning of the course. Everyone, after all, likes a good story, and most students have written narratives in high school and so feel comfortable tackling them in college.

Despite some students' familiarity and seeming ease with the narrative pattern, it's a good idea to keep in mind that narration requires a sophisticated repertoire of skills. Pacing, choice of details, telescoping of time, point of view: all offer a real challenge.

Students seem to have particular trouble understanding point of view. Because they tend to be more familiar with the first rather than the third person, we've found it useful to ask them to write two versions of the same narrative—one in the first and one in the third person. Such an assignment shows students how point of view changes a story and makes them aware of the advantages and limitations of each perspective.

Although each narrative in this chapter is filled with drama and tension, students find special power in the conflicts underlying Orwell's "Shooting an Elephant" and Hughes's "Salvation." While Lorde's piece reminds students of the value of sensory details, it also illustrates careful pacing and strong characterization. With its measured use of dialogue, Gholson's essay conveys the tension and discomfort the author experienced during a mortifying encounter. And Mayblum's powerful account of his harrowing escape from the World Trade Center on 9/11 demonstrates the raw force and immediacy inherent in the narrative form.

ANSWERS FOR PREWRITING ACTIVITIES

Below we provide suggested responses to selected prewriting activities at the end of Chapter 4. Of course, your students are bound to come up with their own inventive approaches. (p. 135)

1. There are numerous ways to use narration to open these two essays. Below we've listed some of the possibilities. In going over this activity in class, we suggest you have students trade responses or read them aloud to each other, so that they are all aware of the diversity of responses to the assignment.

*Topic: **The effect of insensitive teachers on young children***
  Teacher being sarcastic to student making a mistake
  Teacher joking about student's clothes choices
  Child's reading mistakes increasing as teacher corrects
  Child crying after a teacher's cruel remark
  Teacher punishing harshly for small transgression
  Name-calling or labeling of a child for being different

*Topic: **The importance of family traditions***
  Family seated at Sunday dinner
  Sugary donuts for all at breakfast for a family birthday
  Generations gathered at a holiday for a yearly reunion
  Fourth of July kite flying with all the cousins
  Gathering at year's end to view selected family videos

2. Below are possible conflicts for each situation. Dialogue for each conflict will vary according to each student's experiences.

    a. Friend criticizes your food choices as unhealthy

       Friend embarrasses you by snacking on food throughout store

    b. College choice is on the other side of the country

       College choice does not offer the major your parents wish you to take

    c. Counter-demonstrators accost your group

       Some protesters break the law by trespassing and are arrested

    d. Fighting the desire to go to the gym instead of studying

       Telling friends to be quiet or go away

ANSWERS FOR REVISING ACTIVITIES

Below we provide suggested responses to selected revising activities at the end of Chapter 4. Of course, your students are bound to come up with their own inventive approaches. (p. 135)

3. Here are some ways to revise the sentence sets to create first a negative connotation and then a positive connotation. Other versions are possible, of course.

    a. The raucous clanging of the bell signaled that the last day of lectures and homework was finally over.

       With a gentle dinging sound from the school bell, the last day of high school quietly ended.

    b. We strode over to admonish our neighbors for polluting the air with burning leaves.

       We had a neighborly chat with the Joneses, while the autumn leaves burned fragrantly in their yard.

c. The sun slicing through my window jolted me upright in bed, and I was forced to admit that daylight had come.

The lemony-yellow sunshine poured across my bed, and I sat up, grateful the new day was finally here.

4. It's a good idea to set aside some time for students to exchange their versions of the paragraph with others. Seeing how others handled the assignment can open their eyes to techniques they haven't considered.

Students should keep in mind as they revise that this is an introductory anecdote. It needs to be brief and pointed. Here are the main problems in the paragraph:

— The reference to the type of car the writer was driving is irrelevant and should be deleted.
— The speeding car should be described.
— The description "The car didn't slow down . . ." is slow paced and indirect; rewrite to state that the car "sped. . . ."
— Description of car coming, light changing, couple crossing, is too slow; condense and make more dramatic.
— "Dressed like models" is irrelevant, unless other details are added later in the paragraph to indicate how rumpled and bloody their clothes now are.
— The sentence about the man "jump[ing] to the shoulder" is short and choppy.
— Describe man's and woman's locations and injuries more visually, instead of saying he "wasn't hurt" but "it was clear she was."
— Narrator's calling police is a digression; condense events to get to the point: she died.
— Give more visual details of speeding car stopping, driver getting out, instead of saying he "looked terrible"; give us a picture of him drunk.
— Use his repeated offenses as a lead-in or stronger transition to the final sentence, the thesis.

THE FOURTH OF JULY

Audre Lorde

Questions for Close Reading (p. 140)

1. Here is one possible way of stating the essay's implied thesis: "Lorde's eighth grade graduation was supposed to mark the end of her childhood. But it was her Fourth of July graduation present trip to Washington, D.C., that truly marked the end of her innocence, because there she encountered the harsh reality of racism."
2. This picnic is Lorde's mother's idea of what it means to take care of her family, even to the extent that she provides different pickles (one type for the father, another type for the kids), wraps peaches separately so they won't bruise, and puts in a tin of rosewater for messy hands. Being a good mother also means packing the things your family enjoys, like "'marigolds' . . . from Cushman's Bakery . . . and rock-cakes from Newton's" (4). All these domestic details of a caring mother underscore the injustice, the horrific irony of the way the family is treated at the ice cream counter. Although Lorde's mother probably believed in her heart that packing the picnic was

a way to keep her family safe from food touched by the hands of strangers, more importantly, it was also a way to keep her children away from the racist situation they would most likely encounter in the railroad dining car. In short, these elaborate picnic preparations were evidence of the mother's avoidance of unpleasantness at all costs.

3. There are two reasons Lorde gives us for her inability to comprehend her parents' admonitions against white people. First of all, Lorde's parents never gave her any reasons; they just expected her "to know without being told" (7) the logic behind their warnings and the source of their feelings regarding white people. In addition, she has difficulty accepting such a dictate when her mother, as she tells us, "looked so much like one of those people we were never supposed to trust" (7). The fuzziness of the dictate leaves Lorde doubly vulnerable to the experience she encounters at the ice cream counter.

4. In paragraphs 5 and 6, Lorde illustrates her mother's attempt to sidestep racism and her father's attempt to make up for it. By packing an elaborate picnic for the trip, Lorde's mother successfully avoids subjecting her family to the racism they would surely have encountered had they attempted to eat in the dining car. And when Lorde's sister is denied access to her own senior class trip because, truth be told, they would be staying in a hotel that "did not rent rooms to Negroes," Lorde's father tries to offset Phyllis's disappointment by planning a family trip instead. In paragraph 7, Lorde explains her parents' behavior more fully. She writes: "They handled it as a private woe. My mother and father believed that they could best protect their children from the realities of race in america and the fact of american racism by never giving them name, much less discussing their nature."

   In the picture Lorde draws for us in paragraph 18, her family does not so much deal with the situation as ignore it. After the waitress delivered her message, Lorde tells us, "Straight-backed and indignant, one by one, my family got down from the counter stools and turned around and marched out of the store, quiet and outraged, as if we had never been Black before." But when she questions her parents about this obvious injustice, they don't answer her. In fact, they never address the incident, "not because they had contributed to it, but because they felt they should have anticipated it and avoided it" (19). Lorde gets increasingly angry not only because her parents do not share her heated emotions, but also because they seem to accept responsibility for what happened. Also, her sisters mimic her parents' pretense of denial, and this invalidation of her response from all members of the family heightens Lorde's fury and anger. Moreover, while she is given the freedom to articulate her fury in a letter to the president of the United States, because her father insists upon reviewing the letter before she sends it off, we wonder whether she will be permitted to fully express her righteous rage.

5. *fabled* (1): famous; legendary
   injunction (7): order or demand
   progressive (8): favoring progress or reform
   dilated (9): enlarged
   vulnerable (9): unprotected
   travesty (10): a ridiculous representation of something
   decreed (13): ordered
   pretense (19): false appearance

Questions About the Writer's Craft (p. 140)

1. Lorde uses transitions of time and place to let us know when and where events occur. In the first sentence of the essay, Lorde establishes a general time frame when she

writes that events occurred "on the edge of . . . summer." The final sentence of paragraph 1 narrows that time frame down to the Fourth of July. In paragraph 2, we learn that Lorde's family took the trip "during the day" and that it was made by train. We know that the train leaves New York City and passes through Philadelphia; Lorde writes, "I remember it was Philadelphia because I was disappointed not to have passed by the Liberty Bell" (3). In paragraphs 8 and 12, she signals the family's arrival at their destination ("In Washington, D.C., we had one large room with two double beds and an extra cot for me") as well as the family's movement out of the hotel to see the sites ("I spent the whole next day after Mass squinting up at the Lincoln Memorial"). Paragraph 13 reveals the passage of time ("Later that Washington afternoon my family and I walked back down Pennsylvania Avenue"), while paragraphs 15 and 16 set the scene at the ice cream parlor ("Two blocks away from our hotel, the family . . . stopped . . . at a . . . soda fountain. . . . Corded and crisped and pinafored, the five of us seated ourselves one by one at the counter") and indicate Lorde's place in the scene ("There was I between my mother and father"). Paragraph 18 reveals the family's response to the waitress's refusal to serve them ("one by one, my family . . . got down from the counter . . . and marched out of the store"). That day ends with Lorde's writing a letter to the president of the United States, which her father promises she can type out on the "office typewriter next week" (19). The "whole rest of that trip," Lorde writes, she felt sick to her stomach (20).

2. In paragraphs 5–7, 9–11, and 19–20, Lorde moves from the events of the day to other discussions. Nevertheless, the information she provides in these instances is critical. The last sentence of paragraph 5 and the whole of paragraphs 6 and 7 are used to convey the way her parents handle racism and how their behavior affects her. Although the information in these paragraphs does not advance the narrative itself, what she reveals here has much to do with the experience she is describing. Her parents' failure to explain "the realities of race in america and the fact of american racism" leaves her open to the confusion and pain she feels while in Washington.

In paragraphs 9–11, we learn that Lorde has trouble seeing clearly every summer; her eyes are unable to adjust to the "dazzling whiteness" of July. At first, this little aside about squinting seems arbitrary and unnecessary, but later we find that it is actually a metaphor for being blinded to racism: Just as her parents "did not approve of sunglasses, nor of their expense" (thus forcing her to squint her way through each summer, never seeing clearly), they also did not approve of racism discussions, nor of the cost of exposing their children to the reality of racism (thus forcing Lorde into a sort of blindness that made the day of clarity all the more painful).

In paragraph 19, Lorde tells us that her sisters, like her parents, behaved as though nothing was wrong with what happened in the ice cream parlor. In fact, her whole family seemed to have a tacit agreement that denial was the best way to handle—or not handle—racism. Lorde feels alone in her inability to accept injustice. As a result, Washington, D.C., becomes a solid block of whiteness that makes her sick to her stomach, and the trip itself proves to be "[not] much of a graduation present after all" (20).

3. Lorde's use of lowercase letters is appropriate. Given the soul-searing incident she experiences in Washington, D.C., the nation's capital, on the holiday commemorating that nation's declaration of independence and its promise of freedom and justice for all, the use of lowercase letters conveys her lack of respect for a country and a leader that fail to uphold those promises implied in the celebration of the Fourth of July.

4. In paragraph 20, Lorde repeats the word *white* over and over again: "The waitress was white, and the counter was white, and the ice cream I never ate in Washington, D.C., that summer I left childhood was white, and the white heat and the white pavement and the white stone monuments of my first Washington summer made me sick to my stomach for the whole rest of that trip and it wasn't much of a graduation present after all." Like Lorde, who feels overcome by the prevalence of racism, we too are overcome by the word *white* and can understand Lorde's experience: Racism is constant and exists everywhere.

SHOOTING AN ELEPHANT

George Orwell

Questions for Close Reading (p. 149)

1. Orwell's thesis is implied. One possible way of stating it is this: "Members of a ruling imperialistic class feel compelled to behave so as not to lose face or power over the populace, even if that means doing something against their better judgment."
2. Orwell felt pressured by the people, almost overwhelmed by their power over him through their mere presence. In theory, he explains at the start of the selection, he "was all for the Burmese and all against their oppressors, the British" (2). But, in reality, he felt the common people of the country were "evil-spirited little beasts who tried to make my job impossible" (2). During the shooting incident, the people were "happy and excited," he says, and they watched him "as they would a conjurer about to perform a trick." He resentfully saw himself as having to spend his life "trying to impress the 'natives'" (7). He reports later that, as he fired a shot, the crowd emitted a "devilish roar of glee" (11). His choice of words shows that he resented and disliked the Burmese.
3. Orwell shoots the elephant because the two thousand native people standing behind him expect him to. They want vengeance for the man it killed, the meat the carcass will provide, and the entertainment of watching the shooting. "The people expected it of me and I had got to do it" (7), he writes. There is an implication that if he decided not to shoot the elephant, both he and the empire would suffer a loss of prestige, but the main concern in Orwell's mind is the "long struggle not to be laughed at" (7). He is even afraid to "test" the animal's mood by going closer for fear it might attack and kill him before he could shoot, thus giving the crowd a sight it would enjoy as much as the slaughter of the beast.
4. Despotic governments result from the need to maintain power over subtly resistant people; such a government can rule only by fulfilling the people's expectations and responding to every crisis with the expected force. Orwell points to the irony that he stood armed in front of an unarmed crowd, yet he was powerless to do as he wished or as his judgment told him. Instead, he felt himself "an absurd puppet pushed to and fro by the will of those yellow faces behind" (7).
5. *imperialism* (2): a country's policy of gaining power by acquiring and ruling territories
   prostrate (2): lying face down, as in submission or adoration
   despotic (3): tyrannical, all-powerful
   mahout (3): the keeper and driver of an elephant
   miry (5): swampy, muddy

conjurer (7): magician
futility (7): uselessness, ineffectiveness
sahib (7): "Master"; Indian title of respect when addressing Europeans

Questions About the Writer's Craft (p. 149)

1. What Orwell calls a "tiny incident" lasted only a short time, perhaps only an hour at
    most. Orwell uses clear transitions of time to keep us oriented as to what is
    happening, but he provides no specific clock time. "Early one morning," the
    narrative begins (3); after the death of the coolie, the action steps up and the
    transitions indicate things are happening at a rapid pace: "he could not have been
    dead many minutes . . ." (4); "As soon as I saw the dead man . . ." (4); "the orderly
    came back in a few minutes . . ." (5); "meanwhile some Burmans had arrived . . ."
    (5); "As soon as I saw . . ." (6); "I thought then . . ." (6); "But at that moment . . ."
    (7); "I perceived in this moment . . ." (7); "But I had got to act quickly . . ." (8); "For
    at that moment . . ." (9); "When I pulled the trigger . . ." (11); "In that instant, in too
    short a time . . ." (11); "He looked suddenly stricken . . ." (11); "At last, after what
    seemed a long time—it might have been five seconds . . ." (11); "And then down he
    came . . ." (11). In paragraphs 12 and 13, Orwell describes the refusal of the animal
    to die: "I waited a long time . . ."; "Finally I fired . . ."; "but still he did not die" (12).
    The incident ends with Orwell leaving the scene but learning later that the animal
    took half an hour to die.
2. The first two paragraphs introduce us to the alien, far-off world where the narrative
    took place. In addition to setting the scene, Orwell explains what he was doing in
    Burma and, more importantly, gives us an emotional perspective from which to view
    the event. We learn in a general way about the bitterness between the colonialists and
    the native inhabitants and about the psychological effect his job as a policeman had
    on him. His confession that he was "young and ill-educated" and not even aware the
    British Empire was collapsing helps us feel empathy for him in the incident that
    follows. Without this information, we might not be willing to forgive him the
    shooting of the elephant or its horrible death, or comprehend the sense of
    victimization he felt despite his position as an "authority."
3. Orwell uses analogies in three important places. Two of the analogies are from the
    theater and relate to the sense of falseness that Orwell feels about his role in the
    colony. With the crowd watching him, he compares himself to "a conjurer about to
    perform a trick" with "the magic rifle." Then he helps us to understand his own
    psychological state at that moment by using another theater image: "Here was I . . .
    seemingly the lead actor of the piece; but in reality I was only an absurd puppet
    pushed to and fro by the will of those yellow faces . . ."; in the East, he says, the
    white man "becomes a sort of hollow, posing dummy. . . . He wears a mask, and his
    face grows to fit it" (7). Paragraph 10 continues this analogy, as Orwell describes the
    crowd breathing "a deep, low, happy sigh, as of people who see the theatre curtain
    go up at last." The third analogy compares the elephant to an elderly person; as
    Orwell watches the beast in the rice paddy, he feels it has a "preoccupied
    grandmotherly air." After he fires the first shot, he says the elephant "looked
    suddenly stricken, shrunken, immensely old. . . . His mouth slobbered. An enormous
    senility seemed to have settled upon him. One could have imagined him thousands of
    years old" (11).
4. Orwell vividly evokes the suffering of the elephant by carefully observing the
    animal's movements after the shot. He notices the subtle but "terrible change" that
    came over it, in which "every line of his body had altered." The analogy with an old
    man helps structure his observations that the elephant seemed paralyzed, then sagged

37

to his knees and slobbered. Other trenchant details include the image of the animal standing "weakly upright" again and the image of him toppling "like a huge rock," "his trunk reaching skywards like a tree," and trumpeting once (11). In paragraph 12, Orwell provides a graphic description of the beast's death agony. He reports firing over and over; into a picture that has so far been in black-and-white, he interjects colors. He remembers that the elephant's "mouth was wide open" so that he "could see far down into caverns of pink pale throat" and that "the thick blood welled out of him like red velvet." In this paragraph, too, we hear sounds: the "tortured breathing," the "dreadful noise," and the "tortured gasps" that continued "steadily as the ticking of a clock."

CHARITY DISPLAY?

Charmie Gholson

Questions for Close Reading (p. 153)

1. Gholson suggests her thesis in paragraph 3, in which she questions herself: "Did I really want a handout? Should I endure a bit of humiliation to provide some essentials for my kids? I felt as if I had no choice." She alludes to it again in paragraph 12: "Despite the doctor's best intentions, I felt scrutinized—especially with his son there to witness my inability to buy my own kids their damn socks." In essence, Gholson's thesis is that the experience of receiving charity in person from a stranger is demeaning.
2. Although Gholson thinks of herself as the social equal of the doctor, she is reminded in her encounters with him, both on the phone and in person, that in this situation she is below him on the social scale. For example, on the phone she first thinks he is soliciting a charitable contribution rather than offering her one. Then in the store their transaction—which takes place in full view of many others, including their children—is dehumanized with forms and procedures. This conflict between Gholson's self-image as an independent, competent adult and her present reality as a person dependent on charity provides the tension that permeates this essay.
3. Gholson reacts with disbelief to Warm the Children's instruction not to offer the "clients" transportation because it completely undermines her efforts to retain her dignity as a human being, wipes out her individuality, and destroys her pretense that this is an ordinary social interchange. It is the detail that forces her to acknowledge the painfulness of her situation.
4. The title "Charity Display?" has a question mark to reflect Gholson's own uncertainty about the doctor's motive in participating in Warm the Children. She expresses this in paragraph 12, where she indicates she suspects the doctor may have been using her as an example to make his son Jack grateful for his material comfort or to personalize the idea of poverty, but she also concedes he may simply have had his son with him for other reasons. Whatever the reason, Jack's presence made Gholson feel as if she were on display—"scrutinized." The title also raises the larger question, which Gholson does not explore, of whether charity should be extended anonymously to prevent the giver from feeling superior and the receiver from feeling inferior.
5. *humiliation* (3): the feeling of being reduced to a lower position; mortification
    expedite (4): to speed up
    lanky (8): tall and thin

facilitate (10): to make easier
polarized (12): broken up into opposing groups
scrutinized (12): examined closely

Questions About the Writer's Craft (p. 153)

1. Gholson organizes this narrative chronologically, beginning with a telephone call from the doctor. In paragraph 4, the transitional phrase "The night before we were to meet" indicates the next time frame in the action, the evening before the shopping trip. In paragraph 5, the action progresses to "in the morning." The passage of time in the store is indicated by phrases such as "While we waited" (7), "When the doctor arrived" (8), "Once we were in line" (9), "occasionally" (9), and "after the manager" (11). Finally, the essay winds up "Back at home" (12).

2. The descriptions of Gholson's sons add vivid details to the essay, helping to bring them to life and to underscore Gholson's difficulties as their mother in a trying situation. For example, in paragraph 2, Gholson says, "I was shoving pants onto my son Gabriel, who never wants to get dressed." In the next paragraph she relates that "Gabriel took off his pants and ran away." In paragraph 5 the "boys jumped in puddles, soaking themselves to the waist. With mud." She describes seven-year-old Sammy as a stoic, "who never complains, just sitting bleary-eyed in the cart, tolerating his boredom." In paragraph 11, while the whole line at the cash register waits for the complicated transaction to take place, her children continue to draw attention: "[M]y boys...pestered me for some water and got way too close to the doctor." These descriptions help the reader picture the scenes as the narrative develops. Furthermore, all these descriptions underscore the fact that Gholson's resources were stretched so thin that she couldn't even leave the boys home with a babysitter in order to make the clothes-buying expedition go more smoothly.

3. Although the sections in which Gholson tells her thoughts tend to slow the pace of the narrative, they are essential for expressing the tension between Gholson's thoughts and feelings and the experience she was undergoing as the object of charity. Being privy to Gholson's thoughts is necessary for the reader to understand the conflict at the heart of the essay and the thesis. Without them, there would be no tension—the narrative would simply recount events.

4. The dialogue in this essay contributes to its realistic feel, similarly to the way the descriptions of the boys contribute to a full and rich picture of events. It also punctuates the narrative, changing the rhythm and making the writing more interesting. For example, in paragraph 1, Gholson doesn't simply say that she interrupted the doctor on the phone, she demonstrates this through the dialogue: "'Look,' I interrupted, 'I don't have any money to give you. . . .'" The dialogue also gives Gholson the opportunity to present other "characters" in this piece in their own words. For example, the store employee is kind and helpful ("I bet she put it all back"; paragraph 6), and Gholson's friend provides another point of view on Gholson's experience ("You are under an incredible amount of stress; I hardly remember my divorce"; paragraph 13).

SALVATION

Langston Hughes

Questions for Close Reading (p. 157)

1. The thesis in this selection is implied. You could state it this way: "As a boy, Langston Hughes pretended to be saved and lost his faith at the same time." Another way of expressing it is this: "Religious fervor sometimes leads to religious hypocrisy and disillusionment."

2. There are many pressures on the young Hughes. He is the last child left on the "mourner's bench," the only one left unsaved, and he suffers shame (11) and guilt. His aunt, the minister, and the whole congregation pray for him "in a mighty wail" (7) and beg him to be saved. He feels the pressure of time passing (11) and that of the heat as well (6). Finally, Wesley invites him to join in a deception and gives him an example of a person who pretends to be saved without suffering any vengeance from God; Langston comes to understand that perhaps the only way to be saved is to pretend.

3. Wesley does not seem to be a believer, for he chooses deception without any qualms. On the other hand, Langston believes what his aunt has told him about salvation: you see a light, and Jesus comes into your life. Langston is patient and trusting, while Wesley is cocky and profane.

4. Auntie Reed sees only what she wants to see; hearing him crying in his bed the night of the revival, she believes he is emotionally overwhelmed by his religious conversion. She fully accepts the values of her church and takes the external event of walking from the mourners' bench to the altar as proof of salvation. She does not seem to have any understanding of psychology at all. If her nephew told her the truth of his experience in the church, one of two things would probably happen: he would convince her that he is a sinner because he had lied in church, or he would cause her to lose her faith as he has lost his.

5. *revival* (1): a meeting for the purpose of reawakening religious faith
   knickerbockered (11): dressed in knickerbockers, full pants gathered below the knee
   punctuated (14): emphasized, accentuated
   ecstatic (14): rapturously joyful and excited

Questions About the Writer's Craft (p. 157)

1. Hughes creates suspense by drawing out the description of his turmoil as the lone unsaved sinner for almost one-third of the essay (6–11). By this point, we already know the expectations his aunt and the preacher have for him, and he begins the portrayal of his shame by introducing the possibility of deception: Wesley's false salvation (6). We wonder throughout the next five paragraphs whether Langston will hold his ground, be saved, or lie. Another technique that increases the suspense is the use of very specific details about how he was pressured. He tells us the imagery of the songs sung the night of the children's meeting (3, 4). Also, he uses dialogue to show Wesley's irreverent invitation and to present the scene of the minister passionately calling him to the altar.

2. Because he has the role model of Wesley's sacrilege, the narrator understands that lying is a safe option for him to choose. Wesley, in a sense, is his "salvation" from the shame of not being saved. Wesley also serves as a foil to Langston; by contrast, Langston's honest and trusting nature is all the more apparent. Learning that Wesley

is proud about his deception, we can feel more strongly the poignancy of Langston's bitter tears.

3. "The whole room broke into a *sea* of shouting," Hughes writes, and "*waves* of rejoicing" filled the church. Through this metaphor, he portrays the unified and overwhelming force of the congregation as it engulfs the last converted sinner. The image also suggests Langston is helpless and even drowning in the religious ecstasy around him.

4. The hymns sung at the children's revival meeting take on a personal meaning for the young Langston. We are told, for example, that one song is about a hundred lambs, of which ninety-nine are saved and one is left out in the cold (2). A second hymn provides an image of hell ("the lower lights are a burning") to motivate "poor sinners" to be saved. The songs thus threaten the boy with the torments of cold and fire unless he comes to Jesus.

THE PRICE WE PAY

Adam Mayblum

Questions for Close Reading (p. 164)

1. Mayblum's narrative point is that democracy is stronger than terrorism: "If you want to make us stronger, attack and we unite. This is the ultimate failure of terrorism against the United States" (12). Alternatively, some students might rephrase the narrative point along these lines: "Despite the chaos and horror wreaked by the September 11 terrorist attacks, people in the Towers united in their attempt to help each other survive."

2. The main conflict is between people and a life-or-death crisis: getting out of a building that has been struck by an airplane.

3. Mayblum says he is writing so that he and others never will forget what happened (1). His expressions of grief, anger, and guilt suggest that he also is writing to help himself cope with these feelings. In addition, he might be writing to clear up his own confusion about the events of that day.

4. Mayblum refers to the destruction, injuries, and deaths at the World Trade Center as the "price we pay to be free" (12). In other words, the freedoms that Americans enjoy—and, presumably, the dominant international role the United States has assumed as a result of those freedoms—put the country at risk of evoking opposition epitomized by the terrorist attack on September 11.

    Answers to the second question may vary. Some students may agree with Mayblum's analysis, which is optimistic and resilient in nature. Others might disagree, arguing that terrorists wish to kill Americans not because Americans enjoy many individual liberties but because they feel U.S. foreign policy is imperialistic, exploitative, and supportive of oppressive governments.

5. *aka* (2): an abbreviation for "also known as"
    lurched (2): moved suddenly and roughly
    reams (2): large amount
    ticker-tape (2): paper strips released into the air in celebration
    succumbed (3): fallen victim to
    junction (3): place of connection
    ushered (3): led
    retrospect (3): hindsight

nuclear winter (9): life-destroying environmental darkening and cooling caused by nuclear explosion

fallout (9): descending radioactive particles caused by nuclear explosion

debris (9): scattered pieces of something that has been destroyed

engulfed (10): swallowed up

commotion (12): disturbance, confusion

gypsy cab (12): a car for hire, similar to a taxi

Questions About the Writer's Craft (p. 164)

1. While answers may vary regarding the effect of the present tense in the essay, here are some possibilities. Mayblum's present-tense frame (1, 12) makes the opening and the conclusion more immediate and helps readers to identify with the author and his harrowing experiences. Throughout the essay, the present tense adds impact where it breaks chronological order to indicate that a particular person may have died, as in "I do not know what happened to her" (8) and "Pray for him and all those like him" (11). However, where the present tense halts the action for an insignificant statement, it can be seen as diffusing tension and slowing the pace. For example, the statement "Seventy-eight is the main junction to switch to the upper floors" (3) lacks importance and therefore could have been deemphasized. Similarly, instead of removing readers from the time of the attack by stating "In retrospect, I recall seeing Harry" (3), Mayblum could have written simply "I saw Harry." The sentences "I am only thirty-five. I have known him for over fourteen years" (3) would have been less distracting and more effective later in the essay, where Mayblum makes the important statement "I fear that Harry is lost" (11).
2. Sentence fragments and short sentences help to convey the situation's urgency, fragmentation, and sharp impact. Like sentence fragments, the absence of quotation marks also contributes a sense of urgency—as if no time or thought can be wasted on formal correctness.
3. *We* and *our* highlight the unity and cooperation that prevailed at the World Trade Center, underscoring Mayblum's theme that Americans will unite if attacked.
4. Answers will vary. Some students may say these examples represent the comforts and pleasures of life in America. Others, in contrast, may find them problematic since all three examples apply only to privileged Americans. Many Americans cannot find work, let alone decide where they want to work. Many lack adequate food, let alone the option of eating whatever they want. And many either do not take vacations or must take their vacations when their employers permit it. One might argue that more universal and significant examples—such as freedom of speech, freedom from torture, and freedom from imprisonment without due process—would have conveyed Mayblum's point more effectively.

EXEMPLIFICATION

OPENING COMMENTS

When we first started teaching, we were caught off guard by students' seeming inability to provide detailed, specific examples in their papers. But we soon uncovered one reason for the vagueness of their writing. Many of them arrived in college with the notion that good writing is abstract and full of highfalutin language. Warned by dutiful high school English teachers not to pad their papers, many students had come to regard specific details and "for instances" as fluff.

We've found an almost sure-fire way to help students appreciate how powerfully examples can affect a reader. We have them react (see p. 171 in the LR) to two versions of some student writing—one flat, lifeless, and sorely in need of supporting details; the other enlivened with specifics. When we question students about their reactions ("Which version is more interesting?" "Which gives you more of a sense of the writer?"), we actually see them coming to grasp the full importance of vigorous supporting detail.

Next, we spend some class time on prewriting activities. These help students learn how to generate examples for their essays.

That skill mastered, some of our eager-to-please students then give us too much of a good thing. Heaping their papers high with examples, they force readers to wade through a mass of specifics that don't lead anywhere. When this happens, we emphasize that writers need to be selective and choose the most striking examples to support a point.

Varied in subject and mood, the professional selections in this chapter illustrate the power that writing derives from rich supporting detail. Beginning with a dramatic opening illustration, Sykes then uses a variety of example types to reveal a generation headed for trouble. Savan enlivens her essay with numerous examples for each point she makes about how "black talk" has not only infiltrated, but *dominated* pop culture. By piling on instances of how preteens are encouraged to mature too soon, Hymowitz provides a convincing case that the "tween" phenomenon has come to dominate youth culture. Johnson, through a series of poignant personal experience examples, illustrates the precarious nature of the human condition. Finally, Ehrenreich's comical discussion of men's interpersonal talents dramatizes the value of selectivity, of finding just the right specifics.

ANSWERS FOR PREWRITING ACTIVITIES

Below we provide possible responses to selected prewriting activities at the end of Chapter 5. Of course, your students are bound to come up with their own approaches. (p. 182)

1. There are many ways to use exemplification in these two essays; the lists below only begin to name the possibilities. We suggest that you have students share their ideas for examples, perhaps with a partner or in small groups. Seeing what others have come up with clearly makes the point that writing involves invention and individuality.

Topic: Why public school teachers quit
    Teacher who has to work a second job to support family
    Ex-teacher now a mail carrier, better paid
    Science teacher recruited by industry
    Teacher resenting blame and criticism of education today
    Teacher toiling late at night over tests and lesson plans

Topic: Defining a preppie
    Female wearing pearls with baggy shorts on a chilly day
    Male wearing rugby striped shirt with a crest and loafers
    Preppies' conversation centering on grades and careers
    Preppie male going out for crew or tennis
    Preppie female playing intramural lacrosse or field hockey

ANSWERS FOR REVISING ACTIVITIES

Below we provide possible responses to selected revising activities at the end of Chapter 5. Of course, your students are bound to come up with their own approaches. (p. 183)

We suggest you offer students the chance to read each other's reworked versions of the paragraphs in activities 3 and 4. Such exposure to others' work helps them to see new ways of handling the revision and can encourage them to be more creative.

3.   Here are the main problems with the paragraph:

— Needs examples of how stores might be modernized—new signs, more professional window display, interior renovation.
— Nature of the improvements to streets should be shown by examples—potted plants, outdoor sculptures, decorative benches, outdoor cafes.
— Examples needed of how town could be made more "fun to walk."
— Examples of the "attention-getting events" should be provided.

4.   Here are the main problems with the paragraph:

— Vague descriptions ("trendy," "fine") need replacement by vigorous images. A strong example or two are needed here.
— Point about trendy clothes should be tied in to the idea of the costliness.
— Singling out women is sexist; at the very least such a charge needs supporting examples. Indeed, more thought may well show that men are similarly vulnerable.
— Shampoo example should occur at the end of the paragraph, because the movement of the paragraph is from things that don't wear out to things that do wear out. Change the opening words of the sentence to fit it into its new location.
— "Slight changes" is vague; an example is necessary.
— Statement that men are "naive" and are "hoodwinked" is sexist and irrelevant; this point also needs to be more clearly tied in to the point that the desire for the new is costly to the consumer.

THE "VALUES" WASTELAND

Charles Sykes

Questions for Close Reading (p. 191)

1. Sykes's thesis is that the American educational system is not providing students with firm guidelines to help them make moral choices. This thesis is stated directly in paragraph 3 ("A 1992 survey by the Josephson Institute for Ethics of nearly 7,000 high school and college students, most of them from middle- and upper middle-class backgrounds, found the equivalent of 'a hole in the moral ozone' among America's youth") and reiterated elsewhere in the essay: "'I think it is very easy to get through high school and college these days and hardly ever hear, *"That's wrong,'* . . ."* (4); "'Their IDI-ology is exceptionally and dangerously self-centered, preoccupied with personal needs, wants, don't-wants and rights'" (4); "In pursuit of success, or comfort, or self-gratification, the IDI's are blithely willing to jettison traditional ethical restraints, and as a result IDIs are more likely to lie, cheat and engage in irresponsible behavior when it suits their purposes" (4); and "In its place [of moral role models], we provide children a jumbled smorgasbord of moral choices" (5).
2. "At one time," Sykes writes in paragraph 5, "American students used to study historical role models like Benjamin Franklin, Florence Nightingale, Thomas Edison, Madame Curie, Abraham Lincoln, and George Washington—whose stories were used to provide object lessons in inventiveness, character, compassion, curiosity, and truthfulness." Modern education, however, allows students to choose their own values and refuses to teach them that some values are more important, or moral, than others. Sykes maintains that in a misguided fear of "moralizing" and in an attempt to allow students freedom to work out their own value systems, modern educators have failed to give students the ability to distinguish right from wrong and serious moral questions from trivial ones.
3. Sykes feels that educational theorists are responsible for the imposition of this ineffective and amoral system. Specifically, he singles out "developers of Values Clarification and other nonjudgmental approaches to moral decision making" (9) who have imposed upon schools an educational philosophy dedicated to promoting the concept of "individual identity." Central to the development of this identity, such theorists argue, is students' freedom to choose what sort of morality they wish to adopt. To teach that honesty, charity, or patriotism are *a priori* virtues would, according to these theorists, deprive students of the essential opportunity to work out their values for themselves.
4. The object of each exercise is to encourage students to develop their own value systems by examining a situation requiring them to make a moral choice. In both cases, students are presented with a narrative involving a life-and-death situation in which they are required to make a decision about the value of human life, and in both they are asked to recognize the importance of certain human virtues in preserving life. But in the case of the survivors in the cave (15), students are invited to assert the value of their own lives as opposed to—or at the expense of—other people's. Significantly, the exercise does not suggest that opting to be last in line may be the most moral choice. In the exercise positing moral choice in a lifeboat (18), students are asked to judge the value of human vs. animal life, regardless of how cherished that animal life may be.

    Theoretically, there is no "right" answer in the cave situation, and coming to a "successful" result hinges on each student's ability to describe his or her worthiness to classmates. In the lifeboat exercise, however, there clearly is a "right" choice, although instructors may or may not choose to emphasize it, and students are not inclined to condemn classmates who choose "wrongly."

Sykes faults both exercises. They fail to emphasize that "there might be universal and objective moral principles at stake" (18), and they invite children to make moral choices without ultimately indicating which of those choices are morally superior. Interestingly, both situations, although theoretically possible, are essentially artificial—far removed from and not realistic for most students. Asking students what they would do if trapped in a cave or in a lifeboat may not produce more realistic responses than asking children what they would do if they found a genie trapped in a bottle.

5. *unrepentant* (1): feeling no regret for what one has done (or failed to do)
    self-actualization (4): to develop or achieve one's full potential
    precept (5): a rule or principle prescribing a particular course of action or conduct
    emulate (5): to strive to equal or excel, especially through imitation
    perseverance (5): steady persistence in adhering to a course of action
    smorgasbord (5): a varied collection
    bête noire (9): one that is particularly disliked
    moralizing (9): expressing moral judgments or reflections
    cognitive (10): related to the faculty of knowing
    rationalization (14): devising self-satisfying but incorrect reasons for (one's behavior)
    fraught (17): filled or loaded with something (usually something bad)

Questions About the Writer's Craft (p. 191)

1. The opening example of the unrepentant rapist is effective for several reasons. It is vivid, shocking, and graphic—important qualities in any introductory paragraph for drawing readers into the essay. Further, it provides a dramatic personalization of the issues discussed in the essay. Like a "dolly-in" in cinematography, the essay focuses on the Spur Posse member and lets him speak for himself: "'They pass out condoms, teach sex education and pregnancy this and pregnancy that. . . . But they don't teach us any rules.'"

    This opening example is the only one in the essay that establishes a link between student misbehavior and an educational philosophy that fails to teach morality. The examples in the second and third paragraphs (the Rhode Island study reporting on young people's high tolerance for sexual aggression and the write-in survey and Josephson Institute survey indicating that a high percentage of adolescents cheat, steal, shoplift, and so on) simply raise disturbing questions about the morality of America's youth. Unlike the first example, these examples don't posit a connection between schooling and behavior. However, Sykes obviously intends these examples of immoral behavior to shock readers. As such, they pave the way to his argument that values-free education is a poor way to direct young people toward moral behavior.

2. For some classes, it may be sufficient to discuss the ironic and dramatic effect of yoking together two apparently contradictory terms. We notice that the word "Values" in the title is in quotation marks, a standard way of indicating that a word is being used in a special sense, often sarcastically, as it is here. The word *value* implies an exalted absolute, but this "values clarification," according to Sykes, has produced students with no values at all, or none worthwhile—that is, a wasteland. The dramatic juxtaposition of the two concepts catches our attention, as it does in terms like "Christian soldiers" or "tough love." More advanced classes might benefit

from mention of the importance to modern literature of T.S. Eliot's *The Wasteland*. Such a comment would throw further light on the modern concept of "The Wasteland" as a symbolic burial ground of absolute values.

3. Sykes peppers his essay with statistics in paragraph 2 and 3 and makes little use of them thereafter. These statistics, like the strong opening description of the Spur Posse rapist, provide a powerful introductory statement on which the author—and the reader—can chew for the rest of the essay. Moreover, statistics generally seem impressive, particularly to readers concerned about "scientific method" and the supposedly objective nature of truth. By citing numbers—2,000 Rhode Island students, 126,000 teenagers, "more than 60 percent of high school students," etc.— Sykes gives his essay a tone of factuality and objectivity. However, students should not be too willing to accept Sykes's statistics just because they represent numbers rather than words; neither should we dismiss them for the same reason. Much educational theory is framed in vague abstractions and lofty theorizing without many facts (or statistics) to back them up. It is refreshing to find an educational commentator who—instead of offering generalities like "Student morality is on the decline"—reports survey results indicating that a third of high school students shoplift or sixty percent cheat on exams.

4. This is a serious essay on a serious subject. "Youth is going to hell and denying the virtues of its parents and ancestors" has been a common theme in prophetic literature since biblical times. Sykes's commentary shares in this tradition of gloom with an almost prophetic tone of warning and despair. The darkness of Sykes's tone serves to underscore the severity of the problem.

BLACK TALK AND POP CULTURE

Leslie Savan

Questions for Close Reading (p. 200)

1. Savan states her thesis in paragraph 13: "Today, the language of an excluded people [Black talk] is repeated by the nonexcluded [mainstream media and whites] in order to make themselves sound more included."

2. By "pop language" and "pop talk," Savan means the American English of popular culture and the media, especially the words and phrases that are freighted with associations. Examples of pop talk are "slam dunk," "you know what I'm saying?" and "in your face."

3. Savan considers that the Black talk word *cool* is the most emblematic pop word of all time because it expresses the "cool stance that underlies pop culture itself." According to Savan, "pop culture's desire for cool is second only to its desire for money" (9).

4. Savan thinks that the white culture's borrowing of Black talk is selective, a way to appear cool without actually experiencing the full range of blackness, which includes aspects whites do not want to experience (discrimination, for example). In particular, since Black talk originated in slavery, it carries overtones of oppression and guilt, as well as identity and style (32). Another aspect of the use of Black talk that can be exploitative is in marketing products to mainstream Americans. However, Black talk in marketing can also be viewed as progress of a sort, according to Savan, since in the past, companies did not want to associate their products with African Americans at all (15).

5. *vernacular* (1): the normal spoken form of a language
   lexicon (6): the vocabulary of a language
   per se (8): as such
   preeminent (9): outstanding
   template (10): something that serves as a pattern
   catchphrase (12): a popular expression
   minstrel shows (14): performances of Black American jokes, music, and routines, often by players wearing blackface makeup
   loath (15): reluctant
   lucrative (18): profitable
   nexus (18): center; focus
   verisimilitude (19): realism
   colloquial (25): conversational
   spurious (27): false
   argot (28): secret vocabulary of a group

Questions About the Writer's Craft (p. 200)

1. Savan lists so many examples of Black talk in order to support her claim that Black talk has permeated modern American pop language (6). By listing and discussing so many words and phrases, she demonstrates that Black talk has infiltrated American English to a degree of which most people are not even aware. Some of these words and phrases are so commonplace that their origin has been obscured: *24/7, lame, in your face* (7). The purpose of the extended examples is to show the mechanisms of how Black talk makes its way into the mainstream. For example, in paragraphs 18–21, Savan discusses the Sprite marketing campaign that used rappers. Sometimes the Black talk's meaning or usage changes after it crosses over. For example, the word *wannabe* first applied to Blacks who wanted to be white, but then its meaning was generalized to apply to people who want to be something that they are not, and was reversed to mean whites who want to be Black (29, 30).
2. In paragraphs 14 through 21, Savan discusses examples of Black talk and Black culture in marketing in chronological order. In this way, she provides historical background for present usages, showing that white society began by making fun of Black talk in minstrel shows and gradually came to appropriate Black talk in order to sell products, to the extent that today the association of cool Black talk and cultural icons (such as hip-hop) with a product is a major marketing strategy.
3. Although Savan has been describing Black talk and providing many examples, she feels the need to "pause" to clarify her use of terms in this section. Savan takes issue with the various terms used to describe Black talk, which she seeks to define. For example, the term "black slang" is too narrow, because most Black language is standard English. "Black English," "black dialect," and "African American vernacular" are all problematic because they suggest that there is only one variety of English that all Blacks speak, which is not the case. "Ebonics" became too politicized during the late 1990s. Thus Savan favors "black talk" because she considers the term flexible and colloquial, covering more than slang vocabulary. This section demonstrates that Savan has done her research on this topic, but overall, it has the effect of a digression. It could be deleted, and deleting it would not affect the main thesis of the essay at all.
4. *Advertising:* There are several examples of this in the essay, including ads for Buick, BMW, the NBA, and Sprite. The Buick ad used a phrase, "It's all good," from rap; the BMW ad used an interracial couple; the NBA used a phrase from M.C. Hammer's song "It's All Good"; and the Sprite ads featured rappers.

48

MTV: The MTV examples are discussed in paragraph 17 and include the first appearances of Black music videos (Prince and Michael Jackson) and the 1989 debut of *Yo! MTV Raps,* which featured rap videos. MTV thus uses Black music to sell products to its predominantly white suburban audience. Savan's point here is that music videos themselves are advertisements, so the inclusion of Black artists shows how Black culture is moving into the youth advertising mainstream.

Internet: BlackPeopleLoveUs.com presents a fictitious white couple who play at being Black, showing the wide appeal of Black talk and culture among whites (30).

Savan chose these examples because they show Black language or culture being used by various mainstream media in order that some Black "cool" would become associated with the products being sold. Without such specific examples, Savan's essays would be full of claims that she could not substantiate.

TWEENS: TEN GOING ON SIXTEEN

Kay S. Hymowitz

Questions for Close Reading (p. 206)

1. Hymowitz doesn't directly state her thesis. Instead she quotes others stating it: "There is no such thing as preadolescence anymore. Kids are teenagers at ten" (3); "There's a deep trend . . . toward kids getting older younger" (6); "The 12- to 14-year-olds of yesterday are the ten to 12s of today" (6).
2. Tweens like to think of themselves as sophisticated: "flirtatious, sexy, trendy, athletic, cool" (7). Girls project this image by wearing body adornment such as makeup or earrings, attention-getting hairdos, and trendy, often sexually suggestive clothes. Comparably, boys exemplify tweendom in an increased concern with fashion, especially pricey designer wear, as well as in other aspects of personal appearance, such as piercings and ultra-modern hairstyles.
3. A growing number of children under the age of fifteen are committing violent crimes (12); engaging in sexual activity (13–14); using alcohol and drugs, especially marijuana (15); and developing eating disorders (16).
4. She attributes the tween phenomenon primarily to parental absence and "a sexualized and glitzy" marketplace (18). These two factors, in turn, elevate the authority and influence of the tweens' peer group, which results in a vicious circle of negative influences. Another cause that Hymowitz addresses but seems to regard as secondary is the earlier physical maturation of kids today than in the past (17).
5. *glowering* (1): staring with an angry look
   Talmudic (1): relating to a particular collection of ancient Jewish religious writings
   rites (1): religious ceremonial acts
   demographic (3): relating to population trends
   pragmatic (5): practical
   ideological (5): relating to a body of beliefs
   regalia (8): finery
   donning (8): putting on
   ply (8): to participate in
   emblazoned (10): prominently marked
   de rigueur (10): required
   eschewing (11): rejecting
   tentative (14): hesitant

proclivities (14): inclinations
connotations (14): suggested meanings
stigma (15): mark of disgrace
pernicious (16): harmful
correlation (17): co-occurrence, correspondence
augment (18): to increase

Questions About the Writer's Craft (p. 205)

1. The personal nature of this example draws the reader's interest, as do the variety of specific examples Hymowitz presents to illustrate her point. In addition, this anecdote gains Hymowitz credibility in discussing the topic of tweens because it establishes her own personal experience with the phenomenon.
2. Hymowitz draws from a broad spectrum of examples in her essay. She cites specific names, such as of celebrities and retail stores (1, 8), in presenting the kinds of tween preoccupations. Personal anecdotes play an important role; the essay opens with the vivid example of Hymowitz's own daughter (1) and goes on to cite anecdotes from others, such as the fifth-grade Ohio teacher who caught two students in the bushes (14). These anecdotes reinforce the pervasive nature of the tween phenomenon while also demonstrating the author's personal experience with it. Another category of examples that Hymowitz marshals is that of expert opinion. She cites numerous educators and psychologists about the alarming behaviors of tweens (3, 6–9, 13, 15–16)—her thesis is even conveyed in the words of these experts. These citations compellingly establish and explain the tween problem. In the same vein, she cites studies and statistics (4, 6, 7, 12, 13, 15, 17) to help define tweendom and, more significantly, to demonstrate the alarming ramifications of tween behaviors.
3. Hymowitz's tone is concerned and disapproving, somewhat bitter, and sometimes mocking or sarcastic. For example, she dismissively states that her daughter reads movie ads "with all the intensity of a Talmudic scholar" (1). Hymowitz renders the word "empowered" ironical by placing it in quotation marks (5) and sarcastically says that students "showed their respect" by dressing like prostitutes (8). Strongly negative terms such as *vulgar* (5), *crass* (5), *hooker* (9), *painted* (9), and *pernicious* (16) clearly convey Hymowitz's disapproval.
4. In these paragraphs, Hymowitz use female clothing as a way of contrasting the preteens of earlier generations with today's tweens. She demonstrates the gap between the childish, modest clothing such as "little-girl flowers, ruffles, white socks, and Mary Janes" (8) worn in the past and the less-modest or sexually provocative clothing such as tank tops (9), black mini-dresses (8), platform shoes (8), "midriff-revealing shirts" (8), and mini-skirts (8) worn by comparably aged girls today.

BOMBS BURSTING IN AIR

Beth Johnson

Questions for Close Reading (p. 212)

1. The thesis is stated through a metaphor at the very end of the essay: "[Bombs] can blind us, like fireworks at the moment of explosion. . . . But if we have the courage to keep our eyes open and welcoming, even bombs finally fade against the vastness

of the starry sky" (15). In other words, life's unexpected tragedies can seem devastating and insurmountable when they occur; but we must courageously live on, recognizing that even these misfortunes are part of life's greater mystery and beauty.

2. Johnson states directly, "News that reached me today makes me need to feel her [Maddie] near" (2), referring to the revelation that Maddie's five-year-old playmate, Shannon, was unexpectedly diagnosed with a brain tumor. This jarring discovery reminds Johnson of the fragility of life and the randomness of misfortune, for Maddie could just as easily have been the one stricken with the tumor. Compelled by the maternal impulse to protect her child from impending harm, Johnson draws Maddie near. Though Johnson knows she has no power over the bombs that might explode in life, she feels slightly more secure having her daughter nearby.

3. The reactions of Maddie, Sam, and Johnson to the news of Shannon's illness provide a snapshot of the process of evolving maturity. Only five years old, Maddie fails to understand the gravity of Shannon's condition, and she is too young to be "faze[d]" by bombs in general (8). Johnson sees her younger self in Maddie, recalling her own "childhood . . . feeling of being cocooned within reassuring walls of security and order" (8). Maddie declares her certainty that Shannon "will be okay," having learned in school about a boy who recovered from an illness (5, 7). Maddie's confidence in Shannon's recovery and her willingness to change the subject—"Can we go to Dairy Queen?" (7)—contrast with the response of thirteen-year-old Sam, who is "not so easily distracted" (6). Perched between childhood and adulthood, Sam is aware of how serious Shannon's condition is, yet he still seeks his mother's guarantee that the child will recover: "She'll be okay, though, right?" (6). Just like his mother in her adolescence, Sam struggles as "the protective curtain between us and the bombs" (10) is slowly being drawn away from him.

   Finally, Johnson represents the adult stage of awareness, for she is most shaken by the news and is least confident that a happy ending is in sight. This essay itself serves as a testament to how much the news has affected her, for Shannon's "bomb" has inspired Johnson to reflect on life's bombs in general. Having lived through numerous occasions when very bad things have happened to very good people, Johnson lacks any illusions about life's fairness. During Johnson's adolescence, the sudden death of her best friend taught Johnson a life-changing lesson: "[T]here was no magic barrier separating me and my loved ones from the bombs. We were as vulnerable as everyone else" (11). Because the friend died in her sleep without contributing to her own demise in any way, Johnson as a teenager was forced to realize that no rules of logic or fairness govern the bursting of bombs. Nevertheless, as an adult, she demonstrates the need for comfort that characterizes children; she draws her child close to her and takes solace in the conclusion that despite the bombs that potentially may burst, life must be lived and people must be loved.

4. Given the knowledge that "the greater our investment in life, the larger the target we create" for life-bombs, individuals may respond in one of two ways. One option is to withdraw from life and scale back commitments to others, reducing the potential for pain and loss. In Johnson's words, we may "refuse friendship, shrink from love, live in isolation, and thus create for ourselves a nearly impenetrable bomb shelter" (13). The other option is to immerse ourselves in life, willing to brave potential bombs in order to experience life's joys and beauties, "to truly live, to love and be loved" (13). Johnson advocates the latter path, and she marvels at the resilience of the human spirit, which inspires people to live on: "I am moved by the courage with which most of us, ordinary folks, continue soldiering on. We fall in love, we bring our children into the world, we forge our friendships, we give our hearts, knowing with increasing certainty that we do so at our own risk" (13). Those who isolate themselves from life,

she implies, lose far more in the end than those who say "yes, yes to life" and only periodically suffer.

5. *ferrying* (4): transporting
   shrapnel (6): fragments from exploded artillery
   faze (8): disturb; disconcert
   cocooned (8): sheltered; protected
   tremors (9): vibrations
   incantations (10): charms or spells ritually recited
   vulnerable (11): susceptible to harm or injury
   intertwining (12): joined together; interrelated
   impenetrable (13): unable to be entered or understood
   soldiering on (13): bravely moving forward
   prognosis (14): predicted outcome of a disease
   fragility (14): state of being breakable

Questions About the Writer's Craft (p. 213)

1. The first example that Johnson emphasizes—and the one that frames her essay—is the anecdote about Shannon. (Johnson ponders the sad news about Shannon's illness and then delivers the news to her children.) This incident receives so much attention for several reasons. It reminds Johnson of how fragile life is, how randomly calamity strikes, and, therefore, how easily one of her own children could have been the target of a "bomb" like the one that hit Shannon. This news then triggers a series of memories about tragedies that Johnson witnessed in the past and jars her into meditating on the occurrence of misfortune in general.

   These memories are ordered chronologically, beginning with incidents in Johnson's youth that affected her least and progressing to events in her adolescence and adulthood that affected her the most. In paragraph 9, she briefly catalogues "tiny shockwaves"—incidents that were peripheral to her life. She does not describe these memories in great detail because, as she admits, she was unaware of the gravity of these incidents as a child and young adolescent. In paragraph 10, however, she says, "As we got older, the bombs dropped closer." She goes on to catalogue more harrowing events, ones that were closer to her life, such as a peer's suicide and the deaths of a carful of acquaintances. Yet, she says, "we still had some sense of a protective curtain between us and the bombs." But in paragraph 11, Johnson describes the single most destructive bomb, the one that changed her life. Here she develops at great length the example of her best friend's sudden death at the age of sixteen. She focuses on this crisis because of her degree of intimacy with this friend (as opposed to earlier acquaintances) and because this tragedy marked a turning point for Johnson, a rite of passage from innocent childhood into knowing maturity. After this event, she "found [herself] shaken to the core of [her] being" (11), more worldly-wise and less secure in the world around her. Johnson then quickly catalogues bombs that dropped in her late-adolescent and adult life. She does not focus special attention on them because, as an adult, she was more equipped to handle the barrage of misfortune that she witnessed—secondhand, in one instance (her professor's loss of two children), and firsthand, in others (the pain of love, the failure of her marriage, and the death of her father). She says, "I became more aware of the intertwining threads of joy, pain, and occasional tragedy that weave through all our lives" (12); as a result, she came to regard misfortune as part of life's cycle and was not as rattled when it ran its course.

2. In paragraph 6, Johnson contrasts how she wishes life could be with how life actually is. She begins by describing a more ideal world, signaled by a series of sentences

beginning "I want." She wishes she could, in all honesty, assure her son that Shannon will be fine; that her children could "inhabit a world where five-year-olds do not develop silent, mysterious growths in their brains" to begin with; that the medical terms being applied to Shannon were "words for *New York Times* crossword puzzles, not for little girls" (6). However, this fantasy is cut short by the blunt, bleak admission "But I can't," followed by her reason for abandoning illusions: "the bomb that exploded in Shannon's home has sent splinters of shrapnel into ours as well, and they cannot be ignored or lied away" (6). This stark contrast between wish and reality supports Johnson's main idea that in life, we have no control over when and where bombs will drop; all we can do is live fully and love each other in order to weather life's inevitable misfortunes.

3. Johnson uses repetition in these two paragraphs, usually to emphasize magnitude and/or quantity. In paragraph 9, the similarly structured "*There was the* little girl who . . . ," "*There was the* big girl who . . . ," and then "*A* playful friendly custodian . . . ," and "*A* teacher's husband . . ." appear consecutively as Johnson itemizes the different people affected by bombs in her youth. The repetitive syntax emphasizes the number of bomb victims while also demonstrating how a wide range of people were equally vulnerable. Johnson employs repetition for the same reason at the beginning of paragraph 10, where she again itemizes bomb victims: "*A* friend's sister . . . ," "*A* boy I thought I knew . . . ," "*A* car full of senior boys. . . ." Later in the same paragraph, she reiterates "if only" four times to illustrate how she and her peers were powerless in the face of such tragedy, left only to repeat the same futile phrase over and over again.

4. The title, "Bombs Bursting in Air," introduces the central image of bombs, an image that reverberates throughout the essay. The title is derived from the line in "The Star-Spangled Banner" sung expressively by Johnson's daughter, Maddie, at the athletic event that opens the essay (2). Maddie's lively emphasis on the *b*'s triggers a series of painful reflections for the author, who is still reeling from the devastating news about young Shannon's brain tumor. Johnson comes to refer to such unanticipated tragedies in life as "bombs," which burst in air—and in life—without warning and with lasting effect. She goes on in the essay to delineate the impact and aftermath of bombs in her own past, using terms like "exploded" (3), "shrapnel" (6), "shockwaves," and "tremors" (9), in showing how she grew out of youthful naïveté and into painful awareness of life's dark realities. The more one opens oneself up to life and love, she observes, "the larger the target" one becomes for devastation and loss (13). Despite her dark awareness, Johnson emerges with a renewed faith in the human spirit that inspires "ordinary folks [to] continue soldiering on" (13). At the end of the essay, she says that humans are faced with a choice: we may either withdraw from life in order to avoid potential bombs, or we may courageously "keep our eyes open and welcoming," realizing that "even bombs finally fade against the vastness of the starry sky" (15).

   Overall, the metaphor of bombs is effective not only because it captures the explosive impact that life's calamities may have, but also because it is a highly accessible image for readers.

WHAT I'VE LEARNED FROM MEN

Barbara Ehrenreich

Questions for Close Reading (p. 218)

1. Ehrenreich states her thesis directly in the beginning of the second paragraph: "But now, at mid-life, I am willing to admit that there are some real and useful things to learn from men." In paragraph 2, she explains that a main useful thing is "how to get *tough.*" The rest of the essay goes about explaining the "real and useful things" in more depth. Another important statement for the reader seeking orientation to the essay's progress occurs in paragraph 4: "In conversations with men, we do almost all the work. . . . Wherever we go, we're perpetually smiling. . . . We're trained to feel embarrassed if we're praised, but if we seek a criticism coming at us from miles down the road, we rush to acknowledge it. And when we're feeling aggressive or angry or resentful, we just tighten up our smiles or turn then into rueful little moues." The essay then discusses in this order the problems with women's taking too much social responsibility and smiling too much (5–9); their dismissal of praise and embracing of criticism (10); and their weak anger (11).

2. Ehrenreich responded to his inappropriate behavior in the way she had been trained to after "30-odd years of programming in ladylikeness" (3). Although "disgusted," she remained polite and pretended not to notice his advances. Even when he put his hand on her knee, she genteelly moved it away, rather than confront him directly. Finally, he apparently made an attempt to embrace or grab her, "there was a minor scuffle," and she left. She chastises herself for this wimpy, "ladylike" behavior. At the end of the essay (12), she describes her current view of how she should have handled him. She begins by moving her chair away from his side to opposite him so that she can see his face. He chatters, but she does not respond. Instead she stares at him with arms crossed, leaning back, letting him know she feels her time is being wasted. She avoids the typical female responses of "apologetic shrugs and blushes." And then, "at the first flicker of lechery," she says, she stands and coolly rebukes him: "All right, I've had enough of this crap." Then, "slowly, deliberately, confidently," she walks out. This manner of handling him would have been confrontational and impolite, but also "tough"—a sign that she had learned an important skill from men.

3. At the end of paragraph 3, Ehrenreich equates behaving "like a lady" with behaving "like a ninny." In the next paragraph, she elaborates on this negative view of "ladylikeness." Its essence is a "persistent servility masked as 'niceness,'" she says. In other words, women play "nice," but what they are really doing is subjugating themselves to the needs and plans of others.

4. "Macho stars" appeal to women because they contrast with women's typical behavior. The male stars Ehrenreich describes are in control; they have power and use it to take care of themselves. They face down punks; they swagger; they shrug off the law. And they never use the strategies adopted by women to smooth over human relations; they do not "simper," "chatter aimlessly," or "get all clutched up." "Therein . . . lies their fascination for us," Ehrenreich concludes. She goes on to suggest ways in which women can "toughen up," citing the Jean Baker Miller article (6). She advises us to stop smiling (7), gushing, and chattering (8–9), and learn to show our anger (11).

5. *euthanasia* (1): mercifully causing the death of an incurably ill person
   guttural (1): harsh or throaty

lecherous (3): inappropriately and insistently seductive
distractingly (3): in order to divert the attention of another
unconscionable (3): excessive or unreasonable
ninny (3): a fool or simpleton
servility (4): slavish obedience
veneer (4): deceptive outward appearance
moues (4): pouts
marauders (5): raiders, plunderers
aura (6): a pervading quality surrounding a person or thing
brazenly (6): boldly, impudently
deference (9): respectfulness
taciturn (9): silent and impassive
purveyors (10): providers or sellers
emulating (11): imitating in an attempt to equal
basso profundo (11): a deep, low vocal pitch
blandishments (12): statements intended to cajole or coax

Questions About the Writer's Craft (p. 219)

1. Ehrenreich presents this personal example early in order to explain what she means by women needing to learn some new types of behavior and to persuade us that this is so. Many of the later examples in the essay are generalizations about women's behavior, so that including a personal example at the start establishes credibility for Ehrenreich's point of view. We are likely to agree that if she, a mature, convinced feminist, can lapse into this ineffective, self-destructive, incompetent behavior, then the behavior must be epidemic among women. She returns to this personal example at the end in order to show a revised version of her behavior, a version in which she is powerful and effective. This reevaluation of the experience helps us to understand what type of behavior she is recommending.
2. There are numerous contrasting examples in the essay. The introduction humorously posits Ehrenreich's own lifelong failure to get the attention of waiters with how men "can summon a maitre d' just by thinking the word 'coffee.'" The rest of the essay gives more serious contrasts between women's and men's behaviors. Paragraph 4 presents the contrast of how males and females act in conversations; paragraph 5 contrasts typical macho film-star behavior with the coping strategies women typically use. Paragraph 6 implicitly contrasts women's failure to accept and acknowledge their powerfulness with men's power; the next paragraph contrasts women's tendency to smile all the time with Clint Eastwood's two dour expressions. Paragraph 8 contrasts men's and women's conversational styles. In paragraphs 9 and 10, Ehrenreich contrasts two types of female behavior, one actual, the other possible. In 9, she contrasts women's usual perkiness and smiles with the absence of these qualities, noting that serious women's faces cause men to wonder if the women are out-of-sorts or even hostile. Then she contrasts two women's styles of taking credit (10). Paragraph 11 returns to the contrast of male and female styles, this time styles of anger. Finally, the conclusion presents Ehrenreich's fantasy of the ideal response to the lecherous professor, in contrast to her description in paragraph 4 of her actual ineptitude in that situation.
3. Ehrenreich appears to consider her audience to be primarily female. She uses "we" throughout the essay, assuming an identification by the reader. In addition, her frequent jibes at various quirks of male behavior show she isn't writing for men or even a mixed audience. Such remarks convey that she expects her readers to be at least partially sympathetic to her position. She also describes herself as "a full-grown

feminist" (3), and most likely she feels her readers will respect or even share this identity.

4. Ehrenreich's tone is definitely not "ladylike" or "nice." She frequently exaggerates in order to achieve a harsh satiric tone; she uses a blunt or smart-alecky "tough guy" tone in some places, and she clearly does not care, like the macho film stars (5), about whether she hurts people's feelings. Paragraph 1 starts the essay off with this irreverent, unladylike style. She mocks some of men's less appealing characteristics—their tendency to interrupt or perform "conversational euthanasia," their disregard of household neatness even when it could be achieved without effort, and so on. She then comes on strong and uses some unladylike phrasing to establish her thesis: "there are some real and useful things to learn from men. . . . [W]e're just too *damn* ladylike" (2). Later in the essay, she turns her satiric tone on women; she asks whether macho film heroes would "simper their way through tight spots" or "chatter aimlessly" or "get all clutched up" about possibly hurting another's feelings. In paragraph 7, she uses a smart-alecky tone to make a recommendation to women: "if you're not sure what to do with your face in the meantime, study Clint Eastwood's expressions—both of them." Exaggeration again creates the satiric effect in paragraph 8: "the average man can go 25 minutes saying nothing more than 'You don't say?' 'Izzat so?' and, of course, 'Hmmmm.'" Her tone is again irreverent and blunt in paragraph 9—"If you're taking a vacation from smiles and small talk and some fellow is moved to inquire about what's 'bothering' you, just stare back levelly and say, the international debt crisis, the arms race, or the death of God." In paragraph 11, she again presents a humorous, exaggerated picture of male behavior when angry: "they pound on desks and roar . . . the full basso profundo male tantrum." Finally, her concluding image of how she should have handled the lecherous professor is an exaggerated, humorous "tough-guy" portrayal of a woman "playing it like Bogart" (12).

.

DIVISION-CLASSIFICATION

OPENING COMMENTS

We confess. We always feel slightly uneasy about teaching division-classification as a distinct pattern of development. After all, the logic at the core of division-classification comes into play a number of times during the writing process. For example, when students generate thoughts during the prewriting stage, when they outline their ideas, when they prepare process analyses, they instinctively draw on the ordering principles characteristic of division-classification. But even though many students automatically use division-classification, we teach it as a discrete method of development. We do so because the pattern helps students understand the demands of logical analysis.

Working with division-classification causes two problems for students. First, they become confused about the difference between division and classification. They think they're classifying when they're dividing and dividing when they're classifying. On page 222, we state as succinctly as we can the difference between these two related but separate processes: Division involves taking a *single unit* or *concept, breaking the unit down* into its parts, and then analyzing the connection among the parts and between the parts and the whole. Classification *brings two or more related items together* and categorizes them according to type or kind.

Second, some students view division-classification as a pointless exercise designed by overly particular composition teachers. When they learn that they've been using division-classification all along (when brainstorming, when outlining, and so on), they begin to understand that division-classification is a valuable tool for logical analysis. In this connection, the student essay "The Truth About College Teachers" (pp. 229–32) will provide the class with a good laugh (perhaps even at your expense) and help students see how to use classification to make a point.

This chapter's professional essays show how division-classification can help writers analyze different subjects. Ericsson classifies our everyday falsehoods into categories that lend insight into the complexity of human communication. Zinsser and McClintock classify, respectively, pressures on college students and Madison Avenue propaganda techniques. Brooks classifies different abstract elements in the course of explaining his concept of "human capital." To illustrate his point about the deceptive nature of "doublespeak," Lutz organizes his proof into four overlapping categories. In-class discussion of any of these essays is bound to raise provocative questions about contemporary values.

ANSWERS FOR PREWRITING ACTIVITIES

Below we provide possible responses for selected prewriting activities at the end of Chapter 6. Of course, other approaches are possible. (p. 238)

1. Division-classification can be used in a variety of ways in these two essays. Below are a few suggestions. It's a good idea to have students share their ideas on the use of

division-classification with each other; this will provide a concrete demonstration of the possibilities.

Topic: *How to impress college instructors*
Divide brown-nosing techniques into types
Classify students according to their favorite technique
Classify instructors according to what impresses them

Topic: *Why volunteerism is on the rise*
Divide to obtain motivations for volunteerism
Classify people needing help
Classify kinds of people who are apt to volunteer

2. Here are some possible principles of division for each of the topics in Set A. Other principles of division and theses are possible.

   a. **Rock Music**

   Principle of division: According to era
   Thesis: Rock music styles fall into distinct eras: music of fifties, sixties, seventies, and eighties.

   Principle of division: According to audience
   Thesis: Rock music appeals to many audiences: the middle-aged, the yuppie, the college-aged, and the teenaged.

   Principle of division: According to its origin
   Thesis: Rock music has diverse influences: country music, rhythm and blues, and jazz.

   b. **A Shopping Mall**

   Principle of division: According to time of day at mall
   Thesis: At different times of the day, different groups of people inhabit the mall: senior "mall-walkers" in the early morning, business people grabbing lunch at midday, mothers and babies in the early afternoon, and teenagers in the early evening.

   Principle of division: According to what is sold
   Thesis: The types of stores that prosper at Garvey Mall tell much about today's consumer; the majority of shops sell apparel, quite a few sell audio and video tapes, but only one sells books.

   Principle of division: According to places people congregate
   Thesis: The fountain, the fast-food arcade, and the movie theater patio at Garvey Mall are all social spots, but for different types of people.

   c. **A Good Horror Movie**

   Principle of division: According to person being victimized
   Thesis: In *Kennel Horror II*, the victim is either an unsuspecting innocent, a helpless poor person, or a law-enforcement officer.

   Principle of division: According to attack location
   Thesis: The victims in *Kennel Horror II* are attacked in their own homes, in pleasant public places, or in isolated rural areas.

   Principle of division: According to film shots

Thesis: Director Logan Bettari uses extreme close-ups, rapid pans, and jarring cuts to increase the tension in *Kennel Horror II*.

Here are some possible principles of classification and thesis statements for the topics in Set B. Your students, of course, may come up with different ones.

Topic: Why people get addicted to computers

Principle of classification: According to types of people
Thesis: Computer addiction is more likely to affect introverts than extroverts, sedentary people than active people, and single people than married people.

Principle of classification: According to types of computer use
Thesis: Computers can be addictive whether they are used for work, play, or simple correspondence.

Principle of classification: According to circumstances of a person's life
Thesis: Computer addiction can be a consequence of boredom, loneliness, or laziness.

Topic: How fast-food restaurants affect family life

Principle of classification: According to the effects on the different members of the family
Thesis: Frequenting fast-food restaurants affects each member of the family differently.

Principle of classification: According to effects on various aspects of family life
Thesis: Fast-food restaurants seriously affect the financial, emotional, and physical well-being of a family.

Principle of classification: According to types of consequences
Thesis: Fast-food restaurants have short- and long-term consequences for family life.

Topic: Why long-term relationships break up

Principle of classification: According to types of long-term relationships
Thesis: The short-distance long-term relationship, the long-distance long-term relationship, and the live-in long-term relationship all end for different reasons.

Principle of classification: According to levels of commitment
Thesis: The end of a long-term relationship may occur if little commitment is involved, if one person is more committed than the other, or if one person wants a commitment and the other does not.

Principle of classification: According to various aspects of the relationship.
Thesis: Long-term relationships often end when the people involved no longer share the same interests, when the people involved lose interest in each other, when the people involved find the relationship no longer suits their needs.

ANSWERS FOR REVISING ACTIVITIES

Below we provide possible responses for selected revising activities at the end of Chapter 6. Of course, other approaches are possible. (p. 238)

3. The essay is based on a principle of division; "experience" is divided according to areas: employment, academic, social.

    The principle of division is applied incorrectly in the second point. Instead of being about an area of experience, this point focuses on "negative" experiences, a broad division that doesn't fit with the other areas. Second of all, the point refers only to "optimists," while all the other points refer to everyone.

    The problem can be remedied by eliminating the second point, since there are already three other solid points to be made in the essay.

4. Make time for your students to share their revisions with each other. Seeing the work of others helps students see all the possibilities in revising.

    This paragraph divides the concept of "play" using as a principle of division how much the child's peers are involved in the play. The paragraph's organization is based on the chronological appearance of the stages in the child's growth. The principle is applied consistently, but there are some problems in organization and in the support offered.

    Here are the specific problems with the paragraph:

    — The discussion of the first stage ("babies and toddlers") needs a specific example or two of "their own actions."
    — The fourth sentence, about elementary children's play, is incorrectly located in the paragraph, which discusses the play of preschool children. Delete this sentence.
    — The discussion of the second stage ("parallel play") could use an example of the "similar activities" the children engage in and how the children might "occasionally" interact. Note the specific examples provided for the third stage.
    — The last sentence is irrelevant and contradictory because no connection is made between the "special delight in physical activities" and the social aspect of children's play. In addition, the second part of the sentence contradicts the topic (first) sentence. This point must be more thought out and more details should be added.

THE WAYS WE LIE

Stephanie Ericsson

Questions for Close Reading (p. 247)

1. Ericsson's thesis is implied. One way of stating it might be the following: "Lying is common in our society, but an exploration of the types of lies shows that lying is destructive and should be avoided." After the long introduction, in which Ericsson establishes a criterion for determining if something is a lie (1–7), the rest of the essay discusses different types of lying.
2. The lies that Ericsson tells are part of a strategy to smooth out small difficulties for everyone concerned. There's a positive result from these four lies. She protects herself by saying traffic delayed her to a business meeting, when it was her own

fatigue that caused a late start, and she protects her wallet by telling the bank that the money to cover checks drawn on her account is in the mail, when it's not. To protect her obviously tired partner, she hides her day's little disasters from him. She protects her friend's feelings by saying she's too busy for lunch. Even so, she debates whether such small lies are harmless: "Sure I lie, but it doesn't hurt anything. Or does it?" (3). She confesses to having a deep voice inside her that says, "When someone lies, someone loses" (5).

During the week of experimental honesty, Ericsson discovered that telling the truth all the time has "serious consequences" (4) and that lying relieves a person of certain painful effects that descend quickly if the truth is revealed. She cites the consequences of the typical lies she named in paragraph 1: that the bank would levy charges, her partner would become overloaded, her client would fire her, and her friend would be offended (4).

3. In appointing these behaviors as lies, Ericsson examines the "meaning of [the] actions" and applies the definitions from *Webster's Dictionary*, two tests she mentions in paragraph 6. Ericsson grants that while sometimes, "ignoring the plain facts" is not "in and of itself a form of lying," such avoiding of reality can fit the dictionary definition of a "false action done with the intent to deceive" (13). She cites the Catholic Church's ignoring information about a priest's abuse of children as a clear example of this type of lie. "Deflecting" attention away from a topic is an effective way to hide the truth, and therefore constitutes a lie. She provides two serious examples of people who set a false accusation rolling by avoiding a true one about themselves (15–16). "Omission" can create a lie because the partial meaning might "make a difference in how a person lives his or her life" (17). Omissions show the truth of Ericsson's maxim in paragraph 5: "When someone lies, someone loses." She explains how an omission might successfully get you a free pair of replacement glasses (a loss to the optician), or it might affect your whole view of the world, yourself, and religion. She cites the omission of the story of Lilith from the Judeo-Christian Bible as the kind of omission that distorts people's perceptions.

    "Stereotypes and clichés" and "groupthink" are "compound" lies that employ several other techniques of lying. "Stereotypes and clichés" lie by "exaggeration, omission, and denial, to name a few" (23). Her "textbook" example of groupthink involves all these and stereotypical thinking as well—during World War II, Americans denied in the face of plain facts that the Japanese could be smart enough to solve the technical problems of attacking ships in somewhat shallow Pearl Harbor (24).

4. She wonders whether, if she condones lying and practices it herself, she is no better than "slick politicians or . . . corporate robbers" (5). She suspects that "saying it's okay to lie one way and not another is hedging" (5), that is, it's being wishy-washy about a significant moral issue. Her conscience, that "voice deep inside," suggests that "when someone lies, someone loses" (5). Exploring the possible negatives, she wonders if lying protects her at the expense of someone else (6).

5. *travails* (4): burdens and suffering
    hedging (5): avoiding a rigid commitment
    penance (6): punishment received to atone for sins
    pittance (9): a small amount
    façades (10): false fronts
    plethora (11): an overabundant amount
    disenchanted (11): no longer delighted or charmed
    ecclesiastical (12): of the church or clergy
    pedophilia (12): the abnormal sexual desire for children
    irreparable (13): incapable of being repaired or rectified

blatant (14): obvious

demonization (18): act of casting someone as a demon

misogynists (18): people who dislike women

embodiment (18): physical manifestation

archetype (20): original pattern or model from which something is made

obliterated (22): blotted out or erased

dissent (23): difference of opinion

cohesiveness (25): unity

invulnerability (25): immunity to attack

entrenched (25): placed in a position of strength

catatonia (30): mental disease characterized by stupor and rigidity

gamut (31): an entire range

Questions About the Writer's Craft (p. 248)

1. While "white lies" (8–9) and "out-and-out lies" (26–27) are certainly lies, many of the other behaviors Ericsson cites are less obviously examples of lying. In discussing the different types of lying, Ericsson is careful to clarify how each fits the classification of a lie. She establishes how to determine a lie in paragraph 6, suggesting that the underlying meaning of a behavior is the determinant. The "meaning" that creates a lie is the "intent to deceive" or "give a false impression," as the *Webster's Dictionary* definition states (6). As Ericsson goes through the various categories of lies, she shows how each one involves deception or intentional falsity. In paragraph 11, she provides an example of a man with a sparkling façade who constantly cheated his friends. In 12–13, she shows through an example how "ignoring the plain facts" can be lying; the Catholic Church's conscious covering up of the "plain facts" in the case of Father James Porter fits the definition, Ericsson says, of "a false action done with the intent to deceive" (13). Deflecting is shown to be a lie through the example of Clarence Thomas, who was able to deceive the country about whether he sexually harassed a colleague by crying racism (15). Omissions are lies, Ericsson indicates, providing an example of suppression of a truth that deceived Christian and Jewish women into "believing they were the lesser sex for thousands of years" (20). Ericsson supports dismissal as a type of lie by citing psychologist R. D. Laing's investigation of the families of schizophrenics, where "deliberate, staunch dismissal of the patient's perceptions" was a universal and likely causal factor. The other types of lying—stereotypes and clichés, groupthink, and delusion—are compound types, incorporating within them several of the other types of lies (22, 23, 34).

2. By using the narrative in her introduction, essentially "fessing up" to being an everyday liar, Ericsson disarms any negative reaction we might have to the idea she proposes in paragraph 3: "We lie. We all do." Since she has admitted to being a liar, we can't feel accused. Instead Ericsson implies we're all members of the same club. In addition, her listing of ordinary, "I'm just coping" types of lies may ring a bell with readers, again encouraging them to concur that lying is common in our lives. Further on in the introduction, in paragraph 4, Ericsson again uses her personal narrative to sketch in a scenario that is almost humorous: She says she "tried going a whole week without telling a lie, and it was paralyzing." She then describes what dire and off-beat consequences might have occurred had she not told the four lies mentioned in paragraph 1: The bank levies fees, her partner "keels over" upon hearing of her difficult day, her client "fires her," and she loses her friend. Here, the narrative again seduces the reader to accept the implication that lies might actually be necessary in daily life.

3. Ericsson uses a breezy, jaunty tone, especially at the start of the essay, to steer away from sounding preachy; typically, she says what she wants to say and moves on, resisting any urge to over-analyze or become too reflective. The treatment of her four lies in paragraphs 1–2 is an example; other examples of this speedy discussion of topics occur in paragraphs 4, 5, 6, 8, 17, 22, 26, 29, and 32. Even where she develops her examples at greater length, she gets right to the point by using direct sentences, as in paragraphs 11, 12–13, 15, 24–25, and 30–31.

Ericsson also employs lots of colloquialisms and contractions, and she writes as if she's chatting with the reader. This down-to-earth word choice begins right in paragraph 1: "It'd been a rough day," she writes. Other examples of colloquial diction include "one more straw might break his back" (2); "Sure I lie . . ." (3); "my partner keels over" (4); "my friend takes it personally . . ." (4); "slick politicians or corporate robbers . . ." (4); "saying it's okay to lie one way and not another is hedging" (5); "pay my penance because I ducked out" (6); "when he looks like hell" (6); "a vote of no confidence" (8); "quite so cut-and-dried" (9); "putting on another face" (9); "suits rather than sweatpants"; "get the kids off to school" (10); "all talk and no walk" (10); "I saw less than a hundred bucks" (10); "a crowded graveyard of disenchanted former friends" (11); "the victim is fully tamed and crawls into a hole . . . ." (16); "a rowdy game of basketball" (17); "attempted negotiations"; "said adios" (19); "Eve the Rib" (20); "often shuts down original thinking"; "a candy bar of misinformation" (21); "a textbook example" (24); "'good-ole-boy' cohesiveness"; "The rest is history" (25); "the bald-faced lie" (26); "the common thread" (30); "runs the gamut"; "can be quite handy" (31); "I could write the book on this one" (32).

Finally, Ericsson uses a colloquial exaggeration and strong, emotionally tinged language to imbue her essay with feeling, sometimes humorous, sometimes indignant. Exaggerated descriptions include "sit at my computer in my pajamas until four in the afternoon" (10); "fabulous books to read and fascinating insights"; "a crowded graveyard of disenchanted former friends" (11); "from a highly charged subject to a radioactive subject" (15); "a brilliant maneuver" (155); and "information in nanoseconds" (21). Emotionally tinged language includes "actually providing him with a fresh supply of unsuspecting families and innocent children to abuse" (12); "The church became a co-perpetrator with Porter" (13); "Clarence Thomas exploded with accusations"; "it was a brilliant maneuver"; "unlike sexual harassment, which still regards those who can get away with it" (15); "who understandably screams something obscene out of frustration" (16); "I was stunned"; "[it] felt like spiritual robbery . . ." (18); "renegade Catholic feminists" (19); "a patriarchal strategy to keep women weak" (20); "Unfortunately, it often shuts down original thinking" (21); "they are always dangerous. . . . They close minds and separate people" (22); "the slipperiest of all lies" (28); "a powerful lying tool" (32); and "it shamelessly employs dismissal . . ." (34).

4. Throughout the essay, Ericsson admits that most of the types of lies have a harmless or useful side. For example, her introduction presents an everyday scenario in which little lies are told and no great evil results, implying that telling the truth is sometimes more destructive than fibbing (14). In the case of each type of lie, however, she argues that despite the possible practical advantages, that type of lying is damaging and therefore wrong. In paragraph 8, for example, she concedes that the "white lie assumes that the truth will cause more damage than a simple, harmless untruth." By the end of this paragraph, however, she takes a stand against this type of lie, calling it an "act of subtle arrogance." In paragraph 10, she begins by acknowledging that "we all put up façades to one degree or another," but her examples move from the harmless to the destructive, again suggesting that a façade is not an acceptable deception. Her conclusion points directly to this contrast or

tension between the possible "functional" use of a lie and deceitful lying ("living a lie"), thereby clearly establishing the poles of the argument she has been making. Then she firmly takes a side: against lying. She quotes a country music song: "You've got to stand for something or you'll fall for anything."

COLLEGE PRESSURES

William Zinsser

Questions for Close Reading (p. 257)

1. Zinsser states his thesis explicitly in paragraph 7, at the end of his long introduction to the essay: "I see four kinds of pressure working on college students today: economic pressure, parental pressure, peer pressure, and self-induced pressure."

2. The pressures come from the economy, parents, peers, and the individual students themselves. The notes to Carlos reveal the emotional harm students suffer as a result of these pressures, and in the rest of the essay, Zinsser explains that these pressures cause more than just psychological pain; they also inhibit students' intellectual growth and narrow the range of their college activities. He points out such harms as excessive studying and overexertion (27–29), rigid career choices and half-hearted concurrence with parental wishes (19–22), lack of experimentation (33), failure to get a liberal education (11), retreat from creativity (22), rivalry between friends (24), and deemphasis of extracurricular activities (36). As Carlos Hortas puts it, "Violence is being done to the undergraduate experience" (32).

3. The four pressures that Zinsser cites do not exist independently, but are "intertwined" or related to each other. In discussing the "intertwining" of pressures, Zinsser divides the four pressures into two pairs. In paragraph 14, he says, "Along with economic pressure goes parental pressure. Inevitably, the two are deeply intertwined." He means that economic pressure affects students as parental pressure, because the parents pay the bills, for the most part, and often expect compliance in the form of high grades and a practical major. Zinsser introduces the other pair of pressures in paragraph 23: "Peer pressure and self-induced pressure are also intertwined. . . ." The example of two roommates, each of whom suffered feelings of academic inferiority in relation to the other, points out that such peer pressure is often created or imagined by students who feel a great inner compulsion to excel.

4. Students must "break the circles in which they are trapped," Zinsser writes (31). As individuals, they need to stop following their parents' dreams and reacting to their classmates' fears. They must start to believe in their own uniqueness and their own power to achieve a future right for them (31). Zinsser quotes the dean Carlos Hortas, who agrees that students "ought to take chances" (33). Specific remedies are implied rather than stated directly; they include joining extracurricular activities (36–37), risking experimentation and failure (5), going ahead with creative aspirations (22), sampling a wide variety of courses (11), and taking time to relax and enjoy life (25).

5. *privy* (3): made knowledgeable to secret or special information
   venerated (6): worshipped, highly regarded
   exhorted (13): urged
   tenacity (15): perseverance, persistence
   vacillates (22): wavers
   furtively (22): secretly
   circuitous (4): roundabout, indirect

Questions About the Writer's Craft (p. 257)

1. Zinsser's pairing of the pressures on college students is quite logical and reflects the reality of students' lives. The first pair, economic and parental pressure, is external. These two pressures come from society at large and from parents. The other two pressures—mass competitiveness among peers and an inner obsession to excel—affect students psychologically. These pairs make the essay's argument easier to grasp, because they reduce the four points to two larger ones; also, the pairing of pressures helps the reader to understand how the pressures interlock and overwhelm today's students.

2. The pressures on students to drive themselves hard and have a practical goal are essentially causes, and the desperate feelings and compulsive behaviors of the students are the results or effects of these causes. The essay can thus be viewed as an example of a *causal analysis* as well as of division-classification. Zinsser uses a pattern of first discussing effects and then showing the causes. For example, paragraphs 8 and 9 focus on some effects of the economic pressures: the beliefs that grades and decisions about majors determine a student's life; the economic causes underlying these beliefs are revealed in paragraphs 12 and 13. The next section follows this same pattern; paragraphs 15 to 19 present a student reluctantly pursuing an M.D., and paragraphs 20 and 21 discuss the causes of such pragmatic decisions. In the section discussing peer pressure and inner pressures, Zinsser again begins with an anecdote demonstrating the effects of the pressures (29) and follows with an analysis of the causes. Paragraph 27 presents a *causal chain* in which the effects become causes of still further effects.

3. The students' notes to Carlos make an engrossing lead-in to the essay. They capture our attention because they are so colloquial and yet so terse, so packed with emotion and occasional black humor. Also, these notes focus our attention on the theme, that many students today experience college as agony because of the pressures they are under. The self-portraits painted by these notes show that students are not, as a reader might imagine, carefree or rebellious, driven to irresponsible frivolity or to serious challenges of society. They are, instead, overwhelmed and frightened victims. On the positive side, they do maintain a sense of humor ("Hey Carlos, good news! I've got mononucleosis."), struggle valiantly with their problems ("I stayed up all night . . . & am typing. . . . P.S. I'm going to the dentist. Pain is pretty bad.") and are not afraid to reach out for help.

4. Such an exaggerated description of what students want shows sarcasm on the part of the author; the description here is almost a put-down of students who succumb to the idea that they must map out their lives completely. Other examples occur in paragraphs 1 ("Who are these wretched supplicants, . . . seeking such miracles of postponement and balm?"), 9 ("The transcript has become a sacred document, the passport to security. How one appears on paper is more important than how one appears in person"), and 15 ("They go off to their labs as if they were going to the dentist"). This ironic tone is found mainly in the beginning of the essay, as Zinsser is still luring his readers into the article. As he examines the intertwining of pressures, he drops the hyperbole and uses a more analytic tone.

PSST! "HUMAN CAPITAL"

David Brooks

Questions for Close Reading (p. 261)

1. Brooks states his thesis in paragraph 5: "U.S. education reforms have generally failed because they try to improve the skills of students without addressing the underlying components of human capital."
2. Brooks claims that education policies generally focus on improving skills and knowledge, but that without the other forms of human capital, skills and knowledge are not that useful. People must also have the right cultural values, social knowledge, and moral sense, as well as the capacity to think and evaluate, and motivation, in order to succeed, but education reforms do not target these characteristics. Programs such as No Child Left Behind, Title I, and Head Start have disappointing results because they all focus on skills and knowledge to the exclusion of other forms of human capital.
3. Brooks thinks the family plays an especially large role in the formation of human cultural capital, in particular when children are under the age of three. He cites a study by James S. Coleman that found that families shape their children more than schools do, and a study by Heckman and Carneiro that found that "most of the gaps in college attendance and delay are determined by early family factors" (7). Social and moral human capital are also influenced by the family.
4. In paragraph 11, Brooks describes the aspirational capital—the motivation to achieve—that many millionaires possess. According to Thomas J. Stanley's book *The Millionaire's Mind*, on which Brooks bases this paragraph, millionaires tend to be average or slightly below average students. However, many had the experience of being told they were not smart enough to achieve much, and so they had a strong desire to succeed to "prove the naysayers wrong."
5. *capital* (1): in economics, something man-made that can be used in the production of goods and services and that is not used up in the process of production
   revamped (4): remade, revised
   cognitive (10): related to the process of knowing
   aspirational (11): having a strong desire to achieve something great
   naysayers (11): those who are skeptical or cynical about something
   per capita (13): per person
   immersions (14): plunging into something in depth

Questions About the Writer's Craft (p. 261)

1. The benefit of a reference, such as to a character in a film, is that the reader will recognize it and immediately have associations that make the author's intent instantly understandable. This pulls the reader into the essay immediately. On the other hand, the risk of such a reference is that the reader will not be familiar with it, which would make it meaningless and, indeed, off-putting. Students' opinions of the effectiveness of this opening will depend in large part on whether they have seen *The Graduate*. Considering that the movie is four decades old, it's likely that most young people will find it meaningless without the editor's note.
2. Brooks organizes his discussion of human capital by telling the reader he is breaking it down into its constituent parts (5, 6) and then proceeding to identify and explain each part (7–11). Paragraphs 5 and 6 frame the discussion for the reader, and

paragraphs 7–11 each start with the name of the aspect of human capital being discussed. In essence, paragraphs 7–11 function as a list.

3. The pattern of exposition in paragraphs 7–11 is the same, combining definition and exemplification. Each paragraph begins with the type of human capital, follows with a definition, and winds up with one or more examples.

4. This op-ed column is short, but its ideas are big, and any one of them could probably be expanded into an entire essay, chapter, or book. If Brooks had more space, he could support the claims he makes in paragraph 2 with evidence; right now, he just mentions them in quick succession. Then, for each form of human capital, he could develop the definition beyond a single sentence, provide more and deeper examples, cite various types of evidence to support his points, and describe what has been done or can be done to improve that form of human capital. He then could evaluate No Child Left Behind, Title I, and Head Start in more depth, comparing their aims and their results. Finally, he could propose, in much more detail, policies to improve human capital.

DOUBLESPEAK

William Lutz

Questions for Close Reading (p. 268)

1. Paragraph 2, in its entirety, constitutes a statement of Lutz's thesis. And several sentences in paragraph 19 restate the thesis: Doublespeak "is carefully designed and constructed to appear to communicate when in fact it doesn't. It is language designed to distort reality and corrupt thought." The body of Lutz's essay illustrates this thesis by identifying four categories of doublespeak—euphemism, jargon, gobbledygook, and inflated language.

2. The four questions are stated in paragraph 3: "Who is saying what to whom, under what conditions and circumstances, with what intent, and with what results?" In certain contexts, one must consider the desired outcome of language. In such cases, evasive or esoteric language may be permissible—for example, the euphemism "passed away" to express condolences or the special language used within the medical profession. According to Lutz, language is doublespeak when its intent is to confuse, mislead, or deceive—in other words, when it does exactly the opposite of what language is meant to do: communicate. Thus euphemisms such as "radiation enhancement device" (the neutron bomb) and jargon used outside the special group that understands it are doublespeak; gobbledygook and inflated language, which invariably evade or confuse the issue, are *always* doublespeak.

3. Lutz divides doublespeak into four categories—euphemism, jargon, gobbledygook, and inflated language—and illustrates each with many examples. As a result, individual responses to the question will vary, but here are some possibilities. Euphemism is "an inoffensive or positive word or phrase" designed "to mislead or deceive" a listener about a "harsh, unpleasant, or distasteful reality" (4). The State Department uses euphemism when it substitutes "unlawful or arbitrary deprivation of life" for "killing" to cover up damaging political evidence in a human rights report (6). Jargon, "the specialized language" of a particular group, can be used outside that group context to confuse a listener. Lutz points to "the involuntary conversion of a 727" as an example of the legal jargon National Airlines used to conceal the source—a plane crash in which three people died—of a profitable insurance

settlement (11). With gobbledygook, a speaker tries to "overwhelm an audience with words," and Lutz cites long examples from Alan Greenspan (12), Dan Quayle (14), and Jesse Moore (15). Quoting such impenetrable language, Lutz wonders if any of the men "had any idea what he was saying" (15). Finally, inflated language "make[s] everyday things seem impressive," as when mechanics become "automotive internists" and used cars are reborn as "pre-owned" or "experienced cars" (16).

4. In Lutz's schema, gobbledygook and inflated language are *always* doublespeak. In contrast, Lutz suggests that euphemism and jargon *can* have legitimate uses. As a "tactful word or phrase which avoids directly mentioning a painful reality," euphemism respects social convention and demonstrates concern for a listener's feelings (3–5). Euphemism becomes doublespeak only when it is used to thwart expectations and deliberately deceive a listener (6). Similarly, jargon has a useful purpose in the appropriate context. Jargon is the "specialized language" of a particular group, and Lutz concedes that "Within a group, jargon functions as a kind of verbal shorthand," allowing members "to communicate with each other clearly, efficiently, and quickly" (8). Jargon becomes doublespeak only when it is used outside of the group context, either to "impress" listeners or to confuse them willfully (10–11).

5. *variance* (6): difference or disagreement
esoteric (9): specialized and restricted to a small group
profundity (9): intellectual depth or insight
dividend (11): a sum to be divided; money paid to stockholders
initiative (14): a beginning plan of action

Questions About the Writer's Craft (p. 268)

1. Lutz's four categories overlap considerably. For example, the Chrysler corporation's use of the term "career alternative enhancement program" to signal that the company is "laying off five thousand workers" (17) is an illustration of inflated language. But the term could also be considered a euphemism, which Lutz defines as an "inoffensive or positive" wording meant "to avoid a harsh, unpleasant, or distasteful reality" (14). The same is true of "negative patient care outcome," meaning "the patient died" (17). Although Lutz describes this example as inflated language, it also seems euphemistic—as does a "discontinuity," meaning a crack in a beam, which is cited to illustrate jargon (9). In the same vein, "radiation enhancement device," the Pentagon's term for a neutron bomb (7), is classified as euphemism, but it might also be seen as a kind of military jargon. And "rapid oxidation," classified as inflated language (17), could be considered jargon or euphemism as well.

   Lutz's classifications overlap because of the nature of his subject: doublespeak. People who resort to doublespeak, as Lutz shows, may do so in different situations (a corporate or military context), and their specific motivations may differ (to hide something embarrassing, to puff themselves up). But their basic intent is always to deceive, and their basic technique is to use confusing, misleading words. Therefore, it is not surprising that the particular words they choose cannot be strictly or rigidly categorized.

2. In addition to classification, Lutz uses *exemplification, comparison-contrast*, and *definition*. He gives numerous and specific *examples* of doublespeak, such as the Pentagon's use of "backloading of augmentation personnel" (18) for "retreat" and "unlawful or arbitrary deprivation of life" (6) for "killing." These are examples of doublespeak in actual situations, and so they support Lutz's thesis that one can learn to spot doublespeak by paying close attention to the context in which such language is used.

Lutz uses *comparison-contrast* when he "translates" doublespeak into plain language. For instance, he explains that "rapid oxidation" means "a fire in a nuclear power plant" (17). With such contrasts, he not only reveals the truths that euphemism, jargon, gobbledygook, and inflated language are meant to conceal but also points up the absurdity and slyness of doublespeak. Lutz also contrasts harmless doublespeak with dangerous doublespeak: for instance, he makes a sharp distinction between euphemism that is simply tactful or sensitive, such as "passed away" for the harsher "died" (5), and euphemism that is designed to mislead, such as "incontinent ordnance" (7). This contrast emphasizes the purpose of doublespeak: deception.

Lutz uses *definition* as well. At the outset of his discussion of each category, he carefully defines the type of doublespeak under examination (4, 8, 12, 16).

3. Greenspan's words quoted in paragraph 12 are gobbledygook. If they mean anything at all, it seems impossible to say what. But the remark that Lutz quotes in paragraph 13 is plain language—in fact, the only plain language quoted in the entire selection. Lutz probably included it to show two things: first, that Greenspan was capable of speaking coherently if he so chose; and second, that Greenspan, able to speak clearly, was guilty of deliberate deception when he used doublespeak.

4. Unlike an activist or radical reformer, Lutz presents an even, distanced, and objective tone. While he believes that some doublespeak "can have serious consequences" (18), he does not call it "dangerous" or "evil" or "oppressive"; instead, doublespeak is described as "mislead[ing]" (6). Avoiding polemic, Lutz breaks his topic into four constituent parts. He supports his divisions with ample citations from official statements and documents, and it is only in the discussion of these citations that Lutz's distanced voice gives way to something sharper. By the third kind of doublespeak, Lutz seems ready to poke fun at gobbledygook speakers like Alan Greenspan and Jesse Moore, noting that "Mr. Greenspan's doublespeak doesn't seem to have held back his career" (13) and wondering "if Mr. Moore had any idea what he was saying" (15). Generally though, Lutz's tempered tone ensures that his examples stand out; by choosing this tone and restraining his own response to the material, he lets doublespeak will speak for itself. As Lutz notes in paragraph 3, "Most of the time you will recognize doublespeak when you see it or hear it."

PROPAGANDA TECHNIQUES IN TODAY'S ADVERTISING

Ann McClintock

Questions for Close Reading (p. 275)

1. McClintock's thesis is located at the end of the first paragraph: "Advertisers lean heavily on propaganda to sell their products, whether the 'products' are a brand of toothpaste, a candidate for office, or a particular political viewpoint."

2. Propaganda is the "systematic effort to influence people's opinions, to win them over to a certain view or side" (2) in terms of product choices, political candidates, or social concerns. Many people associate propaganda solely with the subversive campaigns of foreign powers or with the spreading of outrageous lies to an unwitting, innocent populace. But actually, propaganda is all around us; it is used by all the special interests that vie for our attention, our dollars, and our votes. American advertising is pervaded with propaganda in its attempt to sell us commercial

products, and our political climate suffers from blizzard after blizzard of propaganda before each election.

3. Advertisers use "weasel words" to "stack the cards" and distort facts so that their products appear superior. Weasel words are words that say more than they mean and suggest more value than they actually denote. For example, an ad might say a shampoo "helps control dandruff," but we might understand this to mean that it cures dandruff (19).

4. Consumers should be aware of propaganda techniques so they can resist the appeal of ads that distort the truth or pull at our emotions. Only when we can separate the actual message and evaluate it for ourselves are we doing the hard work of clear thinking: "analyzing a claim, researching the facts, examining both sides of an issue, using logic to see the flaws in an argument" (23).

5. *seduced* (1): enticed, entranced; misled
    warmongers (5): people who attempt to start wars
    elite (17): an exclusive or privileged group

Questions About the Writer's Craft (p. 276)

1. The definition of *propaganda* informs us about the term's true meaning and also clears up misunderstandings about the extent to which average Americans are subjected to propaganda. The broader purpose of providing us with this definition is to persuade us that advertising is indeed propaganda. McClintock hopes to motivate us to learn more about the various techniques of propaganda, so we can protect ourselves from its daily onslaughts.

2. "Seduced" and "brainwashed" are both words with strong negative connotations; we are likely to be shocked or disbelieving when we read that "Americans, adults and children alike, are being seduced. They are being brainwashed" (1). By using these terms, McClintock challenges our belief in our independence and free will. Through the use of these and other terms ("victims"), she provokes us to continue reading the essay. Ironically, this use of loaded words manipulates the readers' reactions in a manner similar to that of propaganda.

3. Questions appear in the discussions of "Glittering Generalities" and "Card Stacking" and in the conclusion to the essay. In both the sections on propaganda techniques, the questions are rhetorical, in that they need no answers. They are questions used to make a point. For example, McClintock asks, "After all, how can anyone oppose 'truth, justice, and the American way'?" (6). The implied answer is, "No one can." In her discussion of specific empty phrases, the author asks questions to point out the meaninglessness of such statements as "He cares . . ." and "Vote for Progress" (7). These questions are meant not to be answered, but to show the vagueness of glittering generalities. In the section on card stacking (18–20), she suggests that readers ask questions to test the validity of a political accusation such as "my opponent has changed his mind five times. . . ." The questions in the essay's conclusion, however, are real questions to which she provides answers.

4. Tied to McClintock's explanation of why propaganda works is a warning: To remain blind to the power of propaganda is to consent "to handing over our independence, our decision-making ability, and our brains to the advertisers" (24). In order to prevent this fate, McClintock advises us to do the work that clear thinking requires. This ending is an example of a call-for-action conclusion.

PROCESS ANALYSIS

OPENING COMMENTS

Like many of our colleagues, we cover process analysis early in the semester. This pattern of development teaches students a great deal about selectivity ("Which steps should I cover?" "How many examples should I provide?"), organization, and transitional signals. Process analysis also highlights the importance of audience analysis. To explain the steps in a process clearly, the writer must identify what readers need to know and understand.

Students often expect process analysis to write itself; they expect it to unfold naturally and automatically. But once they get feedback on their first draft, they realize that the sequence of steps was self-evident only to them and that they need to work harder to make the process accessible to their readers.

This chapter includes process analyses that vary widely in subject. Shipley's essay gives readers insight into the step-by-step editing process followed at a major U.S. newspaper. By evoking shock and revulsion, Mitford's "The American Way of Death" underscores the effectiveness of highly specific details. In contrast, the essay by Roberts shows students how humor can be used to make a serious point. And Stoll, meanwhile, provides a tongue-in-cheek how-to for computerizing—and dehumanizing— America's schools. Finally, Rego uses directional process analysis to offer a series of pragmatic suggestions for making sure complaints are heard and acted upon.

ANSWERS FOR PREWRITING ACTIVITIES

Below we provide possible responses to selected prewriting activities at the end of Chapter 7. Of course, your students are bound to come up with their own approaches. (p. 294)

1. Process analysis lends itself to these essay topics in several ways. Below are some possibilities. In class, we suggest you have students share their responses. They will be delighted to discover that their neighbors have devised different uses for process analysis in these essays.

    Topic: Defining comparison shopping
    How a person might use a consumer magazine to compare VCRs' quality
    How a person might compare sneakers at a mall
    How someone might call car dealers to get the best price

    Topic: Contrasting two teaching styles
    How two teachers respond to student questions
    How two teachers deal with students who don't understand
    How two teachers convey complex information

ANSWERS FOR REVISING ACTIVITIES

Below we provide possible responses to selected revising activities at the end of Chapter 7. Of course, your students are bound to come up with their own approaches. (p. 294)

3. Encourage students to work together on this activity or have them share their revisions. Other students' responses will help them discover weaknesses in their choices they otherwise might overlook. Here is a revised version of the list:

    > The tone of the opening comments is very important
    > Use a friendly tone in opening comments
    > Don't introduce the product right away
    > Try in a friendly way to keep the person on the phone
    > Keep customers on the phone as long as possible to learn what they need
    > The more you know about customers' needs the better
    > Gently introduce the product
    > Describe the product's advantages—price, convenience, installment plan
    > If a person is not interested, try in a friendly way to find out why
    > Don't push people if they're not interested
    > Don't tell people that their reasons for not being interested are silly
    > Explain payment—check, money order, or credit card payment
    > Encourage credit card payment—the product will arrive earlier
    > End on a friendly tone

    The points that undermine the paper's unity are:

    > Growing rudeness in society. Some people hang up right away. Very upsetting.
    > Many people are so lonely they don't mind staying on the phone so they can talk to someone—anyone
    > How sad that there's so much loneliness in the world

4. We suggest you offer your students the chance to read each other's revisions of this paragraph. Exposure to other versions helps them see many more possibilities in revising. Here are the main problems in the paragraph:

    — To preserve the paragraph's chronology, the sixth sentence (beginning "Before heading to class . . .") and the seventh should come earlier in the paragraph. These two sentences should be placed after "lessen the trauma."
    — Throughout the paragraph, there's a shift in person; for instance, "they" is used in the second sentence, but the third sentence shifts to "you"; it goes back and forth from there. The writer should choose one or the other and stick to it.
    — The tenth and eleventh sentences, running from "A friend of mine . . ." to "volunteers to participate" are irrelevant and should be deleted.
    — The point that you should "never, ever volunteer to answer" should be moved up to occur immediately after the advice about where to sit in sentences 8 and 9.
    — The transition, "however" (sentence 12), doesn't work when the paragraph is reorganized as described above. A transition such as "also" would work well.
    — The last two sentences, though in keeping with the paragraph's light tone, nevertheless seem a bit jarring. Furthermore, since they don't develop the essay's overall point, they should probably be eliminated.

TALK ABOUT EDITING

David Shipley

Questions for Close Reading (p. 299)

1. Shipley states his thesis in paragraphs 2–4: The purpose of editing op-ed articles is to make sure that they are factually accurate and that the writer's argument is clear and sound. In paragraphs 2 and 3, he outlines the editing done to op-ed pieces and the collaboration with the author to finalize the copy. Finally, in paragraph 4, he states that the best way to explain op-ed editing is to walk through the process.

2. *New York Times* op-ed editors check grammar, correct typographical errors, make changes according to the newspaper's style book, check the article's length, fact-check, check assertions, and improve readability (8–17). Shipley devotes the most space to explaining the process involved in checking assertions (four paragraphs) and improving readability (two paragraphs).

3. The relationship between the editor and the writer is a partnership, according to Shipley. Thus the writer gets to see and respond to all the changes that the editor has made or suggested, and nothing is published unless the writer and editor have agreed on all the necessary changes. Shipley focuses on the collaborative nature of this give and take; in paragraph 19, he emphasizes this by saying that "Editing is not bullying." However, he also acknowledges that there can be conflict between editor and writer during this process (20).

4. By "Editing is a human enterprise," Shipley acknowledges that much editing is subjective. Editors may misunderstand a writer's point, may overlook a mistake, or may make a mistake. However, if a mistake is published, the newspaper will correct it as soon as possible.

5. *hardy* (1): robust, strong
   perennial (1): persistent, recurrent
   on-deck circle (6): in baseball, the area where the next batter warms up (in other words, the article is next to be published)
   expletives (9): obscene or profane words or phrases
   assertions (12): declarations, affirmations
   adhering (14): sticking
   readability (16): the quality of being easily read
   venue (23): place, locale

Questions About the Writer's Craft (p. 299)

1. The audience for Shipley's essay is the readers of *The New York Times*. Since the *Times* has a national circulation, and is read by those in government circles, this is a broad group of people, many of them important. The topic is of interest to *New York Times* readers mostly because they gain a better understanding of the vetting that op-ed pieces undergo, but also because some of them may themselves submit articles for the op-ed page and will then undergo this editing process. Shipley's process analysis is informational; he is educating his readers about the process but is not instructing them on how to do it themselves.

2. The first set of tasks involves checking for grammar, typos, style, length, and accuracy, the "clear-cut things" introduced in paragraph 7. When a fact is called into question, the author's assertion about it is checked (12). The second set of tasks involves improving the readability of the essay, introduced in paragraph 16. This

73

includes adding clarifications, smoothing transitions, cutting digressions, moving copy, and simplifying the language. The third set of tasks involves communicating editorial changes to the writer and negotiating any differences between the editor and the writer in order to finalize the piece. Shipley divides the overall editing process into these main components because each is a fundamentally different type of task. The first is largely cut-and-dried; the second involves more editorial judgment; and the third focuses on the communication between the editor and the writer.

3. According to Shipley, if a fact-checker finds a discrepancy between a fact and one of the writer's assertions, the writer will be challenged to prove the accuracy of the assertion. If he cannot, then he has to find some other evidence to support his argument, and the editor will offer guidance. In the example, the writer has made an assertion—that the police in his town have no reason to change their tactics—that is not borne out by the fact that the town crime rate is rising. Since the facts show that the police *do* have reason to change their tactics, the writer must come up with another suggestion for dealing with the crime problem. The example is effective because it adds to the reader's understanding of the depth of the editing an op-ed piece undergoes. Fact checking is not merely a matter of gauging the accuracy of individual facts; it also involves checking the reasoning in an article.

4. Shipley's small joke in the concluding paragraph is that he, too, is subject to the editorial process when he writes an essay for the op-ed page, even though normally he is the one doing the editing. He is acknowledging the writer's, rather than the editor's, point of view on the editorial process by indicating he wouldn't accept all the suggested editorial changes on this article. This brings the article to a satisfying end because it makes it seem that the writer has the last word, after all, even though in fact the *Times* editors have the last word—they can always refuse to publish an article.

THE AMERICAN WAY OF DEATH

Jessica Mitford

Questions for Close Reading (p. 305)

1. Mitford's thesis is implied by her introductory comments that "Embalming is indeed a most extraordinary procedure" (1) and that it is very difficult to obtain information about what goes on behind the "formaldehyde curtain" (3). One way of stating the thesis might be this: "Americans should know exactly what they are paying for when they have a relative embalmed." Here's another possible version: "Knowing the details of embalming is every American consumer's right and responsibility."

2. Ignorance about embalming has a number of causes. On a pragmatic level, bookshops and libraries do not stock texts on the subject, Mitford says (1). Also, while at one time deceased people were prepared for burial at home with a relative standing by, our current custom is to hand over the body to "professionals" who perform their rituals in the mortuary. Mitford suspects that morticians would discourage any family member who wished to witness the procedures because they do not want the information about embalming to become widely known. In addition, the author points out, the law forbids others than the family or mortuary students to watch. Finally, while Mitford says she doubts "the secrecy surrounding embalming can . . . be attributed to the inherent gruesomeness of the subject" (2), since

everything from heart surgery to birth is televised these days, students will probably admit to some squeamishness about the subject themselves.

3. J. Sheridan Mayer reminds us that the goal of mortuary science is to present the deceased in a lifelike manner: "Our customs require the presentation of our dead in the semblance of normality . . . unmarred by the ravages of illness, disease or mutilation" (11). Mitford's treatment of this notion is ironic. After quoting Mayer's guidelines, she makes the wry comment, "This is rather a large order since few people die in the full bloom of health. . . ."

4. The dead person's body can be made to look even better than when he or she was alive by repairing visible damage caused by illness or accident. In paragraph 12, Mitford grimly describes the remedies taken if a body part is missing or if the face is bruised and swollen: replacements are fashioned out of wax, heads are sewn back on with the stitches hidden under a high collar or scarf, and swollen tissue is cut out from the inside. Additionally, emaciation's ravaging can be repaired, Mitford explains in paragraph 13, through the injection of cream, and the effects of diseases on skin color can be rectified through cosmetics, colored lights, and careful attention to color-coded casket interiors (15).

5. *docility* (1): the quality of being easily led or managed
   intractable (3): stubborn
   reticence (3): silence, unwillingness to speak
   raison d'être (3): reason for being
   augers (5): tools for making holes
   distend (5): to stretch, expand, or inflate something
   stippling (12): applying by repeated small touches
   jaundice (15): an illness characterized by a yellowish discoloration of the body

Questions About the Writer's Craft (p. 306)

1. There are two main stages in the process of preparing the body for the funeral. First, it is embalmed. This is the procedure by which blood is replaced with "about three to six gallons" of some sort of embalming fluid (9) and body fluids in the torso with "cavity fluid" (10). The deceased's eyes are closed with cement, the mouth sewn shut, and the face "creamed" to protect it from burns by the caustic embalming chemicals (10). The second stage of the process, restoration, occurs eight to ten hours later. During this stage the mortician, using the combined skills of a sculptor and a cosmetician, repairs the appearance of the body and makes it look lifelike. This process involves making casts of missing limbs (12); modeling the face to be neither too emaciated or too swollen (12–13); positioning the jaw, perhaps by dislocation, so the lips stay shut (14); and finally, washing, shaving (if male), shampooing, and dressing the body (16). The final step of this process is "casketing" (17).

   Mitford uses very clear transition words to delineate the steps of the first two stages, embalming and restoration. Embalming is described sequentially, so she uses transitions of time and addition: "The body is first . . . (4); "another textbook discusses . . ." (7); "a contrasting thought is offered by another writer" (7); "To return to Mr. Jones . . ." (8); "meanwhile" (9); "the next step is . . ." (10). Mitford also employs repetitions of sentence structure to signal she is adding detail to detail: "There are cosmetics, waxes and paints. . . . There are ingenious aids . . . ," she writes in paragraph 5. "If Flextone is used . . ." (8) and "If he should be buck-toothed . . ." (9) are other examples of this strategy. Mitford uses this transition technique again in the section on restoration, where details are added in response to a series of similarly worded questions and conditional clauses: "Is a hand missing?" "If a lip or two, a nose or an ear should be missing . . ." "Head off?"; "Swollen mouth?" "If too much is removed . . ." (12); "If Mr. Jones happens to have no teeth . . ." (14); "If Mr. Jones has died of jaundice, does this deter the embalmer?" (15).

Mitford separates the first two stages of the mortician's job by devoting the end of paragraph 10 to making the transition: "He had been embalmed, but not yet restored." And, in paragraph 12, Mitford orients us to the start of the second stage by stating, "The embalmer, having allowed an appropriate interval . . ." (12). The discussion of restoration uses many transitions indicating contrast: "The opposite condition . . ." (14); "however" (14); "on the other hand" (15, 17); and of addition: "another method" (14). Paragraph 14 begins with a reference to "a problem," so that we know the paragraph will discuss its solution process. Also in this section, there are some transitions referring to process: "sometimes . . . then . . ." (14). Many other details, however, are piled on without transition (16, 17). Paragraph 16 begins with a summation of the process so far and moves us on to the next stage: "The patching and filling completed, Mr. Jones is now shaved, washed and dressed. . . ." And paragraph 17 introduces the last stage by a transition of process: "Jones is now ready . . ." (17).

2. "Mr. Jones" is an "everyman" name; using it for the corpse conveys that this procedure is universally applied in our country. The name also gives the dead man an identity—it is a constant reminder that this is a human being, being subjected to grotesque and dehumanizing techniques. We can feel shock and shame as these processes are performed on a "Mr. Jones" instead of on a "body." The use of the particular name helps Mitford draw her readers over to her point of view. However, Mr. Jones is never given any particular physical characteristics, life history, or cause of death, so that while he is a person, not just a dead body, he could still be any person.

3. The quotations from mortuary science textbooks let us know that Mitford has done her homework; she has acquired some of those hard-to-get books on embalming and studied them. The quotations thus increase her authority on the subject. Since the process of embalming is a mystery to most of us, the quotations verify the almost incredible details of the procedures (12, 15, 16, 17) and convey the theory behind the process as well (6, 7, 11). The particular quotations often combine the subject of barbaric mutilation with a self-congratulatory or sanctimonious tone. The style is usually excessively pompous and marked by terminology designed to underscore the logicality or necessity of the procedures: "It is necessary to . . ."; "removes the principal cause of . . ." (6); "for every hour that elapses . . . will add to the problems . . ."; "we must conclude that . . ."; "In the average case . . ."; "One of the effects of . . ." (7); "Our customs require . . ."; "This is the time . . ."; "all doubts of success vanish . . ."; "It is surprising and gratifying . . ." (11).

4. For the most part, Mitford's tone is reportorial; she describes the odd and fantastic processes without much comment or overt interpretation. Occasionally, however, there are touches of irony and sarcasm, enough so that one can tell that Mitford is not objective about the funeral industry. For example, her discussion of how to place the body in a coffin is clearly meant wryly: "Proper placement of the body requires a delicate sense of balance. It should lie as high as possible in the casket, yet not so high that the lid, when lowered, will hit the nose." She points out that placing the body too low will cause the body to look as if it is in a box. Likewise, the questions in paragraph 12 mock the mortician's blasé attitude toward dead bodies: "Head off?" "Swollen mouth?" Also, her word choice can be evaluative, as in paragraph 5: "*appropriately corrupted* . . . as 'demisurgeon'"; "equipment . . . *crudely* imitative of the surgeon's . . ."; "a *bewildering* array of fluids . . ." (italics added). Finally, her choice of quotations from texts in the field contributes to our sense that practitioners of mortuary science are self-aggrandizing and pretentious, if not actually charlatans.

CYBERSCHOOL

Clifford Stoll

Questions for Close Reading (p. 311)

1. Though Stoll's position is evident from the outset of his essay (when he refers to the "pessimal view of the schoolroom of the future"), he does not express his thesis until the ironic close of the essay's final paragraph: "Yep, jut sign up for the future: the parent-pleasin', tax-savin', interactive-educatin', child-centerin' Cyberschool. . . . No learning. Coming soon to a school district near you." Students may wish to refine this statement using their own words. Here is one possibility: "Though the computerization of the classroom seems to be inevitable, this trend will result in disastrous educational consequences for the students subjected to it."

2. The process of fully computerizing schoolrooms—or creating a "cyberschool"—is as follows: First, the school district buys a computer for every student (5), as well as educational software that matches the curriculum (6). This software will be customized to students' educational levels and personal tastes, but most importantly, to the standardized tests students are required to take (7–8). The computers will track students' progress and convey this information to parents and administrators (9). Classroom desks will be replaced by cubicle workstations, essentially eliminating all student contact (11). Teachers and librarians will be fired or retrained as data entry clerks and replaced by computer specialists and security guards (11–12). "Luxuries" such as art class and field trips will be eliminated to save money, while new profits can be derived from arranging corporate sponsorship of the cyberschool (14). Online extracurricular activities will allow students to "experience" community service and "interact" with people from around the world (18). As a result, test scores will rise dramatically, while costs decrease (13).

   As is made apparent throughout by Stoll's sarcastic phrases, such as "Yee-ha!" (1) and "naw" (4), he opposes the over-reliance on computers in the classroom. Overall, Stoll's dismissive yet cuttingly ironic attitude toward his subject is summarized in the sentence "Yep, just sign up for the future: the parent-pleasin', tax-savin', teacher-firin', interactive-educatin', child-centerin' Cyberschool" (18).

3. In paragraph 3, Stoll points the finger at "harried" school board members and other administrators, especially elected ones. These individuals are pressured to reduce educational costs while improving students' performance and placating taxpayers. In the minds of these individuals, Stoll asserts, the cyberschool model of education presents numerous benefits. First, the computerized classroom allows long-term reduction in education spending achieved through the firing of full-time teachers (3, 11–12, 15), as well as the possibility of future profit through teaming with corporate supporters (14). Proponents also believe computers will allow students more customized learning, especially with regard to standardized test preparation (6–8). They could facilitate instant feedback and surveillance of students' progress to parents and administrators (9, 18) while reducing contact—troublesome and otherwise—among students (10). In the eyes of proponents, computers could even be seen as fostering healthy extracurricular activities such as distance mentoring or international student buddying (17)—all vicariously through the computer and never through firsthand contact.

4. According to Stoll's characterization of the cyberschool, teachers will play little to no role. As he says, tongue-in-cheek, in paragraph 11, "Teachers are an unnecessary appendix at this cyberschool." Rendered "irrelevant" by the new multimedia computer capabilities (11), by a "cadre of instructional specialists, consultants, and hall monitors" (12), and by "real-time instructors" available through "distance learning displays" (15), teachers and librarians will be "laid-off" and some can be "retrained as data entry clerks" (10).

   Stoll's attitude, though tongue-in-cheek, also carries ominous overtones regarding the dehumanization of children's education. This becomes especially apparent in his vision of a Big Brother-esque online instructor available only via "distance learning displays" and "two-way video" (15). Similarly alarming is the idea of the school board's monitoring of everything that students learn "without idiosyncratic teachers to raise unpopular topics or challenge accepted beliefs" (16)— when in fact teachers' fostering of independent thinking among students is what many people value as essential to a good education. Stoll also seems to mock the idea of teachers being replaced by "instructional specialists, consultants, and security guards" (12), as if those functions are the only ones that teachers fill in children's lives.

5. *infrastructures* (1): underlying foundations, especially for an organization or system
   optimal (1): most favorable or desirable
   harried (3): distressed by repeated attacks or harassment
   placate (4): to appease; to allay the anger of, especially by making concessions
   adept (8): very skilled
   standardized (8): conforming to a standard
   cubicles (10): small compartments for work or study
   compartmentalized (10): separated into distinct parts
   cadre (12): small, tight-knit group of trained personnel
   recoup (14): to return as an equivalent for; to reimburse
   idiosyncratic (16): having a behavioral characteristic peculiar to an individual or group

Questions About the Writer's Craft (p. 311)

1. This is a "trick question" of sorts, given the irony at the heart of Stoll's essay. On its surface, the process being described could seem directional in nature, laying out the procedure for implementing the cyberschool model of education. Stoll goes into relative detail regarding the set-up and administration of the cyber-classroom as well as the implications of doing so. The speaker of the essay, in all his ostensible enthusiasm for the cyberschool, almost provides a handbook to interested parties. But on closer look, it becomes apparent that this process analysis is, in fact, informational, primarily because Stoll presents the mechanics of a cyberschool in order to actually advocate *against* its implementation. He does so by offhandedly presenting the cyberschool's serious flaws and defects as though they are benefits; these include the reduction of precious interaction among teachers and students, elimination of independent or creative thinking, concentration solely on learning the content of standardized tests, and so on.

2. Stoll's tone is dismissive and definitely ironic. In presenting the cyberschool, Stoll adopts a persona much like the voice in an infomercial—synthetic, hyper, and ultimately trying to sell junk. However, Stoll's actual cynical agenda comes through in much of the wording that disrupts the pro-cyberschool façade. The phrase "whatever that means" blows the cover on the self-important tech-speak of paragraph 1, as do the artificially enthusiastic "Yee-ha!" (1) and "Naw—it's easy to solve all

these problems" (4). The words "edutainment" (6) and "edu-games" (8) that Stoll coins reveal a cynical view of the education trends he challenges, implying their watered-down nature. This is reinforced by the image of a "chatty pony" or "Fred the Firefighter" assuming the instructional role that trained professional teachers currently occupy—an absurd and demeaning image. In fact, regarding teachers in the cyberschool, he says, "No need for 'em" (11), a phrase that's obviously suspect in its flippancy. And the phrase "Virtual Compassion Corps" (17) is bursting with bitter contradiction, as is the statement "All without ever having to shake hands with a real person . . . or (gasp!) face the real problems of another culture" (17). Overall, Stoll's dismissive yet cuttingly ironic attitude toward his subject is summarized in the sentence "Yep, just sign up for the future: the parent-pleasin', tax-savin', teacher-firin', interactive-educatin', child-centerin' Cyberschool" (18). By referring to educational computers and their supporters in such dismissive terms, Stoll diminishes the stature of computers as a viable vehicle for teaching children, and he reinforces the central idea that computers are flashy distractions from the serious work of learning. The gravity of his message is resoundingly conveyed in the simple phrase "No learning."

Regarding the effect of Stoll's tone on his overall message, students' answers may vary, though it is likely that many will argue his apparent flippancy and humor in handling the topic helps capture readers' attention and send home his point more effectively than a straightforward, dry argument would.

3. Based on the information conveyed about Stoll, he appears to have airtight credibility in writing on the topic of computers and their effect on children's education. As an astronomer and programmer of computers "since the mid-sixties," Stoll has both an intimate working knowledge of computers and a highly informed long-term perspective on their effects on society; this expertise indicates that he is a well-reasoned and well-intentioned computer user, not a fanatical technophobe. As a teacher of children and young adults, he has accumulated firsthand observations of the increasing emphasis on computers in the classroom and the effects of this emphasis on young people. Finally, as a father, he has probably seen the impact of computers on the various facets of children's lives as they grow. His passionate desire to stave off the crippling effects on children of computer overuse is therefore legitimized by his roles as scientist, teacher, parent—and avid computer user.

4. In paragraph 15, Stoll addresses the central argument against the computerization of education when he says, "Concerned that such a system might be dehumanizing? Not to worry." His speaker then goes on to present a series of quasi-human interactions—all involving computers—to "allay" the fear of mechanized learning. These include "interactive chat sessions" among kids (instead of conversation, play, or in-person group work), help from a "trained support mentor" via the Internet (rather than a trained, in-person teacher), and, if necessary, assistance from a real-time instructor via "distance learning display" and "two-way video" (and certainly not in person). Clearly, these examples—all of which demonstrate complete reliance on computer rather than human contact—offer little to no comfort regarding the concern that computerized classrooms will result in dehumanized education for children. For as long as computers are the sole conduit of communication between individuals, the charge of dehumanization will remain valid. Stoll has deliberately selected these examples to sabotage the counterargument because, in fact, his essay seeks to undermine the idea of the cyberschool.

HOW TO SAY NOTHING IN 500 WORDS

Paul Roberts

Questions for Close Reading (p. 325)

1. Roberts states the thesis at the end of paragraph 6: "But there are some things you can do which will make your papers, if not throbbingly alive, at least less insufferably tedious than they might otherwise be."

2. The hypothetical student author of the essay on football seems to assume several things about the assignment: (1) that a student writer should try to hold an opinion that the professor will approve of or agree with, (2) that ending up with the exact number of words is one of the writer's top priorities, and (3) that the intelligence or vitality of the ideas in the essay is not very important.

3. Colorful words are those that create emotions in a reader or that draw a picture. Roberts calls them "dressy," "specific," and "loud" (43). Colored words are those that convey strong favorable or unfavorable associations in addition to their basic meaning; another term for them is "connotative language." Colorless words are so general and vague that they hardly have a meaning at all—words like "nice" (52) or "aspects" (53). Roberts would like students to be more attuned to the qualities of words, and he does wish students to beware of colorless words. He does not, however, indicate a blanket preference for any particular type of word. Instead, he suggests that a writer should decide whether highly colored language is appropriate for the subject matter, the readers, and the purpose of the writing. Writers should use judgment in incorporating colorful words, because, he writes, "it should not be supposed that the fancy word is always better" (36). In paragraph 43, he points out, "The question of whether to use loaded words or not depends on what is being written."

4. The author's main commandments are to avoid stating the obvious, try to hold an unusual position, speak in specifics, pare down your writing, be frank, and avoid clichés. You can look at the headings for sections 2 through 7 for brief statements of his main recommendations.

5. *bromides* (13): hackneyed remarks or ideas
   insufferably (13): intolerably, unbearably
   inexorably (14): relentlessly
   dissent (21): to differ; to disagree
   abolition (24): the act of doing away with something
   adept (28): competent
   euphemism (33): use of an inoffensive term instead of a more accurate, unpleasant term
   insensible (49): unconscious

Questions About the Writer's Craft (p. 325)

1. Roberts first presents the process by which he believes many students write papers— a description "exaggerated a little," he admits, but "not much" (5). Then he describes how students should write a paper; in paragraph 7 he tells how a student should begin, and he follows with advice on how to choose words and edit one's writing. The reader can compare the two processes and see how much more valid is the one Roberts recommends. The description of "how to say nothing" is presented for our information and amusement and to lay the groundwork for the discussion of how to

say something interesting in a composition. This process is intended to be directional and instructive.

2. Writing to the reader directly as "you" helps Roberts establish a personal, friendly rapport with the students he intends as his audience. Most students will say that they come away from the essay with an image of Roberts as an understanding and warm teacher; he seems to speak directly to their concerns and to anticipate their reactions: "Well, you may ask, what can you do about it?" (6). He comes across as someone who knows them and knows how they think, and, most important, respects them while still urging them to improve their work. Note that the headings are in the imperative, as if preceded by "You should. . . ."

3. The tone is warm, human, almost playful at times, but it is also a tone of frankness and directness. The informality and humanness result from a number of different techniques. Addressing the reader directly as "you" is one; in addition, Roberts uses colloquial language: "This was still funny during the War of 1812, but it has sort of lost its edge since then" (13). He has a surprising, sometimes sardonic, way of putting things: "All subjects, except sex, are dull until somebody makes them interesting" (6). He enjoys overstatement, just for effect, as when he provides possible specifics for a paper on college football (15). The sense of directness results from the author's frequent use of short sentences: "Then you go to the heart of the matter" (9) and from his willingness to expand on his points, provide examples, and give specific directions: "Don't say. . . . Say . . ." (18). The tone is quite effective; in fact, it may be the only tone possible for conveying this complex information about the high-level ability of writing to an audience of potentially hostile college students.

4. Yes, Roberts does follow his own advice. His starting recommendations that students seek out unpopular, uncommon, or hard-to-defend topics and points of view for their compositions is itself an example of "avoiding the obvious content" and "taking the less usual side." Roberts also "avoids the obvious content" by choosing to speak in a personal, informal tone, instead of the typical teacherly authoritarian tone most students (and teachers) would expect. He certainly "slips out of abstraction," using numerous examples of weak or potentially successful topics, sentences, phrases, and images. Paragraph 21, for example, illustrates his use of specifics. The essay is quite lengthy, and so it may not be obvious that Roberts has "gotten rid of obvious padding." Yet he does not repeat himself and is certainly not guilty of "circling warily around" his ideas (22). Rather, as he recommends in this section, he conscientiously illustrates and proves his points; see paragraphs 17 and 18 for examples of how he states his idea and then develops it rather than "pads" it. Roberts "calls a fool a fool" by directly confronting the inanities of the typical student composition: "All bloodless, five hundred words dripping out of nothing . . ." (5); "insufferably tedious . . ." (6). In fact, his portrait of the hypothetical student writer clearly reveals the folly of the student's writing process (3–4). Finally, students will have a hard time finding any clichés or euphemisms in Roberts's writing; some may cite his use of familiar expressions, such as "you're off" (3), "good ripe stuff" (3), "the brink of lunacy" (7), and "a general wringing of the hands." These are not really "pat expressions" in the sense that Roberts means, but familiar phrases used in a new context or in an interesting way. They do not "stand like a wall between the writer and thought"; they are colloquialisms that help Roberts make his ideas meaningful to his audience.

THE FINE ART OF COMPLAINING

Caroline Rego

Questions for Close Reading (p. 330)

1. Rego states her thesis in paragraph 4. Noting that many people go to extremes when dealing with annoyances, she writes that both milquetoasts and table-pounders need "a course in the gentle art of *effective* complaining." She proceeds to define this term (5–6) and then to give guidelines on how to achieve this art (7–24).

2. Acting self-important, raising one's voice, and making threats are counterproductive because they are likely to create hostility in the other person. Likewise, Rego suggests that demeaning oneself by begging and explaining is not productive either. Finally, she cautions against apologizing because the problem is not your fault (6).

3. The letter should explain the problem and include facts to convey the seriousness of the problem (12). It should also directly convey what remedy for the problem is desired (16) and what recourse will be sought if the remedy is not provided (19). It should not include details that are not to the point, such as how repairs were attempted (9), and it should not threaten extravagant action or aggression (21).

4. She advises us to keep complaining and to make sure the complaints are always heard by the same person. A single complaint may not be enough to achieve the desired results, and persistent complaining may wear down the person's resistance (23). Finally, she suggests threatening action, as long as it is a reasonable action. Notifying the Better Business Bureau or a consumer affairs agency (21) and taking the case to small claims court are valid recourses that may inspire the company to solve the problem (22).

5. *hapless* (3): unfortunate
   venture (3): to go despite risk or uncertainty
   patsy (3): (slang) a person easily victimized or cheated
   milquetoasts (4): people with meek, timid, or retiring natures
   apoplectic (4): seizure-like
   Neanderthal (4): (slang) crude, boorish person
   indiscriminately (5): randomly; without making any distinctions
   disembodied (7): without or outside the body
   credible (21): believable

Questions About the Writer's Craft (p. 331)

1. Rego provides both information and directions about performing an effective complaint, but most of the essay is devoted to a directional approach. She gives numerous examples of what to do and not to do (5–6), allowing the reader to visualize what it's like to make a complaint effectively. These examples also help persuade the reader that holding the line on emotion and projecting a businesslike image serve a complaining patron well. In paragraphs 7–8, the author provides more in-depth directions for conducting the in-person complaint, and in paragraphs 9–22, she details how to write a letter of complaint. Providing such step-by-step information about complaining and giving a well-developed example of a complaint letter help Rego be all the more persuasive that complaining can be done effectively.

2. Throughout the essay, Rego uses short narrative scenarios to add vividness, variety, and humor to what might otherwise have been a dry set of instructions. The narratives also serve to show exactly what she means at each step of the process. The

narratives begin in the first paragraph, where Rego sketches three brief stories about unappetizing food, a shrunken T-shirt, and a car repair. She then recalls these at the end of the second paragraph. Paragraph 3 provides more mini-narratives about people who flare up and shout in offices, restaurants, and stores as a way of complaining. In paragraph 6, Rego includes a scenario of effective complaining about delayed car repairs. The details in paragraph 9 about a broken vacuum cleaner and its resistance to repair by "Uncle Joe" also convey a narrative. The sample letter of complaint also invokes a more detailed narrative about a balky appliance, poor service, and faulty repairs (13–20).

3. Rego relies upon oppositions to create drama and a touch of humor, as well as to provide clear and persuasive images of what does and does not work in the "fine art of complaining." These oppositions begin in paragraphs 2 and 3, where Rego first describes a wimpy reaction to consumer problems and then an overly combative style. She repeats this contrast between "milquetoasts" and "Neanderthals" in paragraph 4, and invokes it again in paragraph 5, where she discriminates between apologetic and aggressive complaining. In paragraph 5, Rego opposes effective to ineffective complaining by defining what effective complaining is not: it is not "apologetic and half-hearted," nor is it the opposite, "roaring away indiscriminately."

Next, Rego provides details about what an effective complainer is, and opposes each quality to a negative. She defines "businesslike and important" as not "puffing up your chest," but treating your own request as reasonable and fair (6). At the end of this paragraph, she uses examples to contrast a polite, firm request for action with a hesitant, self-effacing style.

In the following paragraph (7), Rego compares the effectiveness of speaking in person and complaining by phone, and in paragraph 8, of complaining to a convenient person instead of to someone who can take or order action. Paragraph 9 introduces the letter of complaint by comparing its use to a personal complaint. Additional contrasts follow the example of the letter. In 21 and 22, Rego contrasts effective and useless threats. By constantly contrasting winning and self-defeating styles, Rego enlivens the essay and makes her strategies for successful complaining irresistible.

4. Rego begins the essay in the second person, giving hypothetical examples that dramatically put the reader right on the scene. In the second paragraph, she moves to the first person plural to describe the typical reactions people—"we"—have in dealing with annoyances and faulty products. Through this switch, she includes herself among those who find complaining an awkward and to-be-avoided eventuality. In paragraph 4, she makes another switch, to the third person, as she labels the two extremes in complaining with pejoratives: "milquetoasts" and "Neanderthals." Her description of how to complain effectively is couched, for the most part, in the third person (4–6). She then returns to the second person in paragraphs 7–9, in order to give advice about the appropriate person to whom one should complain. In paragraph 8, she uses the imperative form to instruct the reader in how to complain: "complain to the right person. . . . Getting mad doesn't help. . . . [M]ake sure from the start that you're talking to someone who can help . . ." (8). The italicized explanations between the paragraphs of the sample letter continue in the imperative, giving instructions about what each section of the letter should contain. After the letter, Rego continues with the use of "you," first, in advising upon the strategy to be used in the postscript (21–22), and then in coaching her readers to persist with complaints, since action may not result immediately. In concluding, she offers an upbeat image of a future devoid of complaint-inducing annoyances and then reminds us that, in the present, complaints are necessary. This final paragraph ends with two sentences that punch home the importance of complaining well. Using

the second person, she asserts, "You can depend upon it—there will be grounds for complaint. You might as well learn to be good at it." The use of multiple points of view allows Rego to inject personality and warmth into the essay and to place the reader and the writer at the center of the complaint process.

.

COMPARISON-CONTRAST

OPENING COMMENTS

Students learn early that comparison-contrast questions are one of the mainstays of essay exams: "Compare and/or contrast the organizations of the Senate and the House of Representatives"; "Discuss the similarities and/or differences between psychotic and neurotic behavior."

But we've found that students' familiarity with comparison-contrast doesn't necessarily mean they know how to structure their answers. On the contrary, students tend to prepare helter-skelter papers that ramble every which way and back. Yet, once they are introduced to some basic strategies for organizing a comparison-contrast discussion, their overall ability to write clearly and logically often takes a quantum leap.

When first using comparison-contrast, students may have trouble organizing their thoughts. Overly concerned about making their ideas fit into a neat symmetrical pattern, they may squeeze their points into an artificial and awkward format. We find it helpful to remind students that comparison-contrast is not an end in itself but a strategy for meeting a broader rhetorical purpose. Our reminder loosens them up a bit and encourages them to be more flexible when organizing their papers. The student essay, "The Virtues of Growing Older" (pp. 343–45), helps students appreciate that a well-organized comparison-contrast paper does not have to follow a rigid formula.

We selected the readings in this chapter because, in addition to being just plain interesting, all of them illustrate key points about the comparison-contrast format. Carson uses the one-side-at-a-time approach to dramatize the difference between two extremes. Suina employs both comparison-contrast strategies to evoke a confusing and painful time of adaptation in his childhood. And Rodriguez organizes his essay around an entire network of comparisons and contrasts. To illustrate his point that men and women view their looks differently, Barry gives both sides equal time, balancing the humorous with the serious in this point-by-point method of analysis. By comparing and contrasting punishments in Islamic and American society, Chapman exposes and questions the values underlying our system of jurisprudence.

ANSWERS FOR PREWRITING ACTIVITIES

Below we provide possible responses to selected prewriting activities at the end of Chapter 8. Of course, other approaches are possible. (p. 348)

1. There are numerous ways to use comparison-contrast in these two essays. Here are some possibilities. In going over this activity in class, we suggest you have students trade responses so that they can see how diverse the responses are.

    Topic: The effects of holding a job in college
    Comparing/contrasting job-holders' and non-job-holders' grades
    Comparing/contrasting on-campus and off-campus jobs
    Comparing/contrasting part-time and full-time jobs

Comparing/contrasting job-holders' and non-job-holders' involvement in campus activities

Topic: *How to budget money wisely*
Comparing/contrasting formal and informal budgets
Comparing/contrasting following a budget to buying on impulse
Comparing/contrasting those who budget and those who don't
Comparing/contrasting reasonable and unreasonable budgets

ANSWERS FOR REVISING ACTIVITIES

Below we provide possible responses to selected prewriting activities at the end of Chapter 8. Of course, other approaches are possible. (p. 348)

3. a. This statement works well as a thesis.
    b. This statement is unworkable as a thesis; it is too vague and broad since "assistance" could refer to academic, financial, or other kind of aid. A possible revision: "This college provides a much more comprehensive job placement service to students than other colleges in the area."
    c. This statement would be effective as a thesis if revised to state an attitude toward the candidates' use of television, for example, if one made legitimate use of the medium and the other none. A possible revision: "Joe Cooper's overwrought campaign tactics gained extensive media coverage, while Cooper's opponent, Nancy Ashbury, conducted a more subdued campaign that emphasized issues and failed to attract much attention."
    d. This statement would not work as a thesis. First of all, it points out the obvious and sets up the writer for a pedantic recital of known information. Secondly, the statement is far too inclusive; in attempting to cover the topic, the writer would have to use a ream of paper. A possible revision: "Applying their technological know-how, Japanese car manufacturers learned how to make small engines more powerful, while American companies, showing very little foresight, simply added power to their cars by reintroducing larger engines."

4. Have students read each others' versions of this paragraph so that they get a stronger sense of what changes need to be made and the revision strategies possible.
    Here are the main problems with the paragraph:

    — Since the paragraph discusses a boss and then a manager, the topic sentence should be reversed to read, "A boss discourages staff resourcefulness and views it as a threat, while a manager encourages creativity and treats employees courteously."
    — The second sentence ("At the hardware store . . .") begins abruptly; a transition, such as "for example," would be helpful here.
    — The boss's helter-skelter system is introduced awkwardly: "What he did was . . ." Something like this might be more effective: "He organized overstocked items . . ."
    — The phrase "created chaos" is vague, possibly a bit extreme, and also somewhat slangy. Briefly describing the actual problems his system created would be helpful, as long as the paragraph doesn't veer off-track and focus entirely on the chaos.

- Some language is possibly too judgmental: "helter-skelter" (4), "slapdash" (7), and "eccentric" (9). Students may want to describe the system with enough telling details so the readers can see for themselves the system's inefficiency.
- No reason is given for the boss's anger at the new system—or perhaps there was no reason other than that his ego was deflated. In either case, the source of his objections should be clarified.
- Some ideas are repeated at the end; sentences 8 and 9 ("I had assumed he would welcome my ideas . . .") repeat material conveyed at the beginning of the paragraph.
- The phrase "to scrap" is perhaps a bit slangy in tone.

A FABLE FOR TOMORROW

Rachel Carson

Questions for Close Reading (p. 351)

1. Carson's thesis comes at the end: "A grim specter has crept upon us almost unnoticed, and this imagined tragedy may easily become a stark reality we all shall know." Carson is referring to the potential devastation of plant and animal life by herbicides, insecticides, and other environmental hazards.
2. The lovely sights include orchard blossoms (1), autumn foliage (1), wildflowers (2), and birds (2).
3. She is adopting the point of view of the townspeople, who find the spreading illness "mysterious" and "unexplained" (3). The people are "puzzled and disturbed" (4).
4. Plants, animals, and humans die; an eerie silence replaces bird-song and other customary animal sounds; the landscape turns increasingly ugly ("browned and withered vegetation"); and animals fail to reproduce normally.
5. *viburnum* (2): a tree or shrub of the honeysuckle family
   alder (2): a tree or shrub of the birch family
   moribund (4): dying
   specter (9): something fearful that appears unexpectedly

Questions About the Writer's Craft (p. 352)

1. The one-side-at-a-time method enables Carson to highlight the drastic difference in conditions before and after the blight. The selection is so short that a point-by-point comparison would only reduce the impact.
2. The first paragraph is developed primarily through lush visual description, such as "white clouds of bloom drifted above the green fields" and "a blaze of color that flamed and flickered across a backdrop of pines." It refers, as well, to foxes' barking and deer's silence. Paragraph 2 is dominated by visual description. Paragraphs 4, 5, and 6 all mention sounds no longer present: "chorus of robins" (4), "no bees droned" (5), and "silent roadsides" (6). Paragraphs 4, 6, and 7 each contain at least one visual detail that creates a harsh, disturbing image unlike the luxurious, peaceful description that opens the essay. All of the sensory images reinforce Carson's thesis by making the reader experience the fullness of life before the blight.
3. The biblical tone adds an air of authoritative prophecy.
4. In the last paragraph, Carson steps outside her fable and writes direct argumentation-persuasion. She no longer shows, using description and narration, but instead warns the reader directly that the situation is a dangerous one. The effect of the last

paragraph is to base the fable in reality by stating that "every one of these disasters has actually happened somewhere."

AND THEN I WENT TO SCHOOL

Joseph H. Suina

Questions for Close Reading (p. 358)

1. Suina's thesis is implied by the comparison of his preschool lifestyle with his life after school begins. It could be stated as "Attending school began the destruction of Suina's strong Indian self-image and of his attachment to Indian customs and values." Paragraph 16 also provides a thesis-like statement: "life would never be the same again. . . . [T]he ways of the white man . . . would creep more and more into my life."

2. Values were instilled through story-telling, praise, and direct instruction. Suina mentions several typical storytelling sessions; for example, his grandmother would tell him about "how it was when she was a little girl" (3). When the relatives gathered, a nightly occurrence, they too would tell stories to "both children and adults" (4). Praise was showered upon him by his grandmother so that he would be proud of his accomplishments; "her shower of praises," he writes, "made [him] feel like the Indian Superman of all times" (6). Finally, his grandmother teaches him about his culture by taking him along with her to various ceremonies and teaching him "appropriate behavior" for these occasions. She also models how to pray, so that he learns both the words and the proper attitude (7). When Suina goes to school, he is shocked by the very different methods of teaching. Instead of praise, he receives "a dirty look or a whack with a ruler" when he speaks his native language (13). Personal hygiene is impressed upon him through a cruelly administered shampoo and caustic, embarrassing comments about his background (12). The language barrier meant that he couldn't comprehend all the lessons, but "yet [he] could understand very well when [he] messed up. . . . The negative aspect was communicated too effectively. . . ." (11).

3. The village begins to take in some non-Indian influences. There are automobiles, albeit very few of them. Suina's grandmother possesses a dresser in which she keeps some of her possessions; the dresser, a European type of furniture, was acquired by trading some of her famous handmade pottery. And, in the dresser, she keeps goodies, which include "store bought cookies and Fig Newtons." (3). Even the tradition of going nightly to visit relatives to chat and tell stories is on the decline as radios and televisions cause people to stay home instead of going out (4). And the children have access to some ten-cent comic books, which they read and use as the basis for fantasy games when their families get together at night. They imitate the cowboys-and-Indians plots in the comics, with, ironically, all the children wanting to be cowboys because they always won the conflicts. Suina sums up the encroachment of white culture in paragraph 16: "The schools, television, automobiles and other white man's ways and values had chipped away at the simple cooperative life I grew up in. The people of Cochiti were changing."

4. In paragraph 13, Suina indicates that the adults around him wanted him to attend school so that he "might have a better life in the future" (13). This idea is in itself confusing to him, because he felt he "had a good village life already" (13). Near the end of the essay, he recognizes that "there was no choice but to compete with the white man on his terms for survival" (16).

Many elements of the school lifestyle are confusing to him. The teaching style, with whacks of a ruler, dirty looks, scoldings, and embarrassing comments, is very alien to him. "The strange surroundings, new concepts about time and expectations, and a foreign tongue" were other elements that bewildered him (8). The teacher is so different in appearance from his grandmother that he thinks she is ill; she is also unfriendly and, he thinks, not very smart, because she cannot speak his language. The classroom is so large it seems cold and ominous; the artificial building style and the fluorescent lighting also seem forbidding and alien. Instead of running freely, he must sit all day long. The most confusing thing to him, however, is that he must give up his language and speak English.

Going to the boarding school clinches his separation from his native village culture. He lives in a white-style building and learns the comforts of indoor plumbing, spacious rooms, and ventilation. By the time he returns for a four-day break at Thanksgiving, the village lifestyle does "not feel right anymore" (15). Now living with whites twenty-four hours a day, he finds himself unaccustomed to the culture he was raised in. He soon "gets back with it" (15), he says, and then finds returning to school extremely difficult. His life has been transformed; he "could not turn back the time just as [he] could not do away with school and the ways of the white man" (16).

5. *adobe* (5): sun-dried clay, usually in bricks
    ego (12): sense of self-importance
    belittled (15): to criticize something as unimportant or trivial

Questions About the Writer's Craft (p. 358)

1. The essay is predominantly organized according to the *one-side-at-a-time* pattern. First, Suina discusses his life as a preschooler residing in his grandmother's house (1–7). Then, he discusses what life was like for him after he was required to attend school (8–16). This pattern works well because the essay compares "before" and "after" stages of Suina's childhood, stages that occurred one after the other. The *one-side-at-a-time* strategy allows Suina to maintain the chronological order of events.

    There are some places within the description of his school life where Suina returns to talk about Indian ways; in these places he uses the *point-by-point* strategy. For example, at the start of paragraph 9, he describes his teacher, comparing her with his grandmother. In paragraph 10, he compares the fluorescent lighting to "the fire and sunlight that my eyes were accustomed to" and sitting at a desk all day with his previous life of "running carefree in the village and fields." In paragraph 13, he compares the attitude of the school toward his native language and his own childhood view of it: "This punishment was for speaking the language of my people that meant so much to me. It was the language of my grandmother and I spoke it well. With it, I sang beautiful songs and prayed from my heart" (13). Later, Suina compares the beloved home cooking that his family brings to him once a month with the school food: "I enjoyed the outdoor oven bread, dried meat, and tamales they usually brought. It took a while to get accustomed to the diet of the school." Finally, the last paragraphs of the essay use *point-by-point* organization to express the conflicts he felt when he returned home from boarding school for four days. In paragraph 16, he describes how disappointed he felt with his old home: "Home did not feel right anymore. It was much too small and stuffy. The lack of running water and bathroom facilities were too inconvenient. Everything got dusty so quickly and hardly anyone spoke English. I did not realize I was beginning to take on the white man's ways, the ways that belittled my own."

2. The numerous places where Suina evokes the pueblo lifestyle and values include paragraph 3, where he describes the inside of his grandmother's one-room house in great detail. Most of the details here are visual, although Suina does mention the "sharp odor of mothballs" in the dresser and the flour sack containing the " goodies," which made a "fine snack" at night. We also learn that he frequently hears stories or a softly sung song from a ceremony in the house. There are further references to the foods they shared with relatives in paragraph 4, and in the next paragraph he notes the sound and glow of the fire and the smell of stew cooking. He contrasts these sensory descriptions with details about the school he attends. There, he notices the teacher's appearance is very different from his grandmother's; he smells her odor, which makes him sick (9). He provides details of the classroom: its "huge" size and medicine-like smell, its artificial walls and ceiling, its "eerie" and blinking fluorescent lights. He feels the hardness of the desk to which he is confined. Towards the end of the essay, he returns to some beloved details about his Indian culture, things that he savors when his parents visit him at boarding school: "outdoor oven bread, dried meat, and tamales" (14). Yet, once home for a four-day break, he discovers he longs for some of the conveniences of the school, for his home "was much too small and stuffy. The lack of running water and bathroom facilities were too inconvenient. Everything got dusty so quickly. . . ." (15).

3. Into the simple factual information of the first two sentences, Suina inserts a word with strong negative connotations: *invade*. This word is used metaphorically to suggest that the coming of electricity to the pueblo began a conquest of the Indian culture by that of the whites. Portraying the Indians as "unsuspecting" suggests their innocence in not being aware that they were being transformed. These images establish an ominous tone and convey Suina's ambivalence about the material goods and other elements of white lifestyle that altered his native culture. However, while suggesting negative forces are at work in the pueblo, Suina's tone remains calm, almost matter-of-fact. There is no sense of blaming or rage; because of this tone, the changes seem to be inevitable.

4. The last four sentences of paragraph 14 all begin with the phrase "I longed for. . . ." This repetition drums into the reader the grief and yearning Suina felt at being parted from his home culture. The sentences seem to cry out with pain. In addition, the shortness and simplicity of the sentences effectively convey the depth and sense of unalleviated need. The final sentence moves away from specific needs for his grandmother and siblings, his home, and the familiar ceremonies to asserting that he needs to be free to be himself, instead of being confined in the alien world of the boarding school.

WORKERS

Richard Rodriguez

Questions for Close Reading (p. 366)

1. The thesis of "Workers" is implied. One way of expressing it might be this: "A summer of hard physical labor is not enough to teach a young middle-class college graduate what it is like to be poor or Mexican, or what it means to make construction work one's livelihood."

2. Rodriguez writes that desire for the job "uncoiled" in him as soon as he heard about it. This surprised him, although he was in need of money at the time (1). In the

weeks leading up to the job, he realized that he felt challenged to learn, after four years in college, what it was like to work hard physically (3). In doing so, he would overcome his father's scorn that the young Rodriguez did not know what "real work" was. He was also intrigued by the thought of the sensations that would come from working in the open, under the sun, and by the chance to become "like a *bracero*" (4).

3. Very quickly the contrast between the "real laborers" and Rodriguez becomes apparent to him. He is only flirting with being a construction worker before going on to graduate school, while the other men do construction work for a living. Unlike them, he appreciates the sheer physicality of the work. When the older men try to show him how to shovel efficiently, so as not to waste energy or strain his back, he feels resistant to their instructions. "I liked the way my body felt sore at the end of the day," he writes (7).

4. Rodriguez comes to recognize he has little in common with *los pobres*, the Mexican aliens who occasionally cut trees and haul debris, although at first he seems to think there might be some natural kinship between himself and them. After all, they are Mexicans, like Rodriguez's parents; he is "physically indistinguishable" from them (17). He even speaks a rudimentary Spanish and can communicate with them in their native tongue. They treat him as an outsider, however, and he realizes he is of a different world. He earns a wage, while they are paid "for the job," as if they had no individual identities. They stay apart from the regular workers, work with little rest, converse rarely, and are powerless to change their situation. "They lack a public identity. . . . They depend upon the relative good will or fairness of their employers each day" (19). In addition, they must be submissive to retain the good will of employers; they are vulnerable in a way Rodriguez will never be. Rodriguez has a self-determined future ahead of him, the result of his college education. He says he can "act as a public person—able to defend [his] interests, to unionize, to petition, to speak up—to challenge and demand" (18). He states the difference philosophically at the end of paragraph 17: "What made me different from them was an attitude of *mind*, my imagination of myself."

5. *menial* (1): servile, subservient
   skepticism (4): doubt
   luxuriating (5): wallowing in pleasure
   diversity (9): variety, quality of difference
   ludicrous (16): laughable, absurd
   nouveau riche 18): the newly rich
   pathos (20): quality of arousing pity or sorrow

Questions About the Writer's Craft (p. 366)

1. The author is more like the American construction workers than the Mexican laborers; the details provided in paragraph 9 make his similarity to the Americans clear. He is able to find other workers that he can relate to, because some, like himself, have college degrees; one is an abstract painter in the off-hours. Also, these workers accept him, while the Mexicans do not. "I felt easy, pleased by the knowledge that I was casually accepted, my presence taken for granted by men (exotics) who worked with their hands," he writes (9). Other details reveal that these workers are "middle-class Americans," like himself, who follow football, vacation in Las Vegas, and consider the merits of different campers, presumably in view of purchasing one (9). The details about the Mexicans, on the other hand, show them to be alienated, silent, and submissive (11, 15).

2. There are four narrative segments in the piece: the stories of how Rodriguez heard about the job and how he came to take it (1–3, 4); the story of the older workers teaching him how to shovel (6–8); the narrative of his Spanish conversation with the Mexican workers (12–15); and the description of how the boss pays the Mexicans (16). The anecdotes about the Mexicans come last because the experience of working with them generates Rodriguez's most important point—that he will never be like them, that his attempt to recover a more elemental, ancestral self was a failure. The anecdotes occur in chronological order at first: hearing about a job, getting it, and learning to do the work. In putting the Mexican anecdotes last, Rodriguez switches to emphatic organization.

3. The subjective descriptions of how it feels to do hard physical work occur mostly in paragraph 5. Students will probably find two phrases especially striking: "my chest silky with sweat in the breeze" and "a nervous spark of pain would . . . burn like an ember in the thick of my shoulder."

4. Rodriguez mixes in a few Spanish words to suggest his origins. In terms of the theme, these foreign words express the author's uncertain identity: as a highly educated American of Mexican descent, he feels neither like an "all-American worker" nor like a Mexican laborer; the Spanish terms convey his middle position between the two groups. Also, Spanish in general and the words he chooses in particular (such as *bracero*) represent his desire to vindicate himself in terms of his father's value system, which celebrates "real work."

THE UGLY TRUTH ABOUT BEAUTY

Dave Barry

Questions for Close Reading (p. 370)

1. The selection's main idea is expressed in the fourth paragraph: "The problem is that women generally do not think of their looks in the same way that men do." Throughout the essay, Barry addresses a serious topic—the way men and women develop their self-images—with tongue-in-cheek humor. Most men, he argues, "think of themselves as average-looking," and "being average does not bother them" (5). He illustrates this claim with the humorous observation that men's "primary form of beauty-care is to shave themselves, which is essentially the same form of beauty-care that they give to their lawns" (5). Most women, on the other hand, believe that their appearance is simply "not good enough" (6) and obsessively seek to narrow the gap between themselves and the images of ideal beauty that pervade society. Women "grow up thinking they need to look like Barbie, which for most women is impossible" or "like Cindy Crawford, who is some kind of genetic mutation" (8).

    Though he pokes fun at the behaviors of both men and women regarding how they view themselves, Barry implies that women's obsession with how they look can be highly detrimental to the psyche as well as a colossal waste of time.

2. The reason for men's unwavering unconcern with their appearances, Barry states, is that men are not inundated with images dictating how they should look. For instance, while girls grow up subjected to an impossibly proportioned, utterly unrealistic model of female beauty—the Barbie doll—boys, through their "hideous-looking" but "self-confident" action figures, are socialized to value physical perfection to a much lesser degree (7). So, as women grow up "thinking they need to look like Barbie,

which for most women is impossible" (8), men aren't encouraged to spend much time at all considering their looks. In fact, to look presentable—which, Barry implies, is good enough for most men—men only need engage in a "four-minute . . . beauty regimen" of shaving, "which is essentially the same form of beauty care that they give their lawns" (5). Ultimately, Barry argues, men can content themselves with an average appearance because, unlike women, they are not subject to a "multibillion-dollar beauty industry devoted to convincing [them] they must try to look perfect" (8).

3. From a woman's point of view, Barry argues, personal beauty is a matter of measuring up to the "difficult appearance standard" that pervades society (7). He says that "women grow up thinking they need to look like Barbie, which for most women is impossible, although there is a multibillion-dollar beauty industry devoted to convincing women that they must try" (8). TV shows, such as *Oprah,* perpetuate these negative values in featuring "supermodel Cindy Crawford" and her ludicrously detailed lessons on make-up application (8). Eventually, women become convinced they must strive for what is actually an unattainable image, and they "spen[d] countless hours . . . obsessing about the differences between [themselves] and Cindy Crawford" (13), whose apparent flawlessness Barry identifies as "some kind of genetic mutation" (8). Because the image that women pursue is virtually impossible to achieve, most women feel they fall far short of the mark when it comes to attractiveness. Thus, women believe that their appearance is simply "not good enough" (6), and they often wind up developing a negative self-image and low self-esteem (7).

In addition to Barbie dolls, the all-powerful beauty industry, and the media (represented by TV shows like *Oprah*), Barry addresses another potential source of women's obsession with their appearance: men. He says that "many women will argue that the reason they become obsessed . . . is that men WANT them to look that way" (10). But he then undermines this claim in two ways. First, he says that women should know better than to be misled by men, that "just because WE'RE idiots, that does not mean YOU have to be" (11). Next, he claims that "men don't even notice 97 percent of the beauty effort you make anyway" (12). Ultimately, despite his humorous take on his subject, Barry seeks to point out the negative consequences of women's obsession with beauty and to persuade women away from this misguided mentality.

4. Barry implies that, ideally, women should not align their sense of self-worth with their appearance and should reject the unrealistic beauty standards with which they are bombarded in society. Though this is not an easy feat, Barry implies that women have the intelligence and strength of character to resist society's damaging messages about beauty: "just because WE'RE [men are] idiots [in appreciating supermodels], that does not mean YOU have to be" (11). In fact, though Barry cautions that he's "not saying that men are superior" (9), he does imply that men's indifference to matters of their own appearance is a worthwhile model for women to emulate.

5. *regimen* (5): routine or process
municipal (6): community or public
societal (7): shared by society or by the group
dispensed (8): handed out
genetic (8): inborn, hereditary
mutation (8): alteration or deviation from the norm
demeaning (9): humiliating
bolster (9): reinforce, strengthen

Questions About the Writer's Craft (p. 370)

1. Barry uses the point-by-point method of organization to contrast how men and women perceive their personal appearances. Paragraphs 4 and 5 explore how men evaluate their appearance, and then paragraph 6 looks at how women do. Paragraph 7 begins by exploring how girls' toys affect their self-perception and ends by showing how boys' toys affect theirs. Paragraph 8 illustrates women's embracing of beauty role models, while paragraph 9 outlines men's rejection of the same. This animated alternation between women's and men's attitudes toward personal attractiveness both heightens and lends immediacy to the contrast between the two. Barry's point-by-point contrast, maintained with a great deal of humor, encourages both women and men to laugh at themselves and their efforts (or lack thereof) to be good-looking. Yet the sharply delineated disparity between men's and women's self-evaluations emphasizes the fundamental absurdity of what women put themselves through.

2. Throughout the selection, Barry tends to overstate ideas in order to maximize their impact on readers. For example, to demonstrate men's quandary when women ask how they look, Barry suggests that men should "form an honest yet sensitive opinion, then collapse on the floor with some kind of fatal seizure" (3). In this and other instances, Barry's humor draws upon highly exaggerated visual images. For example, when illustrating men's unchanging, generally positive opinion of their looks, he says that men who decide early on that they are "stud muffins" remain steadfast in this opinion "even when their faces sag and their noses bloat to the size of eggplants and their eyebrows grow together to form what appears to be a giant forehead-dwelling tropical caterpillar" (4). Barry likewise employs exaggeration in demonstrating that women are perpetually dissatisfied with their appearances. He says that "no matter how attractive" a woman may be, "when she looks at herself in the mirror, she thinks: woof" and that "at any moment a municipal animal-control officer is going to throw a net over her and haul her off to the shelter" (6). To demonstrate the negative impact on women of Barbie's unrealistic figure, he provides another humorous overstatement: If the doll were a human, "it would be seven feet tall and weigh 81 pounds, of which 53 pounds would be bosoms" (7). Similarly, in conveying the unattainable beauty standards set by supermodels, Barry calls Cindy Crawford "some kind of genetic mutation" (8). And in dismissing the claim that men encourage women's painstaking efforts to be beautiful, he claims that "[t]he average woman spends 5,000 hours per year worrying about her fingernails, while [m]any men would not notice if a woman had upward of four hands" (12).

   The most obvious purpose of this repeated exaggeration is to engage readers by making them laugh. At the very least, Barry shows, people should laugh at themselves for taking their looks and society's standard of beauty too seriously. Yet Barry's overstatement has a serious purpose: to demonstrate how women's obsession with society's inflated beauty standards undermines women's and, by extension, men's psychological well-being. Sadly, Barry's exaggerations may have much in common with many people's distorted mindset about the subject of personal beauty.

3. Barry points out a number of cause-effect relationships in order to make us aware of how our self-perceptions are formed and to persuade us to stop subjecting ourselves to society's impossible standards. The central causal analysis of the selection explores the reasons for, and effects of, women's appearance-consciousness. Barry begins by illustrating some of the effects of this fixation, the first of which is women's need to have the answer to the question "How do I look?" (2). This question, which strikes fear in the hearts of men who don't know how best to respond, reflects women's need for external affirmation of their appearance. Barry goes on to state that, unlike men, women generally appraise their appearance as "not

good enough" (6) and that most women suffer from "low self-esteem" (7). He then proceeds to explore the complex psychological and societal reasons for women's poor self-image, which, he half-jokingly proposes, are summed up in the Barbie doll (7). The doll, complete with its outrageous, unnatural physical proportions, brainwashes young girls about the way a real woman should look. It is no wonder, then, that women would "grow up thinking they need to look like Barbie, which for most women is impossible" (8). Other sources of women's beauty ideals include the "multibillion-dollar beauty industry" (8) as well as the media (represented by the *Oprah* show), which fuel women's insecurity and beauty-obsession by constantly imposing new standards of beauty. As a result, women squander "countless hours"—and, presumably, dollars—as well as precious self-esteem in "obsessing about the differences" between themselves and the newest unattainable beauty ideal (13).

Since Barry's thesis is that "women generally do not think of their looks in the same way that men do" (4), he offers a second series of cause-effect chains; these focus on men's relative comfort with their appearance and provide a crucial counterpoint to his analysis of women. Unlike women, men "never ask anybody how they look" (5). This is because most men, Barry argues, see themselves as "average-looking" (5); they "form an opinion of how they look in seventh grade, and they stick to it for the rest of their lives" (4). The reason for this mentality, Barry reveals later, is that young boys, unlike young girls, are *not* taught to emphasize their physical appearance. He illustrates this claim with the example of his son's "hideous-looking" but "extremely self-confident" action figure, which contrasts sharply with the inhumanly beautiful Barbie dolls with which girls are socialized to play (7). As a result, men are not conditioned to obsess about their appearance. Unlike women, men spend very little time and energy on grooming, their greatest exertion being a "four-minute beauty regimen" of shaving, "which is essentially the same form of beauty care that they give their lawns" (5). In fact, men's freedom from beauty-brainwashing causes them aggressively to reject any models of male beauty. Barry argues that men would recognize as "pointless and demeaning" (9) women's eager desire for Cindy Crawford's beauty tips on the *Oprah* show. If men were presented with the challenge to look like Crawford's male equivalent, Brad Pitt, they would respond by making reference to their capabilities—"Oh YEAH? Well, what do you know about LAWN CARE, pretty boy?"—*not* by trying to mirror the beauty standard placed before them (9).

Barry does acknowledge an intersection point between the female and male causal chains when he addresses women's claim that men "WANT women to look like supermodels" (10). Barry, however, debunks this claim by humorously arguing that women should know better than to listen to men and that "[m]en don't even notice the beauty efforts women make anyway" (12). Yet despite Barry's light-hearted dismissal of women's claim, the fact still remains that men are indeed a cause of women's beauty-mania. Ultimately, a larger effect of both women's and men's attitudes is their different expectations regarding beauty—hence, Barry's advice that when a woman asks "How do I look?" a man would do best to "collapse on the floor with some kind of fatal seizure because he will never come up with the right answer" (3).

4. The title, "The Ugly Truth About Beauty," suggests that our concept of beauty itself is not beautiful. Throughout the essay, Barry outlines the highly detrimental psychological effects to women of the appearance-consciousness they are taught. Women's obsessive pursuit of beauty, in effect, has disastrous—and ugly—consequences for their mental and emotional well-being. Thus, in spite of the humor with which Barry addresses his subject, his title indicates that he takes the matter seriously and wants his readers to do the same.

THE PRISONER'S DILEMMA

Stephen Chapman

Questions for Close Reading (p. 376)

1. Chapman's thesis statement is implied in his discussion of how the American justice system compares with that of Islamic countries. The thesis might be stated this way: "Although we consider the Islamic punishment system cruel, our own is just as frequently cruel, even barbaric, and often unfair." In paragraph 3, Chapman presents the "single device" of our punishment system, incarceration, and through examples of its use, strongly implies its unfair, cruel, and even ludicrous nature. These examples include that (a) some states do not impose a sentence of a specific length on certain convicts, but instead permit parole boards to decide the sentence length during the course of the imprisonment and (b) extremely long sentences can be imposed for small crimes because of multiple offenses or of the use of a weapon.

2. Chapman gives several examples of Islamic punishments: flogging for such crimes as prostitution (1), stoning or scourging for sexual crimes or drinking alcohol, amputation of the hands for thievery, and death for murder or leaving the Islamic religion (2). These punishments are barbaric to us not only in themselves but also in the manner in which they are inflicted. Many punishments are carried out in public, with hordes of viewers, as many as 10,000 at a time, entertained by the spectacle of other people's agony (1). The accused are often punished after summary, immediate trials, and, in the case of flogging, are stripped, marked with red, and virtually attacked by burly, strutting, stave-wielding convicted murderers (1). As Chapman says, these punishments seem barbaric in two ways, by being cruel and by seeming "pre-civilized" (1). Much later in the essay (11), Chapman returns to the issue of why Americans might find the Islamic system barbaric. He cites the lack of due process, that is, of an elaborate and protective legal system such as ours, and the numerous offenses pertaining to what Americans consider personal morality, such as drinking, adultery, and religious offenses. He also points out that the Islamic legal system is full of "ritualistic mumbo-jumbo pronouncements," which Americans find irrelevant and peculiar.

3. There are five goals of imprisonment, according to criminologists cited by Chapman in paragraph 6. These are, first, retribution, the idea that the criminal should pay for the crime. A second goal is "specific deterrence," the idea that the criminal should be discouraged by the punishment from repeating the crime at a later date. There is also the goal of "general deterrence," by which the criminally inclined will take note of the punishment meted out to others and turn away from crime. The fourth goal is prevention, the idea that while in prison, the criminal cannot commit other similar crimes. The fifth and most important goal is supposed to be rehabilitation, by which the criminal is reformed so that he will return to society an upright citizen (6). In terms of success, only on the score of punishment does Chapman believe American prisons achieve their goals. He cites statistics on the increase of crime over the last twenty years to indicate that few criminals are reformed and few are deterred, in specific or in general. In addition, he pronounces that "almost no one contends any more that prisons rehabilitate their inmates" (17).

4. Chapman concludes that both systems are cruel and barbaric, and that ours may be the worse one. The main difference is that our system is hidden from our eyes, and

so we find it easy to ignore how cruel it is, whereas the Islamic one is inflicted in full view of the public (12). Chapman finds us admirable in our reluctance to sanction cruelty and violence in the style of Islamic societies. He sees that this revulsion for deliberate cruelty both forces us to hide our punishment of criminals and might prompt us to someday discover a better way to deal with criminals (13). However, this hidden nature of our cruelty also perpetuates it and causes us to be self-congratulatory about our civilized methods. In other words, we have become unknowing hypocrites.

5. *barbaric* (1): crude and unrestrained
   stipulated (2): specified
   penological (2): having to do with the punishment of crime
   malefactors (2): people who do evil or violate the laws
   effusive (2): unrestrained in expression of feeling
   brazen (3): shockingly bold
   genteel (3): refined; free from vulgarity or rudeness
   indeterminate (3): not specified; not known in advance
   superfluous (3): more than sufficient or necessary
   extortion (4): the use of force to compel someone to hand over valuables
   criteria (7): standards of measurement
   ostensible (8): apparent, professed, or stated
   recidivism (9): relapsing into or returning to criminal behavior
   corporal (9): affecting the physical body
   blasphemy (11): impious statements about God
   sanctioned (13): authorized or approved

Questions About the Writer's Craft (p. 377)

1. Chapman helps the reader keep track of the goals by using transitional questions as he moves from one function of imprisonment to another. Only with the first goal does he use the numbering system that he relied upon in paragraph 6: "First, do they punish?" The other transitional questions that cue the reader's memory of his earlier list include "Do they deter crime?" (8); "Do flogging and amputation deter recidivism?" (9); "Do these medieval forms of punishment rehabilitate the criminal?" (10). Note that in paragraph 8, he disregards the difference between specific and general deterrence, and discusses deterrence in response to the question "Do they deter crime?" (8). By thus collapsing two functions into one, he needs only to contrast four aspects of punishment in the two cultures.

2. In the first paragraph, Chapman defines "barbaric" for us, although it is a word with which most readers would already, in some sense, be familiar. But Chapman spells out two dimensions of this word because he believes both are relevant and need to be acknowledged. To Americans, he says, Islamic punishment seems "barbaric" in two ways: "cruel" and "pre-civilized." He then provides a definition of what "flogging" is in Pakistan, even though the reader most likely has a basic understanding of the term. But by providing an extended definition, involving a horrifying, vivid picture of flogging in action, Chapman dramatizes what Americans would find so barbaric. These definitions establish the reader's agreement with Chapman's opening point, that Islamic justice is cruel beyond our conception. In the next paragraph (2), Chapman solidifies the reader's revulsion to Islamic ways by defining "scourging."

   In paragraph 6, Chapman uses definition to clarify what is meant by the five separate goals of punishment in the American system. He spells out the five goals carefully, defining them and differentiating them from each other. Later in the essay, he will argue that the American system is a failure by its own standards, meeting only one of five goals (retribution), and that by American standards, the Islamic system may, shockingly enough, be more successful.

3. Chapman uses emphatic organization in arranging both these paragraphs. In paragraph 3, he begins with a fairly standard or "typical" example of our punishment system at work, the sentencing of people to three to five years' imprisonment for grand theft and to six to thirty years for armed robbery. He points to longer sentences for repeat offenders and begins to give additional examples, but these examples begin to display the illogicality and cruelty that can crop up in our system. These examples of prison sentences, thus, are arranged from those that seem acceptable to those that seem unfair and even absurd (receiving life for thefts of less than $300 of property or the sentence of "life plus a day," once a sentencing option in Maryland).

In paragraph 4, Chapman offers examples of what it's like to be an American prisoner. Again he moves from the moderate, almost expected negatives to those which are horrific. The first examples consist of routine cruelties, such as overpopulation and overcrowding, unhealthy conditions conducive to infectious diseases, and poor medical treatment. He moves from these fairly mundane examples to those that dramatize the extent of violence and other crimes rampant in our prisons. These last examples, enumerating the numbers of stabbings and fatalities and specifying a list of horrific crimes, are shocking.

4. In paragraph 3, Chapman begins with a judgment on Islamic justice that hints of sarcasm: "Such traditions, we all must agree, are no sign of an advanced civilization." This seems a put-down of the Islamic systems, but as we read the paragraph that follows, describing the application of the "single device" of American justice, imprisonment, we may feel that the entire paragraph is tinged with irony. The examples offered demonstrate that our justice system produces cruel and unfair results equal to those in Islamic countries.

Paragraph 4 begins with a sarcastic question: "What are the advantages of being a convicted criminal in an advanced culture?" The details provided in the paragraph show plainly that "advantages" is hardly the word for the conditions in our prisons and that the term "advanced culture" is misapplied to such a cruel system.

Chapman summarizes these ideas more neutrally at the start of paragraph 5, but then inquires of the reader, "Skeptical? Ask yourself: Would you rather be subjected to a few minutes of intense pain and considerable public humiliation, or be locked away for two or three years in a prison cell crowded with ill-tempered sociopaths?" The tone of this question and that following is teasing. The academic-sounding term "ill-tempered sociopaths" ironically mocks our complacent distance from the violence within our prisons.

In paragraphs 8–9, Chapman speaks mockingly of the debate about punishment continuing "in all the same old ruts." Throughout these two paragraphs, his word choice and phrasing are occasionally ironic. He asserts that Islamic punishment succeeds "in a uniquely painful and memorable way" and dryly suggests that "presumably no Western penologist would criticize Islamic punishments on the grounds that they are not barbaric enough" (8). He wryly notes that "it is hard to imagine that corporal measures could stimulate a higher rate of recidivism than already exists [in our culture]" (9). Chapman's use of irony adds passion to his argument and could be effective in creating indignation in a reader newly aware of the flaws in the American justice system.

CAUSE-EFFECT

OPENING COMMENTS

Along with comparison-contrast, cause-effect writing (often called "causal analysis") is frequently required of college students—especially in exams ("Analyze the causes of the country's spiraling divorce rate"; "Discuss the impact of the revised tax laws on middle-income families"). Since students can't deny that an ability to write sound causal analyses will serve them well, they are generally eager to tackle this rhetorical pattern.

Not surprisingly, though, many students run into problems with their analyses. Although they enjoy the intellectual challenge of tracing causes and effects, they sometimes stop at the obvious—overly concerned as they are about getting closure on an issue.

We've found a classroom activity that helps counteract this urge to oversimplify. Here's what we do. We put on the board a broad, non-controversial statement (for example, "In the United States, many people work hard to keep physically fit"). Then we ask students to take five minutes (we time them and announce when the time is up) to brainstorm the reasons *why* (causes) people are so involved in physical fitness. Then we ask students to spend another five minutes brainstorming the *consequences* (effects) of this concern with physical fitness. Next, we put students in pairs and then in groups of four; each time they exchange, first, their causes and then their effects. As you'd expect, this activity generates a good deal of energy. We hear a number of comments such as, "That's interesting—I never thought of that." Such a reaction is precisely what we hope for. The activity sensitizes students to the complexity of cause-effect relationships and encourages them to dig deeply and not settle for the obvious.

For this chapter, we chose professional selections that dramatize the power of causal analysis to make the reader think. In his essay "Why We Crave Horror Movies," King, a master of horror himself, considers both the obvious and the underlying reasons for the horror film's popularity. With reflective eloquence, D'Amboise identifies dance as a major component in character development. Walker explores a complex causal chain to conduct an in-depth inquiry of human nature. Darley and Latané's "Why People Don't Help in a Crisis" provides a well-researched analysis of the causal factors behind bystanders' typical inaction. Bissinger examines the causes and effects surrounding the professionalization of high school sports.

ANSWERS FOR PREWRITING ACTIVITIES

Below we provide possible responses to selected prewriting activities at the end of Chapter 9. Of course, other approaches are possible. (p. 395)

1. There are many ways to use cause-effect in these two essays; the lists that follow suggest only a few of the possibilities. We suggest that you have students share their ideas on ways to use cause-effect in these essays. Seeing others' ideas makes the point dramatically that writing involves invention and individuality.

Topic: The need for a high school course in personal finance
Causes of many young people's casual attitude to money
Causes of parents' reluctance to teach about finance
Effects of a young person bouncing checks
Effects of overspending

Topic: How to show appreciation
Causes of people's callous disregard for each other
Causes of an appreciative approach to good manners
Effects of appreciation in everyday life
Effects of not showing appreciation

2. Here are some possible causes and/or effects for the various topics. Others are possible. Students' thesis statements, purposes, and outlines will vary widely.

a. **Pressure on a student to do well**
Causes:
High career ambitions
Parental demands
Inner pressure; self-esteem
Effects:
Restricted social, campus, and physical activities
Emotional instability, anger
Less effective academic performance

b. **Children's access to soft-core pornography on cable TV**
Causes:
Lenient parents
Failure to purchase a TV lock
Children visiting friends' homes
Effects:
Children grow up too soon
Children get unrealistic view of adult relationships
Children dating at too early an age

c. **Being physically fit**
Causes:
Media attention to health concerns
Trend to engage in sports
Desire to look attractive
Effects:
Better health
Growing enrollments in health clubs
Preoccupation with fitness

d. **Spiraling costs of college education**
Causes:
Growing costs of faculty and staff
Modernization going on: computers, for example
Inflation
Cutbacks in state and federal funds

Effects:
    Students burdened with more loans
    Concern about paying back loans influences career choices
    More students work during college
    Some students drop out

ANSWERS FOR REVISING ACTIVITIES

Below we provide possible responses to selected prewriting activities at the end of Chapter 9. Of course, other approaches are possible. (p. 396)

3.   a. The growing Latin American immigrant population and the crime rate may be correlated; that is, there may be some connection between the two. That both figures are increasing, however, does not mean that the rise in immigration has *caused* the rise in crime. To say so is *post hoc* thinking.

     b. This statement shows *post hoc* thinking because it assumes that one of two parallel events is causing the other; that is, that more women working is causing the divorce rate to rise. However, there are other possible reasons for the increase in the divorce rate: a change in American values regarding the family, for instance, or the "sexual revolution." Moreover, one could cite the same two facts—more women working and the divorce rate rising—and argue the opposite, that the divorce rate is causing more women to work outside the home. In any case, disregarding these other possible points of view and arguing that a clear-cut relationship necessarily exists is an example of *post hoc* thinking.

     c. These two parallel situations do not have a proven causal relationship. To say that one has caused the other is *post hoc* reasoning, unless other proof exists. Such proof might consist of information about what chemicals exist in the landfill, whether they are cancer causing, whether the chemicals have leached into the soil, water, or air of the town, and whether other causes for the cancer might exist.

4.   It's a good idea to provide time in class for students to read over each other's revisions of this paragraph. Seeing how others handled the activity can give students a stronger sense of their revision options.

Here are the main problems with the paragraph:

— Overall, the paragraph asserts that the bank machines have *caused* certain behaviors and attempts to support such a claim with broad generalizations stated in absolute terms. For example, the fourth sentence asserts that automatic tellers have negatively influenced the "average individual." Similarly, the next three sentences state—almost categorically—that people, once they have cash readily in hand, invariably spend their lunch hours shopping. Equivalent absolutes can be found throughout. The paragraph could be rescued if the writer toned down the absolute tone and provided qualifications that suggest that "for *some* people" or "for *many* people" these machines present problems.

— The writer assumes causation explains the circumstances (use of ATM cards and people shopping during lunch hour) when these may simply be correlated, that is, they may happen at the same time because they are two results of some other earlier event. Or, the simultaneous appearance of increased spending and ATM card use may be a coincidence, meaning that the writer has committed the *post hoc* fallacy.

— Another problem with the paragraph is its lack of supporting examples. Although it isn't necessary for the writer to provide hard evidence in the form of research, he or she should have supported the paragraph with specific references to friends, family, etc., for whom automatic tellers have created problems.

— The point that children don't appreciate the value of money is an unfounded generalization; it also digresses from the paragraph's point and so should be eliminated.

— The last sentence categorically asserts ("There's no doubt . . .") that banking machine fraud is a *cause* of the "immoral climate in the country." This is an unsupported causal statement and would need evidence to be considered valid. It should be deleted.

WHY WE CRAVE HORROR MOVIES

Stephen King

Questions for Close Reading (p. 399)

1. King states the *topic* of his essay clearly in the title, which proposes to explore not only why we watch or enjoy horror movies, but why we *crave* them. He does not, however, state his *thesis* explicitly but, rather, develops over the course of the essay his main idea: that the horror movie satisfies a type of "insanity in us." He begins with the provocative opinion, "I think we're all mentally ill; those of us outside the asylum only hide it a little better" (1). For King, sanity is only "a matter of degree," and we are all on the same continuum as "Jack the Ripper or the Cleveland Torso Murderer" (8). While King is sure that "the potential lyncher is in all of us" (9), he also knows that society works very hard to hide or repress this fact. As a result, "every now and then, [the lyncher] has to be let loose" (9). It is what King calls the "dirty job" of horror movies to satisfy "all that is worst in us" (12). Watching these movies is like "throwing a basket of raw meat to the hungry alligators swimming around in that subterranean river beneath" (12). King concludes that horror movies keep the dangerous psychological gators "down there" and a more ostensibly sane "me up here" (13).

2. In paragraph 8, King wants to collapse the separation between the sane and the insane. Watching a horror movie, we are all invited to "lapse into simplicity, irrationality, and even outright madness" (7) as we enjoy the spectacle of "seeing others menaced—sometimes killed" (6). Our eager participation in this "modern version of the public lynching" (6) proves that "we are all insane" and that, by extension, "sanity becomes a matter of degree" (8). The infamous killers are now invoked to demonstrate this point. Using the second person, King directly addresses the reader, placing him or her on a continuum with famous killers. King writes, "[I]f your insanity leads you to carve up women like Jack the Ripper or the Cleveland Torso Murderer, we clap you away in the funny farm. . . . [I]f, on the other hand your insanity leads you only to talk to yourself"—or to crave horror films—"then you are left alone" (8). The extreme examples of the serial murderers are necessary to illustrate King's main thesis: the presence of a shared "insanity of man" that the horror movie. satisfies (11). Linking the psychopath and supposedly normal, everyday people (like us) is King's project, and the references to the murderers in paragraph 8 establish this uncomfortable bond.

3. What King calls the "conservative" nature of horror movies should not be understood in terms of politics. Instead, King uses the term more strictly to mean "cautious," "traditional," and "staid." While horror films may challenge us to face the darkness, they provide no new understanding of it. King argues that horror movies "re-establish our feelings of essential normality" (4). By watching monsters on the screen, we reassure ourselves that we are not monsters ourselves. As King writes, horror movies remind us that "no matter how far we may be removed from the beauty of a Robert Redford or a Diana Ross, we are still light-years from true ugliness," such as that of the grotesque creatures featured in many films (4). Furthermore, King argues that horror movies encourage us to "put away our more civilized and adult penchant for analysis" and to see the world in "pure blacks and whites" (7). In reinforcing basic definitions like "us" and "them," horror movies touch on the "reactionary," restoring us to primal, absolute attitudes and emotions.

   Yet some of these same impulses inspired by horror movies render the films "anarchistic, and revolutionary" (11)—quite the opposite of conservative. Reveling in the dark fun of horror movies, we "exercise" our inherent, universal "anticivilization emotions" (11)—the ones that society attempts to quash out of us, as in the example of the child being punished for deliberately hurting "the little rotten puke of a sister" (10). The "dirty job" of horror movies is highly subversive in nature: "It is morbidity unchained, our most basic instincts let free, our nastiest fantasies realized (12). As we watch these films, we may allow our emotions a free rein . . . or no rein at all" (7). So, while horror films may restore our conservative sense of humanity (as opposed to the extreme monstrousness on the screen), they also incite an anarchy of the psyche, where our delight in the grotesque is free from regulation. In spite of the "civilized forebrain," horror movies feed "the hungry alligators swimming around in that subterranean river beneath" (12).

4. Alligators symbolize the latent, uncivilized tendencies that King argues we all possess but are compelled, by society, to repress. Throughout his essay, King develops his theory that sanity is only "a matter of degree" and that we are all on the same continuum as "Jack the Ripper or the Cleveland Torso Murderer" (8). Society, however, militates against "the potential lyncher . . . in all of us" (9). It encourages actions based on feelings like "love, friendship, loyalty, kindness" while actively discouraging their opposites (10). To King's mind, however, sanctioned emotions are only half of the equation; the rest of our emotions—the aberrant ones—won't disappear, and they too "demand periodic exercise" (11). So, while love may be the sort of emotion endorsed by society, this and other benevolent sentiments cannot be sustained unless we periodically satisfy the other, darker elements in our psyche— the "gators." King argues that one safe way to "feed" these gators is to indulge in watching horror movies, which function as a safety valve for our potentially destructive emotions.

5. *hysterical* (1): characterized by nervous, emotional outbursts
   reactionary (4): extremely conservative; opposed to progress
   voyeur (6): one who is highly stimulated by watching others
   lynching (6): an illegal mob action against a person; a murder carried out by a mob
   penchant (7): a strong preference, inclination, or liking
   immortalized (9): made eternal
   anarchistic (11): lawless, wild
   morbidity (12): an interest in gloom, disease, and death

Questions About the Writer's Craft (p. 400)

1. King may be seen, at different points in the essay, as encompassing each of the three purposes. In explaining why we crave horror movies, King proposes a theory of the human psyche. Unlike a scientific researcher, he offers no statistical, biological, or clinical data. He does not aim to inform us about new psychological discoveries. Instead, he acts like a philosopher and *speculates* about the nature of human emotions and, more specifically, about why we crave horror movies. He develops a theory about the existence of a shared "insanity of man" that the horror movie satisfies (11). But he then attempts throughout the rest of the essay to *persuade* us of this claim's validity, providing an abundance of vivid examples and analogies. His purpose may also be interpreted as *informative*; King wants to show us the dark, repressed part of ourselves as well as a benign means of keeping it at bay: watching horror movies.

   King's theory also functions as a defense of his own craft—of not only why we crave horror movies, but why King writes them. In persuading us of our psychological need for horror movies, he simultaneously (and implicitly) seeks to persuade us of our practical need for horror writers—like King himself.

2. The task of King's essay is to spell out the dark psychological tendencies satisfied by horror movies. In order to explain the "simple and obvious" (3) reasons for the horror films attraction, King begins by comparing it to a roller coaster. Like roller coasters, horror movies pose a challenge. As King argues, in both cases "we are daring the nightmare" (2), and we do so "to show that we can, that we are not afraid" (3). In both, we enjoy the sheer thrill of the ride—the possibility that a movie, like a coaster ride, might "surprise a scream out of us" (3) or might just be "fun" (5). But, according to King, horror films fundamentally differ from roller coasters in the source of all that fun. Our enjoyment of horror movies, he demonstrates, originates in a far darker and more complex part of the psyche. In the horror movie, the fun comes not from twists and turns but from "seeing others menaced—sometimes killed" (6). The horror movie returns us to child-like thinking, shutting down adult analysis and recasting the world in "pure blacks and whites" (7). In this way, horror movies invite us "to lapse into simplicity, irrationality, and outright madness" (7). Roller coasters, by implication, do not serve nearly as complicated a function.

   King then turns to a second comparison-contrast to explain our response to horror movies. He says that "the horror film has become the modern form of the public lynching" (6). In both cases, spectators derive "a very peculiar sort of fun . . . from seeing others menaced—sometimes killed" (6). This malignant pleasure in morbidity always lurks beneath our socially adjusted surfaces, King argues, but society systematically represses these "anticivilization emotions" (11). The implied difference between the two is that public lynchings are no longer sanctioned by society, while horror movies still are, even though they exercise the same emotions. As King concludes, horror movies keep the dark side "from getting out, man" (13).

   King develops a final comparison-contrast to explain the phenomenon of horror movies: the same "anticivilization emotions" that fuel our enjoyment of the films also incite us to delight in "sick jokes" (11). Sick jokes "may surprise a laugh or a grin out of us even as we recoil" (11)—a response much like the one King attributes to horror-movie watching. He goes a step further, stating, "The mythic horror movie, like the sick joke, has a dirty job to do. It deliberately appeals to all that is worst in us" (12). Our morbid enjoyment of the two serves as evidence of King's larger observation that "we're all mentally ill" (1) and "share in an insanity of man" (11). Another similarity between them is that they both are particularly attractive to young people. Early in the essay, he identifies horror movies as "the special province of the young" (3). Later in the essay, King cites the example of the dead baby joke that he heard "originally from a ten-year-old" (11). Ultimately, both horror movies and sick jokes attest to the "potential lyncher" (9) that we all harbor within.

3. In explaining our attraction to horror movies, King builds a theory about the shape of our emotional life, a theory that fundamentally includes children. He begins by observing that "horror movies, like roller coasters, have always been the special province of the young" (3). Ostensibly, this youthful appeal owes to the raw thrills provided by both, but King goes on to suggest several less innocuous reasons for young people's attraction to horror films. In discussing society's repression of malignant human emotions, he cites the example of our youthful reactions to a little sister (10). King demonstrates how "society showers us with positive reinforcement" (often in the form of sweets) when we exercise valued emotions like love or kindness—"emotions," King explains, "that tend to maintain the status quo" (9). However, when we deliberately hurt "the rotten little puke of a sister," "sanctions follow" (10). King explains the problem of such sanctions in paragraph 11, reminding us that, even after a series of punishments, "anticivilization emotions don't go away." We still harbor destructive desires, a fact evidenced in King's example of the "sick joke" told by a ten-year-old. The child's implied enjoyment of the gory "dead baby" joke points to the shared "insanity of man"—King's main point. "We're all mentally ill" (1), he believes, and the perverse impulses that society tries to repress in its young nevertheless remain with us forever. In King's view, children are not innocents; instead, they are an amoral nature run amok. The use of children as examples simply underscores King's belief that "the potential lyncher is in almost all of us" (9).

4. Each of these paragraphs consists solely of one brief sentence or, in the case of paragraph 14, one sentence fragment. In each case, King's compressed writing style adds emphasis and directs our attention to a single idea. In paragraph 2, King places us in the darkened theater, "daring the nightmare," in order to establish the horror movie's conscious and unconscious challenge to viewers. Not only does the film dare us to sit through it, as King will explain in paragraph 3, but the horror movie also dares our darker side to come out and express itself (9). The second brief paragraph—"And we go to have fun" (5)—forces us to think about the unconscious challenge to seek the kind of fun that excites "the potential lyncher . . . in almost all of us" (9). This short paragraph introduces King's thesis about the inherent pleasure involved in "seeing others menaced—sometimes killed" (6). King hopes to deliver the same kind of punch in his sentence-fragment conclusion. In the preceding paragraph, he acknowledges that you, the reader, are taught to believe that civilized emotions are "all you need" (13). But, as his striking conclusion asserts, this is true only "[a]s long as you keep the gators fed" (14). This pithy conclusion, with its vivid imagery, memorably captures King's thesis and promises to resonate in the minds of readers.

SHOWING WHAT IS POSSIBLE

Jacques D'Amboise

Questions for Close Reading (p. 406)

1. D'Amboise states his thesis explicitly in paragraph 8: "When you learn to move your body on a note of music, it's exciting. You have taken control of your body and, by learning to do that, you discover that you can take control of your life." D'Amboise

restates and broadens his thesis—that learning dance teaches discipline, control, confidence, and respect—elsewhere in the essay, specifically in paragraphs 16, 22, and 27.

2. Madame Seda is wise in the ways of human nature and in knowing how to find the best in and for her students. For instance, instead of disciplining him and thereby possibly encouraging his misbehavior, Madame Seda involves young Jacques in the class. Then, knowing that a very active seven-year-old boy would bristle at the suggestion that girls can perform actions that he cannot, Madame Seda challenges Jacques to attempt the *changements*. Finally, knowing also that Jacques needs encouragement to continue and to improve, Madame Seda praises him and then lets him join other dancers during part of the lesson—teaching him patience and self-control as he awaits his turn. She continues to praise and to set further challenges, all the while pulling him into the group of dancers. Finally, in an act of unselfish wisdom, she recommends that Jacques and his sister go to a better dance teacher.

3. D'Amboise relates qualities of the special environment that teaching dance requires in paragraphs 7, 15–16, 19–22, and 27–29. Those special qualities include the following: challenging and praising students; participating actively in students' learning and their struggles; demanding "precision, order and respect"; and, most importantly, continuing to encourage students and never "polluting" them with negativity, bad manners, and disrespect. In short, the ideal environment seems to be one that demands students' best while at the same time nurturing and respecting them.

4. D'Amboise is quick to point out that "polluting" does not refer only, or even necessarily, to unhealthy air or drugs. The kind of personal pollution he has in mind concerns a metaphorical poisoning of the soul and spirit and sense of self—in short, those qualities that humanity has developed over thousands of centuries that make it civilized. For D'Amboise, these kinds of personal pollution would include violence, disrespect for oneself and for others, "foul language, dirty books and ignorance."

5. *diabolically* (1): wickedly, devilishly
   flaying (5): in a lashing motion or manner
   accessible (8): easily entered or understood
   choreography (11): the art of creating and arranging dance movements
   inevitably (12): unavoidably, certainly
   triathletes (23): athletes who compete in a race involving bicycling, swimming, and running

Questions About the Writer's Craft (p. 406)

1. D'Amboise uses both sequences. He begins chronologically, recounting his own childhood experiences, explaining what he learned in Madame Seda's classes, continuing through his later training and professional career, and concluding by examining his later years as a dance instructor. Throughout this chronology, he illustrates the influences that dance had on students, including himself. Complementing the chronological sequence is an emphatic sequence, which moves from immediate effects (self-knowledge and self-confidence) to longer-term effects (control, life-long discipline, and an appreciation for "the best that is available to you from the wealth of human culture").

2. The introductory narrative serves at least two functions. First, as an autobiographical story, it engages readers' interest in the potential conflict developing between the fidgeting seven-year-old and the "wise" Madame Seda. Second, the short narrative introduces one of the themes of the essay—how an "exceptional teacher got a bored little kid, me, interested in ballet" (7). In conjunction with this theme, the narrative

106

illustrates the instructional process Madame Seda—and later the author—employed: setting an initial challenge, complimenting students on completing that challenge, and then further encouraging students by setting a new challenge.

3. The two sentences of paragraph 21 could have gracefully concluded paragraph 20. However, by placing the climax and the point of his brief anecdote in a short, separate paragraph, D'Amboise succeeds in emphasizing more fully his dual point: that dance teaches self-discipline and that children want (and need) to learn such control over their minds and bodies.

4. In paragraphs 30–31, D'Amboise establishes an analogy between a trunk and a person. He says that whatever people put into a trunk in an attic will be what those people leave behind. Similarly, whatever people fill a child with—violence, foul language, ignorance—will determine what that child will be left with, what he or she will become. But if a child, like a trunk, is filled with good, valuable interests or qualities—"music, dance, poetry, literature, good manners and loving friends"—then the result is a happy, well-adjusted person. These good things, D'Amboise argues, can be taught and learned through the study of dance.

BEAUTY: WHEN THE OTHER DANCER IS THE SELF

Alice Walker

Questions for Close Reading (p. 414)

1. Walker's thesis is not stated explicitly. The following, however, approaches a thesis statement: "[F]or all it [the defect] had taught me of shame and anger and inner vision, I *did* love it" (49). The main idea of the piece is that a physical loss can lead to a spiritual gain. Having suffered from people's negative, superficial judgments of her, Walker eventually overcomes her own tendency to judge by appearances.

2. Before her disfigurement, Walker is garrulous, chattering at her siblings until they demand silence. Three years later, she delivers a long Easter speech "without stammer or pause" (6)—further evidence of self-assurance. After the "accident," however, Walker alternately answers with a monosyllable or "rants" with self-hatred. After her surgery, Walker is once again articulate, with her classroom lessons flowing "faultlessly" from her lips (32). Finally, with her realization that being able to *see* beauty is more important than being thought beautiful, Walker experiences a poetic outpouring.

3. After Walker has developed a strong bond with her cat, she is prevented from being with the cat. Eventually, she is even told the cat cannot be found. Similarly, she becomes attached to a teacher who soon afterward marries and departs for Africa. Both the cat and the teacher, then, represent Walker's feelings of loss, perhaps even betrayal.

4. The title's meaning is not obvious. At the end of the piece, Walker's dream, in which she is dancing with herself, follows her revelation that her daughter's love for her transcends physical appearances. Because of this context, the title seems intended to convey a sense of joy and fulfillment. Walker writes that both dancers are "beautiful, whole and free." It would seem, then, that she intends to communicate a newfound sense of personal autonomy, self-sufficiency, and self-acceptance. At last, she loves herself. At last, she needs no outside approval, no admiring partner.

5. *subversive* (1): rebellious
chronic (2): habitual
flocked (4): tufted

crinoline 4): a stiff petticoat
cataract (13): an opaque area of the eye's lens
abscess (25): a localized swelling containing pus

Questions About the Writer's Craft (p. 415)

1. The "accident," of course, is the physical cause of Walker's disfigurement, but her brother was first motivated to aim his gun at her. As a result of the physical event, Walker's self-esteem diminishes. Her father, classmates, and others treat her differently after her disfigurement, but her own changed attitude may be a contributing factor. The same is true after her cosmetic surgery—this time, with positive consequences. Those who accept Walker without censure—her lover, her favorite teacher, her daughter—help her to be less affected by externals.
2. The present tense adds immediacy. It also emphasizes how an event or statement can have lasting effect.
3. Walker signals the ages at which some significant change in her life occurred by repeatedly using the phrase "I am" followed by her age: "I am eight years old . . ." (8), "I am fourteen . . ." (32), and "I am twenty-seven . . ." (47).
4. The repetition creates irony and ambiguity. Despite her relatives' claim that she did not change, Walker relates a process of both social and spiritual change. In addition, people *do* appear to treat her differently after her disfigurement. On the other hand, her relatives seem to be speaking sincerely, because Walker tells us they respond with puzzlement to her question. Perhaps, then, Walker wants us to understand that her relatives are right insofar as she remains "fundamentally Alice" whatever her social and physical vagaries. Some support for this view occurs in paragraph 32, where Walker writes that after the corrective surgery she was transformed, or so she *thought*.

WHY PEOPLE DON'T HELP IN A CRISIS

John M. Darley & Bibb Latané

Questions for Close Reading (p. 421)

1. Darley and Latané state their thesis at the end of their introduction, as an answer to the question, "Why, then, didn't they [witnesses to an emergency] act?" (8). They write, "There are three things the bystander must do if he is to intervene in an emergency: *notice* that something is happening; *interpret* that event as an emergency; and decide that he has *personal responsibility* for intervention" (9). They then indicate that the rest of the essay will explain the research that has led the authors to this conclusion: "As we shall show, the presence of other bystanders may at each stage inhibit his action" (9).
2. People need to notice that a problem is occurring before they can help, which means they must be disturbed out of their mental distractions. In addition, Americans are taught to keep their eyes to themselves, to "close our ears and avoid staring," the authors write (10). This principle of polite behavior can cause people to ignore or not really see a critical situation happening near them (10).

   Then, after an event has attracted their attention, people must realize that someone needs help. But the presence of others can delay the realization that a problem is going on. Darley and Latané explain that people take their cues from those around them—"if everyone else is calm and indifferent, [a person] will tend to remain so" (14). People simply get the message that there's no problem because, in our culture, people usually try to remain cool and calm in public: "it is considered embarrassing to 'lose your cool'" (15). The collective nonchalance of a crowd can suppress anyone's urge to help, that is, to go against the prevailing passivity and rush to aid.

Finally, even when a person has determined that aid is required, he or she will not feel the personal requirement to perform the assistance if there are many others nearby. Darley and Latané call this the "diffusion of responsibility theory" (21). Such people are not hard-hearted but just confused about what to do when others around them are doing nothing (27). People's "reactions are shaped by the actions of others," be it response or passivity.

3. The researchers wanted to eliminate the possibility that the presence of others would prevent awareness of the emergency, so they designed an experiment in which an obvious crisis occurred and in which the subjects' awareness would not be blunted by others being in the room with them. The subjects were told to discuss with each other over headsets, used with the rationale of protecting everyone's privacy. In this way, the researchers could determine whether, even when one of the students reported a medical crisis, the knowledge that several people knew it was happening and could take responsibility would blunt the individuals' willingness to act. The experiment showed that, indeed, the response of subjects to the emergency deteriorated rapidly when the number of people linked by microphones increased. "The responsibility diluting effect of other people was so strong that single individuals were more than twice as likely to report the emergency as those who thought other people also knew about it" (25).

4. The authors indicate that any one of us could be that unresponsive bystander, because being unresponsive is not a defect of character or a sign of the decay of civility in urban life (5). Rather, the failure to respond occurs in particular situations which could befall any of us. When people are surrounded by others, they notice less (10), they conform to norms of public behavior (14), and they take less responsibility for events around them (20). As Darley and Latané write, "If we look closely at the behavior of witnesses to [emergencies], the people involved begin to seem a little less inhuman and a lot more like the rest of us" (7). Any person could be influenced by the "apparent indifference of others" to "pass by an emergency" (28). "We are that bystander," they conclude (28) and suggest that being aware that groups or crowds might encourage our passivity could help us to "see distress and step forward to relieve it" (28).

5. *megalopolis* (5): an urban region consisting of several adjoining cities
    apathy (5): lacking involvement or interest
    indifference (5): without interest or concern
    alienated (6): to cause to become indifferent or hostile
    depersonalized (6): to make impersonal
    inhibit (9): to block or hold back
    corroborates (11): supports with additional proof
    coronary (13): of the human heart
    slavish (14): deliberately dependent or slave-like
    nonchalance (15): coolly unconcern or indifference
    diffused (20): spread widely or thinly
    blandly (27): unemotionally or indifferently

Questions About the Writer's Craft (p. 422)

1. From the way the thesis is introduced to the way the essay is organized, the authors make it easy for the reader to determine the causes of inaction. Darley and Latané introduce their thesis in a dramatic way, as the answer to a one-paragraph question (8). Setting off the question in one paragraph creates surprise in the reader. They then follow this with a clear and direct answer. In this sentence, the three causal factors are italicized to call attention to them (9). The writers follow up this listing with a direct announcement of their intentions in the essay: "As we shall show, the presence of other bystanders may at each stage inhibit his action" (9).

   The rest of the essay is divided into sections, the next three of which reflect the three causes: "The Unseeing Eye," "Seeing Is Not Necessarily Believing," and "The Lonely Crowd." Each one of these sections begins with an anecdote about a hypothetical situation in which help is needed. Then after presenting the ambiguities in this situation, the authors present a hypothesis suggesting why people avoid or delay acting and then cite psychological research that has shown the hypothesis to be valid. In addition, the authors use bridging sentences, the beginnings of which link back to previous material. For example, paragraph 13 begins with "Once an event is noticed . . . ," which repeats the idea of the previous section. And paragraph 20 uses the beginning clause "Even if a person defines an event as an emergency . . ." to remind the reader of the previous point.

2. Using the present tense creates a dramatic introduction to draw readers in—or at least, not scare readers away—from a serious and analytic essay. Narratives of crime and danger are intrinsically interesting, but the style used here heightens the shock effect of the situations. Each narrative begins bluntly, with no lead-in, using a direct statement of the victim's situation: "Kitty Genovese is set upon by a maniac"; "Andrew Mormille is stabbed in the head"; "Eleanor Bradley trips and breaks her leg." The present tense adds a sense of urgency, while the direct style seems almost like a narrative voice-over, telling us events as they happen. In addition, the present tense circumvents the need to provide background data, such as the year of occurrence and so on, data that would slow the reader down and introduce the analytic style too early in the essay. Finally, the present tense conveys the timelessness of the events, in the sense that given human nature, these past responses would hold true at any point in time.

3. The experiments are described in paragraphs 11–12, 16–19, and 22–25. Each experiment is introduced by a clear announcement, and throughout the description of the experiment and the results, numerous transitions make each stage of action crystal clear. In paragraph 11, Darley and Latané write, "Experimental evidence corroborates this. We asked college students to an interview. . . ." Paragraph 16 begins, "To determine how the presence of other people affects a person's interpretation of an emergency, Latané and Judith Rodin set up another experiment." And the third experiment is introduced in paragraph 21: "To test this diffusion-of-responsibility theory, we simulated an emergency . . ." and is picked up again in paragraph 22: "For the simulation. . . ."

   Within each description of an experiment, the authors use numerous clear signals to indicate the stages of the process. In paragraphs 11–12, they use signals of time, as well as the colon, effectively: "<u>as</u> the students waited. . . . <u>As</u> part of the study, we staged an emergency: smoke was released. . . . <u>Although eventually</u> all . . . —<u>when</u> the atmosphere grew so smoky. . . ."

   In the injured-researcher experiment (16–19), narrative and spatial signals help the reader along: "An attractive young market researcher met them . . . and took them to . . . <u>where</u> they . . ."; "<u>Before</u> leaving, she told them she would be working

110

next door in her office, which was separated from . . . "; "She then entered . . . where she . . . "; "After four minutes. . . ."

In the group-discussion experiment (21–25), narrative transitions predominate, along with spatial indicators and enumeration: "Each student was put in an individual room. . . ."; "Each person was to talk in turn. The first to talk . . ."; "Then . . ."; "Other students then talked . . . in turn"; "When it was the first person's turn . . ." (22–23). The authors interrupt the process to explain the hidden reality of the experiment, using transitions of contrast: "But whatever the apparent size . . . only the subject; the others, as well as the instructions . . . were present only on . . . tape" (23). Returning to the process of the experiment again in paragraph 24, the authors use a narrative transition plus an enumeration and a signal of repetition: "When it was the first person's turn to talk again. . . ."

The authors also often use balanced sentence structure to compare the reactions of subjects who were alone with those who were in groups of various sizes. In the leaking-vent emergency (11–12), they write, "Solitary students often glanced idly about while filling out their questionnaires; those in groups kept their eyes on their own papers" (11); "two thirds of the subjects who were alone noticed the smoke immediately, but only 25 percent of those waiting in groups saw it as quickly" (12). In the injured researcher experiment, the results are presented in two separate paragraphs—one for those who were alone (18) and one for those who were in groups of various sizes (19). Short direct sentences that put in the foreground the percentages of how many subjects responded in what way make the data easy to follow, and signals of contrast help the reader sort out the details: "Seventy percent . . . offered to help. . . . Many pushed back the divider . . . ; others called out to offer their help" (18). "Among those waiting in pairs, only 20 percent . . ." (19).

In reporting the results of the group-discussion simulation, Darley and Latané again rely upon direct statements that list the percentages explaining who responded how: "Eighty-five percent of the people who believed themselves to be alone. . . . Sixty-two percent of the people who believed there was one other bystander. . . . Of those who believed there were four other bystanders, only 31 percent reported. . . ."

4. At the start of the essay, the reader is likely to think of witnesses who do not help a victim as monsters, as aberrant and mean-spirited human beings. Darley and Latané wish to show that inaction is in fact a natural result of ordinary human psychology; as they write in paragraph 7, "If we look closely at the behavior of witnesses to these incidents, the people involved begin to seem a little less inhuman and a lot more like the rest of us." One of their goals is to show that the failure to take action is typical in certain situations, situations, in fact, in which there are multiple bystanders. "As we shall show, the presence of other bystanders may at each stage inhibit his action" (9).

At the end of the essay, they indicate that their ultimate purpose is to create the awareness that inaction is the norm when people are in a group. With this awareness, people might be able to counteract the paralyzing effect of other people and get involved in helping in a critical situation. "Caught up by the apparent indifference of others, we may pass by an emergency without helping or even realizing that help is needed. Once we are aware of the influence of those around us, however, we can resist it. We can choose to see distress and step forward to relieve it" (28).

INNOCENTS AFIELD

Buzz Bissinger

Questions for Close Reading (p. 427)

1. Bissinger states his thesis in the first sentence of the third paragraph: "[H]igh school sports in America has become an epidemic of win-at-all-costs in too many places, just as corroded as college and the pros; actually more so because none of the ends can possibly justify the means when many of those involved are still too young to vote."

2. The "supposed virtues" of high school sports include innocence, valor, and healthy competition (1), as well as "the magnificent foolishness of youth" and the idea of noble sacrifice (2).

3. According to Bissinger, money has corrupted high school sports by raising the expectations for these sports (3). The extravagant spending on stadiums, travel, equipment, and training puts a lot of pressure on young athletes to perform, sometimes with deadly effects such as those caused by steroid abuse. The pressure comes from coaches, schools, families, and the community that supports the teams. In addition, the money lavished on sports means that less money goes to core educational programs and to the majority of students who do not play on competitive teams (8).

4. In paragraph 10, Bissinger describes a report, issued by the National Association of State Boards of Education, which called for greater oversight of high school athletic programs. The association cited steroid use, predatory agents, coaches, recruiting practices, and gifts as being problems in many sports programs and declared that the exploitation of high school students needed to be stopped. Bissinger does not believe this proposal will succeed in solving the problems of high school athletics because too many people have a stake in sports as they are played today. In paragraph 12 he describes sports as an institution as powerful as "corporate America or the Catholic Church" and suggests that society is still in thrall to the myth of sports rather than the reality of sports.

5. *valor* (1): personal bravery
   zeal (2): eager interest; fervor
   unsullied (2): spotlessly clean and fresh
   social stratification (3): the hierarchical arrangement of social groups (from sociology)
   repercussions (3): widespread effects
   careening (5): swaying from side to side; lurching
   queasy (5): uneasy, delicate, squeamish
   monolith (8): a huge, massive structure
   conjure (8): to summon as if by magic
   nirvana (8): the final dream or bliss (from Buddhism)
   siphoning (9): drawing off (as through a siphon or tube)
   ancillary (12): supplementary
   emulate (13): imitate

Questions About the Writer's Craft (p. 427)

1. According to Bissinger, money is the main cause of the professionalization of high school sports (3–6)—money for overpaid coaches, travel teams, sports arenas, and field houses. In addition to mentioning money, Bissinger cites recruiting practices and travel teams as other causes of the professionalization of high school athletics (9). The money invested in high school sports has the effect of upping the ante for all involved, and the pressure is felt most acutely by the athletes, who are expected to perform and who are too young to deal with this type of exploitation (3). The money invested in high school sports also affects non-athletes by diverting resources away from them and the main educational mission of the high schools (8).

2. In paragraph 3, Bissinger contrasts the imaginary things that high school athletics money might buy (televised Super Bowls and Bowl Championship series games) with the actual things it does buy (booster clubs, coach salaries, divisions between athletes and nonathletes, and steroid abuse). He introduces the imaginary purchases by starting each sentence with the word "no": "*No* Super Bowl with television ratings through the roof. *No* Bowl Championship Series games with millions watching." He then goes on to contrast them with the actual results of this spending, introducing each with the word "just": "*Just* millions of dollars spent by certain school districts. . . . *Just* coaches . . . making close to $90,000 a year. . . . *Just* steroid abuse. . . ." This repetition at the beginning of each sentence is effective because it helps the reader categorize each factor that Bissinger discusses.

3. Bissinger supports his argument that high school sports have gotten worse since he published *Friday Night Lights* in 1990 by citing a news story from *USA Today* that listed huge school sports building projects taking place around the nation, along with their price tags, in the millions of dollars.

4. Bissinger's prediction is that high school sports will continue on its present road of "shameful overemphasis," becoming more and more like college sports until the pleasure of sports is destroyed for teenagers. He is pessimistic about the future of high school sports because he feels that sports is such a powerful institution that it will not correct itself until it is completely ruined.

DEFINITION

OPENING COMMENTS

In high school and certainly in college, students frequently answer questions that ask for definitions: ("Define *mitosis*"; "Explain what *divestiture* means"). Even so, we hold off discussing definition as a method of development until the last quarter of the course. Here's why.

Since extended definitions can be developed through a variety of patterns, students need to be familiar with those patterns before they can prepare a well-supported definition essay. At the very least, they need to know how to marshal well-chosen *examples* so that their definitions can be grounded in specifics. Similarly, the *comparison-contrast* format can show students how to go about organizing a definition by negation. And *process analysis*, explaining how something works, is often critical when developing a definition. Once students feel comfortable with these and other rhetorical strategies, they can approach definition essays with confidence, knowing that they have a repertoire of techniques to draw on.

For this chapter, we selected readings that illustrate a variety of approaches for writing definition essays. Touching on a wide range of topics, the pieces show how definition can explain difficult-to-understand scientific concepts, as well as demonstrating that the pattern can challenge the meaning we attach to common everyday words. We often start with Cole since she mixes a number of strategies (examples, facts, personal anecdotes) to develop her definition of entropy. Gleick, in a careful analysis of behavioral research, asserts that the traits typically associated with Type A behavior are actually characteristics we all exhibit, directly related to the world we live in today. Angier defines the concept of cuteness from the perspective of biology. With the help of abundant examples, Robbins and Wilner coin a new term—"the quarterlife crisis"—and make a case for its pervasiveness in contemporary culture. Finally, Raspberry's essay relies on a series of definitions to compare the positive and negative effects labels can have on a person's self-image.

ANSWERS FOR PREWRITING ACTIVITIES

Below we provide possible responses to selected prewriting activities at the end of Chapter 10. In many cases, other responses are possible. (p. 443)

1. There are many ways to use definition in these two essays. Here we've listed some of the possibilities. In classroom use of this activity, we suggest you have students share their responses. They will be surprised and often delighted to discover that their neighbors have quite different answers.

    Topic: How to register a complaint
    Define "effective" complaining
    Define a "no-win situation"
    Define "conflict resolution"
    Define "diplomacy"

Topic: Contrasting two stand-up comics
Define "black humor"
Define "improvisational humor"
Define "political humor"
Define "put-down humor"

ANSWERS FOR REVISING ACTIVITIES

Below we provide possible responses to selected revising activities at the end of Chapter 10. In many cases, other responses are possible. (p. 444)

3. Here's our appraisal of the effectiveness of the definitions:

    a. This definition is circular because it repeats the words of the term itself. In addition, the "is when" format is awkward if not ungrammatical. Here's one way to revise the definition: "Passive aggression is a personality disorder in which a person chronically performs poorly as a way of unconsciously showing resentment of the demands of an employer, teacher, or other person."
    b. This definition is also ineffective because of its circularity. One way to rewrite it might be this: "A terrorist uses violence against innocent people to intimidate those in power."
    c. This definition is effective and clear.
    d. This is a circular definition that tells us nothing about the term being defined. A better version would be the following: "Pop music typically contains simple lyrics, a strong beat, and appealing harmonies."
    e. This definition needs rephrasing to eliminate the awkward "is when"; otherwise, it is a workable definition. "Standing by another person during difficult times is the essence of loyalty."

4. It's a good idea to have your students read each other's revisions of this material. Doing so gives them helpful exposure to alternative ways of rewriting a problem paragraph.
    Here are our recommendations for rewriting the paragraph:

    —   The opening sentence is weak; relying on the dictionary only tells us (boringly) what we already know. The sentence should be rewritten to catch the reader's interest.
    —   Since the second sentence states the obvious, it should be deleted.
    —   The listing of times people feel tense (sentences 3, 4, and 5) consists of obvious, general situations. Dramatic examples would be appropriate here.
    —   Similarly, "Wear and tear on our bodies and on our emotional well-being" is overly general. "Wear and tear" is a cliché as well. Specifying some actual damage that can result from tension would be an effective revision strategy.
    —   The thesis (how to relieve tension with walking) seems tacked on. A transitional phrase or lead-in is needed to build more naturally to the thesis.

ENTROPY

K. C. Cole

Questions for Close Reading (p. 448)

1. Cole's thesis is located at the start of paragraph 3, after her two-paragraph introduction: "Disorder, alas, is the natural order of things in the universe."
2. Entropy is unique in being irreversible; most physical properties "work both ways" (3). In nature, things fall apart and decay, and they do not naturally reverse themselves and come together. The "arrow of time" image helps us understand that entropy occurs in relation to time; as time passes, disorder naturally accompanies it. Entropy is the "arrow" also in the sense that it is the weapon time uses to destroy things.
3. The creation of life is the ordering of the particles of matter into a living thing, be it a plant or a person, and so represents the major contradiction to entropy. Such creation, however, requires energy in the form of nutrients such as, for a plant, soil, sun, carbon, and water, and for a person, "oxygen and pizza and milk" (9). Cole's other examples show that countering entropy does generally require energy in the form of physical work, the work of cleaning up children's rooms, painting old buildings (4), or maintaining skill at flute playing (12). Creating order and countering entropy require energy whose expenditure causes an increase in entropy in another part of the system; Cole uses as an example our society's creation of electricity by burning oil and coal, only to produce smog.
4. Entropy is "no laughing matter" because it is inevitable, and it operates not only in nature, but in society as well. There are "always so many more paths toward disorder than toward order," Cole writes (14), and unless we are diligent, entropy will get the better of us individually and societally. This ever-present threat of disorder is especially distressing in the area of social institutions and international events. Cole believes that the ultimate randomness of entropy endangers us—the "lack of common purpose in the world" (15) threatens to create more and more disorder.
5. *futility* (1): sense of uselessness
   dissipated (6): scattered, spread out
   buffeted (7): hit, slapped, pushed
   tepid (7): lukewarm
   atrophied (12): deteriorated

Questions About the Writer's Craft (p. 448)

1. Entropy is a phenomenon we surely have noted—rooms getting messy, wood rotting, metal rusting—but it is not likely we have understood it to have a name or be a "principle" of the universe. So Cole's definition is informative about this scientific law. In explaining the need for energy to counteract entropy (10–12) and in relating entropy to societal and world events, however, Cole adopts a persuasive tone. In paragraph 16, she cautions, "Friendships and families and economies all fall apart unless we constantly make an effort to keep them working and well oiled." Clearly, she is making a pitch for us all to work harder at keeping order in our world.
2. Speaking like a common person with average concerns, such as her refrigerator breaking and her tooth needing root canal work, Cole encourages a reader to follow her into a discussion of entropy as an explanation for these ordinary problems. She achieves a friendly, almost breezy tone by using the first person, contractions, short

sentences, and colloquialisms such as "lukewarm mess" (5), "to get ourselves together" (10), and "the catch is" (10). The question in the second paragraph is another example of her personable, casual tone.

3. These terms are blunt and jarring and carry an intense impact. Throughout the essay, Cole uses these emotional words to keep us aware of the personal dimensions of entropy. While entropy is a scientific concept, she wants us to understand that it also pertains to our personal lives and has effects we can respond to emotionally. Some other similar terms are "unnerving" (4), "lost and buffeted" (7), "distressed," "afraid," "terrified," and "upset" (15).

4. This sentence pattern emphasizes contrasts—it contains an inherent opposition between the elements of the first and second half. Cole may find this pattern useful because she is trying to dramatize the effects of entropy and convince us to counteract its power as best we can. The first example compares the two "roads" to disorder and creation, finding one downhill, the other uphill. The second example compares ways to do "a sloppy job" and a "good one." Other examples occur throughout the essay: "Once it's created, it can never be destroyed" (3); "When my refrigerator was working, it kept all the cold air ordered in one part of the kitchen. . . . Once it broke down the warm and cold mixed into a lukewarm mess that allowed my butter to melt . . ." (5); "Though combating entropy is possible, it also has its price"; "That's why it seems so hard to get ourselves together, so easy to let ourselves fall apart" (10); "creating order in one corner of the universe always creates more disorder somewhere else"; "We create ordered energy from oil and coal at the price of the entropy of smog" (11); "The chances that it will wander in the direction of my refrigerator at any point are exactly 50–50. The chances that it will wander away from my refrigerator are also 50–50" (13); "there are always so many more paths toward disorder than toward order. There are so many more different ways to do a sloppy job than a good one, so many more ways to make a mess than to clean it up" (14); "The more pieces in the puzzle, the harder it is to put back together once order is disturbed" (17).

LIFE AS TYPE A

James Gleick

Questions for Close Reading (p. 454)

1. The thesis is clearly stated in the first sentence of paragraph 4: "We believe in Type A—a triumph for a notion with no particular scientific validity." Prior to paragraph 4, Gleick illustrates the cultural pervasiveness of the Type A category and traces its identification to Friedman and Rosenman's studies; these studies attempted to link heart disease to a set of personality traits clustered around the "theme of impatience" (2). Following the statement of his thesis, Gleick challenges the scientific validity of Type A, while observing its compelling cultural relevance. He concludes the essay in paragraph 12 by reiterating the thesis; he says that linking the Type A phenomenon to cardiac problems "made for poor medical research," but "it stands nonetheless as a triumph of social criticism."

2. Friedman and Rosenman's study, "Association of Specific Overt Behavior Pattern with Blood and Cardiovascular Findings," looked at connections between heart disease (including high blood pressure) and Type A behaviors. Gleick gives several reasons why the study was "obvious and false" and "a wildly flawed piece of research" (5). First, only a small number of people were studied. Group A consisted

117

of only 83 people. Second, the subjects were all men. Third, the research subjects were not chosen at random. Instead, Friedman and Rosenman selected subjects who shared similar professional and personal characteristics. They were generally "white-collar male employees of large businesses" (5) who exhibited stressed behavior, who smoked, and who were overweight. Fourth, rather than acknowledging these shared characteristics and the possibility that they might be associated with heart disease, Friedman and Rosenman instead claimed that the Type A personality—rather than the subjects' unhealthy behaviors—was responsible for Group A's medical problems. Gleick also cites the researchers' amorphous definition of Type B as evidence of their flawed understanding of Type A.

3. "The notion of Type A has expanded, shifted, and flexed to suit the varying needs of different researchers," writes Gleick in paragraph 7. He calls Type A a "grab-bag" of traits; researchers pick and choose those characteristics that reinforce their predetermined conclusions. Such researchers, each with a definite agenda, jump on the Type A bandwagon, producing sometimes alarming, sometimes ludicrous, but usually problematic results. For instance, researcher V. A. Price associated hypervigilance with the Type A personality. And researcher Cynthia Perry applied her interest in the study of daydreams to the Type A phenomenon and was able to conclude that Type A's daydream less often than other people. Similarly, National Institutes of Health researchers looking at the effects of petlessness on particular groups connected the incidence of heart disease in Type A people with the condition of petlessness. Further, researchers interested in the behavior of children—even babies—have extended the reach of the phenomenon to include this group: babies who cry more are Type A (7).

    Gleick concludes that even before they begin their studies, these researchers already have in mind how Type A will be tied into their findings, and they manipulate the studies "until they find some correlation, somewhere" (8). He concludes: "The categorizations are too variable and the prophecies too self-fulfilling" (9).

4. Gleick demonstrates that the Type B personality has been "defined not by the personality traits its members possess but by the traits they lack" (10). He remarks somewhat disparagingly that Friedman and Rosenman were able to find only eighty men—municipal clerks and embalmers—"in all San Francisco" who, unlike Type A sufferers, did *not* feel that they were under any time constraints (10). The researchers labeled these men as having the Type B personality. Gleick implies that this identification by default of a small, nonrepresentative sample is further evidence of the researchers' unscientific practices. As the "shadowy opposites" of Type A's, Type B's, according to Gleick, "do *not* wear out their fingers punching the elevator button. They do *not* allow a slow car in the fast lane to drive their hearts to fatal distraction; in fact, they are at the wheel of the slow car" (10). In essence, Gleick implies that scientists' vague, amorphous definition of Type B reinforces the dubious scientific validity of Type A.

5. *coinage* (1): an invented word or phrase
    harrying (2): harassing, annoying
    canonical (2): authoritative, officially approved
    circuitously (2): indirectly
    sanctimoniously (4): in a hypocritically righteous manner
    overt (5): open, observable, not hidden
    incipient (5): beginning to exist or appear
    sedentary (6): inactive
    hypervigilance (7): excessive watchfulness
    correlation (8): the mutual relation of two or more things

strident (9): loud, harsh, grating, or shrill
staccato (9): disjointed, abrupt
foil (10): an opposite
totem (12): a venerated emblem or symbol

Questions About the Writer's Craft (p. 454)

1. Although Gleick questions the scientific basis of Friedman and Rosenman's link between heart disease and Type A behavior, he seeks to show the universality of many of the Type A personality traits ascribed to Paul. Gleick counts on the fact that we've all met a Paul and could well have some of Paul in us. As Gleick goes on to argue, Paul's Type A personality is shaped not by personal psychology, but by the society in which he lives—the same society that, to some extent, has engendered Type A traits in us all.

2. The three fragments—"Excessive competitiveness. Aggressiveness. 'A harrying sense of time urgency'"—are, according to Gleick, how Friedman and Rosenman describe the Type A personality. Gleick probably intended these choppy, clipped fragments to mimic the hurried, fast-paced lifestyle of the Type A person.

3. Gleick uses the personal pronouns "we," "us," and "our" throughout his essay. In the first paragraph of the essay, for instance, he asserts that Type A "is a token of our confusion" and asks, "[A]re we victims or perpetrators of the crime of haste? Are we living at high speed with athleticism and vigor, or are we stricken by hurry sickness?" These queries involve and hook us; they are *about* us; they cause us to want to read on. Because he knows that most readers will identify with these Type A characteristics, he seeks to show that Type A is less a medical condition than a cultural one. We are members of the society that has embraced the Type A phenomenon. We are Type A people because of the high-intensity society in which we live. It is also important to note that the pronouns "us," "we," and "our" also include Gleick himself; he, too, is a member of the society that has embraced and perpetuated the Type A lifestyle.

4. Gleick's sarcasm reflects his frustration and annoyance with the medical establishment's attempts to find scientific correlations where no valid ones exist. Other examples of sentences, phrases, and words that strike a similar tone include the following: "standard medical knowledge untainted by research" (4), "cardiovascular comeuppance" (4), "the original Type A grab-bag" (7), "This is sweet, but it is not science" (7), "even more bizarrely" (11), and the last sentence of paragraph 11, which asserts "No wonder they omitted Type C from the subsequent publicity." Considered together, these sentences and phrases establish the author's stance: one of bemused dismay, even disappointment, at the unscientific treatment the scientific community has given the Type A phenomenon.

THE CUTE FACTOR

Natalie Angier

Questions for Close Reading (p. 461)

1. Angier states her thesis in the second paragraph: "Scientists who study the evolution of visual signaling have identified a wide and still-expanding assortment of features

and behaviors that make something look cute." She then restates and expands this thesis in paragraphs 11 and 12.

2. Visual signaling involves features and behaviors that are meaningful in some way and that elicit a certain response. The article focuses on the visual signaling associated with cuteness. Visual signaling cues that indicate cuteness include "bright forward-facing eyes set low on a round face, a pair of big round ears, floppy limbs, and a side-to-side, teeter-totter gait" (paragraph 11) or "anything remotely resembling a human baby or part thereof" (paragraph 12).

3. According to the article, the reason humans respond so readily to cuteness is that features we consider cute are those of human babies. Since babies are so vulnerable, we have evolved to respond quickly to their needs. Without this response to the needs of babies, the human species would die out. The fact that humans consider other animals and things cute derives from the resemblance of those things to babies.

4. In Japan, cuteness (*kawaii*) is everywhere, even on truckers' dashboards. There, cuteness (of little dolls and perky mascots) is used as a means to soften the hierarchical boundaries of a fairly rigid society where power and authority can be threatening. In contrast, in the United States cuteness is associated with youth and Americans' desire to be youthful, and these associations are exploited in branding (Google), advertising (cute graphics), and fashion (youthful clothes).

5. *gamboling* (1): skipping about, frolicking
   rapture (1): great joy
   sonorous (7): full-sounding; deep-toned
   despoiled (15): pillaged, robbed
   cosegregate (15): to be inherited together (from genetics; the tendency for closely linked genes and genetic markers to segregate [be inherited] together)
   homeliness (15): plainness
   aesthetics (20): the science or theory of the beautiful
   blatantly (22): conspicuously, obtrusively
   unadorned (24): plain, without ornament
   primal (26): primary, original
   redoubts (27): areas of secure retreat
   hierarchical (28): having to do with rank
   inherent (31): inborn
   salient (31): noticeable, standing out
   winsomely (40): attractively

Questions About the Writer's Craft (p. 461)

1. The lead of Angier's article starts with a description of a cute panda cub in a zoo and the crowd of visitors exclaiming over it and taking pictures. In addition to drawing the reader in with this vivid description, Angier addresses the reader directly, suggesting that the reader also, if present at the scene, would be responding to the panda cub in the same way. The combination of vivid description and direct address is designed to engage, or hook, the reader's interest.

   Angier then goes on to frame the contents of the remainder of the story with her thesis statement: "Scientists who study the evolution of visual signaling have identified a wide and still-expanding assortment of features and behaviors that make something look cute." The rest of the story consists of examples and explanations that expand on this statement.

   In this article, the thesis statement is the "framework" part of the lead. The lead contains more than the thesis statement; it also contains the description designed to engage the reader's interest and make him or her want to continue reading the article.

2. The tone of the article is somewhat humorous; Angier gently pokes fun at the human tendency to overreact to cuteness. Even in the more objective, scientific passages, such as the description of a baby's features, she injects some lightness, describing how Disney ducks and mice have forward-facing eyes, contrary to nature. Angier adopts this tone to keep readers entertained and reading. She does not take a strictly informative approach in this article because she is writing for a general audience and must hold their interest. Therefore, the scientific findings she reports are interspersed with vivid examples of cuteness, such as the panda bear cub, as well as examples of cuteness in the culture at large. These examples serve to make the scientific findings interesting and relevant to ordinary people's experience.

3. In paragraph 15, Angier sharpens the contrast between cuteness and beauty by juxtaposing their characteristics and separating them with the word *over* as in "rounded over sculptured, soft over refined, clumsy over quick." In the next sentence, she juxtaposes the two concepts, using only a semicolon to separate them. Finally, the last set of contrasts consists of two full sentences with no transition between them.

4. The purpose of the lengthy description of a baby's features is to explain why similar features elsewhere evoke the same swift, positive response in adults. A baby's features may have evolved for other, more specific functions, but they also have the effect of arousing the response of adults because that response is necessary to the baby's survival. This description of babies is largely objective. For example, "Baby eyes and ears are situated comparatively far down the face and skull" (32), "cartilage tissue in an infant's nose is comparatively soft and undeveloped" (34), "baby skin sits relatively loose on the body" (34), and "the toddler gait consists as much of lateral movement as of any forward momentum" (35).

WHAT IS THE QUARTERLIFE CRISIS?

Alexandra Robbins & Abby Wilner

Questions for Close Reading (p. 468)

1. In paragraph 4, the authors provide a series of statements that could be identified collectively as the thesis: "[This crisis] may be the single most concentrated period during which individuals relentlessly question their future and how it will follow the events of their past. It covers . . . an age group that can range from late adolescence to the mid-thirties but is usually most intense in twentysomethings. It is what we call the quarterlife crisis, and it is a real phenomenon." However, students might want to refine and slightly expand this thesis using their own words; one possibility is: "The quarterlife crisis, a period of intense confusion and anxiety about the future typically experienced by twentysomethings, is a real phenomenon that should be acknowledged in our society."

2. The authors say that individuals anywhere from "late adolescence to the mid-thirties" are prone to this crisis. However, they specify that twentysomethings—the twenties being the age when people typically complete their education and are confronted with the "real world"—are most vulnerable.

3. Robbins and Wilner commence their comparison-contrast in paragraph 4, before they've officially named the "quarterlife crisis," calling it the "other crisis" and saying it "can be just as, if not more, devastating than the midlife crisis." What the two crises have in common is that they "stem from the same basic problem," which is major life change (5). And both result in tremendous anxiety and upheaval in the

lives of their sufferers. But in every other way, the quarterlife and midlife crises are opposites.

The contrast begins on the most fundamental level: the age of the sufferers, indicated by the name of each respective crisis. On one hand, uncertainty about the future causes quarterlife crisis sufferers to fear change and instability (6), while the feeling of stagnancy experienced by middle-agers causes them to seek out change (5). As the authors observe, "the midlife crisis revolves around a doomed sense of stagnancy" while "the quarterlife crisis is a response to overwhelming instability, constant change, too many choices, and a panicked sense of helplessness" (8). In addition, the responsibility levels that characterize each of the two groups contribute to their differences. Midlifers have more responsibilities, which they may seek to flee, while quarterlifers have fewer commitments, resulting in a dizzying array of possibilities (17). Another key difference between the two crises is the level to which they are acknowledged in society. Midlife crisis, the authors assert, is the "widely acknowledged" subject (8) of "hundreds of books, movies, and magazine articles" (3). As a result, midlifers know about and even expect this crisis; they can choose from a variety of helpful resources, including "support groups, books, movies, or Internet sites" (8). In contrast, despite its pervasiveness, the quarterlife crisis remains unacknowledged in society and unexpected by young people, causing them to be blindsided when it strikes (8). In fact, no crisis-related statistics exist for this younger age-group; quarterlifers and their specific issues have not been studied by the mental health or the medical communities.

4. The authors state in paragraph 18 that the feeling of doubt is the "most widespread, frightening, and quite possibly the most difficult manifestation of the quarterlife crisis." Doubt is especially threatening because it can strike anyone in any situation, from the most to the least socially and professionally successful, regardless of "levels of self-esteem, confidence, and overall well-being." While doubting oneself is a normal, healthy part of life, the excessive self-doubt that characterizes a quarterlife crisis can immobilize a person. And because this doubting as it relates to the quarterlife crisis remains unaddressed in society, people's anxiety is increased by the feeling they are alone in self-doubt, sending them "spiraling downward."

5. *pertinent* (3): relevant
    chaotic (4): disorderly; confused
    disarray (4): disorder
    interval (4): the time between two periods
    phenomenon (4): an occurrence, circumstance, or condition that can be perceived
    stagnancy (5): motionlessness; state of lacking vitality
    nexus (7): a place of connection
    monotony (8): tedious sameness
    ramifications (8): consequences
    trepidation (9): apprehension
    virtually (17): practically
    ramen (15): Japanese dish of noodles in broth, usually very affordable
    excruciatingly (17): very painfully; agonizingly
    manifestation (18): obvious demonstration
    barrage (18): an overwhelming outpouring

Questions About the Writer's Craft (p. 468)

1. The authors do not seek to define their term in a vacuum; rather, there is a distinctly persuasive aspect to their essay, one which seeks social change. Robbins and Wilner posit that the quarterlife crisis is an unacknowledged social phenomenon whose

effects are rendered more acute because it is undiscussed. This lends immediacy and importance in their attempts to define the term and "get the word out" about its existence. To deliver home to readers the importance of their mission, the authors use high-impact words and phrases in explaining the dire effects of the quarterlife crisis: "Twentysomethings . . . face a crisis that hits them with a far more powerful force than they ever expected" (8); "The slam is particularly painful because today's twentysomethings believe that they are alone . . ." (8); "[T]he ramifications can be extremely dangerous" (8). In addition, in paragraph 13, the authors provide a compelling quote from an expert, Robert DuPont, to validate their claim that the quarterlife crisis is a pervasive and potentially serious condition.

2. This narrative anecdote, presented and discussed in paragraphs 1 through 3, serves multiple purposes. First, its familiar, stereotypical subject matter—of a man having a midlife crisis—is an inviting way to draw readers into the essay. But the mere familiarity of the anecdote's subject also serves a more pointed purpose: It proves the authors' point about midlife crisis being common knowledge in society. This, in turn, sets up the contrast with the quarterlife crisis, which, the authors argue, is as pervasive but remains unacknowledged. Additionally, the humor implicit in the opening anecdote sets the comfortable, conversational tone of the piece. This, too, draws readers into the essay and helps make them more sympathetic to what the authors have to say.

3. It would not be inaccurate to say that an exploration of causes and effects of quarterlife crisis is at the heart of the authors' definition of the term. While other patterns of development allow the authors to set up the term and explain the importance of defining it, causal analysis provides the structure and content of the definition itself.

    Robbins and Wilner logically begin their causal analysis with an exploration of the causes of the quarterlife crisis. In a nutshell, they say that it is "a response to the overwhelming instability, constant change, too many choices, and a panicked sense of helplessness" (8) and then proceed to explain each of these causes in subsequent paragraphs. They discuss causes including the feelings of uncertainty and instability following completion of school (6–7), as well as the sense of being overwhelmed by the massive amounts of options suddenly available to them (7–8) and the "whirlwind of new responsibilities, new liberties, and new choices" (9).

    The effects of the crisis, briefly stated, are "overwhelming senses of helplessness and cluelessness, of indecision and apprehension" (8). Whole paragraphs are devoted to explaining how the following conditions can result from the quarterlife crisis: hopelessness (12); depression, anxiety, and even addiction (12–14); disappointment (15); and self-doubt (18).

4. In discussing the similarities between the two crises, the authors use signals including "same" and "both" (5), and then later, "Just as . . . so, too" (8). But overwhelmingly, the authors focus on contrasting the two crises, a shift clearly marked by the phrase "In contrast" at the beginning of paragraph 6 and marked by the following signal devices: "while" (8), "by contrast" (8), and "But" (17).

THE HANDICAP OF DEFINITION

William Raspberry

Questions for Close Reading (p. 473)

1. Raspberry implies the thesis when he introduces the concept of "handicap of definition" in paragraph 1. The thesis might be stated as "Black youth are handicapped by the associations of the word "black" in our society." The rest of the essay explains through examples what "black" has come to mean—something limited rather than something open-ended. He asserts this position clearly in paragraph 7: "My point is the harm that comes from too narrow a definition of what is black." Near the end of the essay he includes a statement that crystallizes the situation: "But the real problem is not so much that the things defined as 'black' are negative. The problem is that the definition is much too narrow"(14). This sentence is the clearest statement of the thesis in the essay.

2. Black culture, according to Raspberry, includes assumptions that certain talents are "black"—that is, that Blacks possess them in abundance—while other talents are not Black, or are "white." The Black talents are athletic, musical, and performance based, while whites own all the talent in business, language, reasoning, academics, and so on (6). As a result, Blacks do not strive to achieve in "white" fields, even if they have ability, and so failure is all but guaranteed. Another effect of this limited view of blackness concerns the way being a "man" is defined in Black culture. Blacks are led to assume that maleness is related to "physical aggressiveness, sexual prowess, the refusal to submit to authority" (13). The prisons, Raspberry comments, "are full of people who, by this perverted definition, are unmistakably men."

3. "Positive ethnic traditions" are "myths" (9) or assumptions (11) that portray ethnic groups as having innate talents or traits. Raspberry cites the beliefs that Jews are strong in communication and that the Chinese have a facility for mathematics. He believes that such talents result as much from the assumption they exist as from actual genetic inheritance. The assumption that Blacks excel in sports and entertainment is another example of a "positive ethnic tradition." He would like Blacks to expand their sense of what is naturally Black. He writes, "Wouldn't it be wonderful if we could infect black children with the notion that excellence in math is 'black' rather than white, or possibly Chinese? Wouldn't it be of enormous value if we could create the myth that morality, strong families, determination, courage and love of learning are traits brought by slaves from Mother Africa and therefore quintessentially black?" (9)

4. Raspberry perceives that the assumptions about what it means to be Black are inhibiting African American youngsters from success. Too many of the qualities necessary for success are attributed to white heritage and not to Black. Raspberry believes that the African American community needs to convey to its youth that Blacks are naturally competent, smart, and capable. Once it is accepted that academic achievement, success, hard work, and so on are not limited to whites, African American children will be freed from the inhibiting narrowness of the definition of "black" (15). Then they will be able to succeed in mainstream culture instead of becoming "failures—by definition" (16).

5. *diction* (3): clarity of enunciation
    scrimping (5): economizing in the extreme
    array (6): an impressive display of numerous items
    quintessentially (9): most typically or most purely

elocution (10): the art of public speaking; vocal ability
sustained (10): prolonged or repeated
inculcated (11): instilled or taught by frequent repetition
concede (12): to yield or grant

Questions About the Writer's Craft (p. 473)

1. Raspberry defines three additional terms besides "black": "white" (5–6), "positive ethnic traditions" (11), and "man" (13). Raspberry defines "white" as a term that Blacks use to describe qualities which they feel they do not have but which whites do. The effect of this definition is that "white" has become a negative label among Black youth, who criticize each other for speaking well (talking "white") and striving academically (acting "white") (5–6). Describing this use of "white" helps Raspberry explain through contrast what he means by the "narrowness" of the word "black."

    The second term that Raspberry defines is "positive ethnic traditions" (11). By giving examples, he explains that such traditions are assumptions about talents supposedly innate to various ethnic groups: communication ability for Jews, math ability for the Chinese. The qualities associated with ethnic groups are merely assumptions; they are in the realm of psychology, not genetics (11). He believes these myths have the effect of encouraging hard work and dedication in the ethnic youth who believe themselves talented in these areas. Thus, by discussing the term "positive ethnic traditions," Raspberry shows by contrast the negative effects of the narrowness of the meaning of "black."

    Finally, in paragraph 13, Raspberry explains the definition of "man" in the Black community. This definition is a parallel to the definition of "black," for it consists of assumptions about innate qualities, assumptions that aren't necessarily true and that are very limiting and even damaging in their effects. For Black youth, a "man" is physically and sexually aggressive and combative toward authority. The tragic effect of this "perverted definition," according to Raspberry, is that such "men" often wind up in prison.

2. In his introduction, Raspberry discounts the effects of a series of commonly recognized negative factors—"bad schools, mean politicians, economic deprivation, and racism"—on Black youth, suggesting they are not the "heaviest burdens." Rather, he says, there is a different burden that is especially influential, and this is the "handicap of definition," the burden imposed by the associations commonly held with the term "black." This refutation of the sociological factors affecting Black achievement creates a credible tone; here is a writer, the reader might think, who knows the facts, the reality, and the explanations, and can cut to the essence. Raspberry shows himself to be forthright and direct, someone who doesn't "soft-pedal" the truth. Also, beginning with this refutation permits Raspberry to present his thesis right away, without a lot of beating around the bush; this would be very important for him stylistically, since the essay first appeared as a newspaper column.

3. Although the readership of *The Washington Post* is predominantly white, Raspberry appears to be addressing Blacks rather than whites. He uses the first person to emphasize he is a participant-critic of Black culture and uses "we" and "our" to join with Black readers in thinking about their own culture. Raspberry uses "I" in paragraphs 1, 2, 7, and 11; since the essay is critical of the Black community for its narrow, handicapping use of the words "black" and "white," Raspberry uses the personal pronoun "I" to keep the readers aware that he is a Black writer. Especially for Black readers, knowledge of Raspberry's race might defuse resistance they feel

toward his criticism of an aspect of Black culture. Raspberry shows his awareness that people might be upset by his thesis when he begins the second paragraph by saying, "Let me explain quickly what I mean." He doesn't want readers to get the wrong impression, that he is "anti-black."

The pronouns "we" and "our" occur in paragraphs 9, 12, 15, and 16. In paragraph 9, the "we" could refer to Americans as a whole: "Wouldn't it be wonderful if we could infect Black children with the notion that excellence in math is 'black' . . . ? Wouldn't it be of enormous value if we could create the myth that morality, strong families, determination, courage and love of learning are traits brought by slaves . . . ?" But the references to "we" at the end of the essay clearly refer to the Black community: "many of the things we concede to whites . . ." (12); "we have to make our children understand that they are intelligent, competent people. . . . What we seem to be doing, instead, is raising up another generation of young Blacks who will be failures . . ." (15–16). By creating this link with the Black community, Raspberry includes himself among those who are responsible for the attitudes of the future generation.

4. Raspberry makes use of several techniques to keep us interested in his subject. He includes numerous recognizable examples, establishes a personal tone, employs balanced sentences for dramatic effect, and chooses informal transitions. His specific examples begin in paragraph 2, where he refers to basketball star Larry Bird and well-known singer Tom Jones. He also names Teena Marie, a singer some readers might recognize, and refers to a rock group called "The Average White Band"—a humorous reference even if we have no familiarity with the group. In addition to these and other specifics later in the essay, Raspberry establishes a lively, personal, forthright tone that keeps us involved. "Let me explain quickly what I mean," he writes in starting off paragraph 2, showing his directness. He then uses parallel structure and the imperative form to draw the reader in: "Tell pop singer Tom Jones he moves black. . . . Say to Teena Marie or The Average White Band that they sound 'black'. . . ." In the next paragraph he continues this tone: "But name one pursuit. . . . Tell a white broadcaster he talks 'black'. . . . Tell a white reporter he writes 'black'. . . . Tell a white lawyer he reasons 'black'. . . ." He returns to this memorable style in paragraph 5: "Think of all the ways black children put one another down. . . ." Finally, Raspberry uses informal transitions that keep the essay moving, such as "But" (3, 14), "And" (7), and "So" (13).

ARGUMENTATION-PERSUASION

OPENING COMMENTS

First-year composition courses often end with argumentation-persuasion. There are good reasons for this. Since an argumentation-persuasion essay can be developed using a number of patterns of development, it makes sense to introduce this mode after students have had experience using a variety of patterns. Also, argumentation-persuasion demands logical reasoning and sensitivity to the nuances of language. We've found that earlier papers—causal analysis and comparison-contrast, for example—help students develop the reasoning and linguistic skills needed to tackle this final assignment.

When teaching argumentation-persuasion, we stress that the pattern makes special demands. Not only do writers have to generate convincing support for their positions, but they also must acknowledge and deal with opposing points of view. Having to contend with a contrary viewpoint challenges students to dig into their subjects so that they can defend their position with conviction. Students should find the material on pages 486–90 helpful; it illustrates different ways to acknowledge and refute the opposition.

Despite their initial moans and groans of protest, students enjoy the challenge of argumentation-persuasion. To help them become more aware of the characteristics of this rhetorical pattern, we often ask them to look through current newspapers and magazines and clip editorials and advertisements they find effective. In class, these items provide the basis for a lively discussion about the strategies unique to argumentation-persuasion. For example, the endorsement of a health club by a curvaceous television celebrity raises the issue of credibility, or *ethos*. An editorial filled with highly charged language ("We must unite to prevent this boa constrictor of a highway from strangling our neighborhood") focuses attention on the connotative power of words.

We often conclude our composition courses with an assignment based on a controversial issue. Depending on the time available and the skill of our students, the assignment may or may not require outside research. If it does call for research, we begin by having the class as a whole brainstorm as many controversial social issues as they can. Then, for each issue, the class generates a pair of propositions representing opposing viewpoints. Here are a few examples of what our classes typically come up with:

Controversial Subject	*Propositions*
School prayer	Prayer in public schools *should / should not* be allowed.

Controversial Subject	*Propositions*
Drug abuse in professional sports	Professional sports *should / should not* implement a program of mandatory drug testing.

Adoption	Adopted children *should / should not* be given the means to contact their biological parents.

If the assignment does not include research, we focus attention on more immediate local problems. Using the sequence described above, we start the activity by asking the class as a whole to brainstorm as many controversial campus problems as they can. Here are some argumentative-persuasion topics that have resulted from this activity:

Controversial Subject	*Propositions*
Cheating	A student found guilty of cheating on an exam *should / should not* be suspended.
Fraternities and sororities	Fraternities and sororities *should / should not* be banned from campus.
Drinking	The college pub *should / should not* be licensed to serve liquor.

Once the propositions have been generated, the activity can go in one of two directions. We might ask students to pair up by issue, with the students in each pair taking opposing positions. Or, unconcerned that both sides of an issue be covered, we might have students select a position on any issue identified by the class. In either case, students base their argumentation-persuasion essays on the proposition they have selected. Though they may eventually qualify their propositions, starting with a definitive thesis helps focus students' work in the early stages of the activity.

We try to schedule the assignment so that there is enough time at the end of the course for students to deliver their arguments orally. The presentations take about one class; we call this class either "Forum on Contemporary Social Issues" or "Forum on Critical Campus Issues." Students tell us that they enjoy and learn a good deal from these brief oral presentations. (We do not, by the way, grade the talks—just the papers.)

We have been pleased by the way this final activity energizes students, pulling them out of the end-of-the-semester slump. The forum creates a kind of learning fellowship— not a bad way to end the course.

This chapter's professional readings illustrate the mix of logical support and emotional appeal characteristic of argumentation-persuasion. To develop her assertion that the threat of failure should be regularly utilized to motivate students to work up to their potential, Sherry relates her experiences as a teacher and a mother and thus establishes her *ethos* on the subject. Yuh uses a synthesis of personal anecdote, statements by credentialed authorities, and analysis to create an eloquent plea for multicultural education. In arguing his case against distance education, Barszcz dismantles the claims of the pro-tech position using appeals to logic as well as to emotion. With scathing examples, Twain counters the common assumption that humans are superior to other animals. The remaining essays are particularly helpful for illustrating different ways of dealing with opposing arguments. Citing compelling examples, Fish argues for a clearer definition of free speech. Paglia accuses feminists of spreading ignorance and falsehood regarding men and sex, and Jacoby directly refutes Paglia's position, charging her with being an apologist for rapists. On opposite sides of the debate about using torture against terrorism suspects, both Alter and Porter support their viewpoints by aggressively discrediting the opposition. Finally, Rodriguez and Parker both refer to racism and civil rights in establishing their opposing points of view.

ANSWERS FOR PREWRITING ACTIVITIES

Below we provide possible responses to selected prewriting activities at the end of Chapter 11. Of course, your students will devise their own inventive approaches. (p. 510)

1. Listed below are some possible approaches to each of the topics. We recommend that you have students share their responses to this activity in groups or pairs. Seeing how others handled the assignments can provide inspiration for their own work.

    ### Topic: *Defining hypocrisy*
    Possible Audience: Employers
    Essay might argue the merit of these ways of behaving:

    > Some employees react negatively to the hypocrisy of bosses not practicing what they preach. Employers should be careful to dispense advice that they themselves are willing to follow. For example, they shouldn't reprimand staff for taking office supplies if they also "borrow" such supplies; they shouldn't write memos outlawing personal phone calls if they themselves make such calls.

    ### Topic: *The difference between license and freedom*
    Possible Audience: College students
    Essay might argue the merit of these ways of behaving:

    > While license involves nothing more than indulging one's every whim, freedom means acting with thoughtful regard for consequences. Students, then, should think before going out to party before an exam, should reconsider substituting an easy course for a difficult one, and so on.

2. Below is an audience analysis for each thesis. Persuasive points for thesis will vary from group to group.

    a. College students: Hostile
       Parents: Wavering or hostile
       College officials: Wavering or supportive

    b. City officials: Hostile
       Low-income residents: Supportive
       General citizens: Wavering

    c. Environmentalists: Supportive
       Homeowners: Hostile
       Town council members: Wavering

    d. Alumni: Wavering or supportive
       College officials: Supportive
       Student journalists: Hostile

ANSWERS FOR REVISING ACTIVITIES

Below we provide possible responses to selected revising activities at the end of Chapter 11. Of course, your students will devise their own inventive approaches. (p. 510)

3. a. ***Begging the Question***. The statement that "Grades are irrelevant to learning" requires proof, but this argument skips over this debatable premise. The second statement is also debatable; some students—those wishing to attend graduate school, for example—are in college to "get good grades."

   b. ***Either/or; Begging the Question***. Both statements are debatable; for example, that jail provides a "taste of reality" is questionable, and that juvenile offenders will repeat crimes "over and over" unless jailed needs to be proven. Moreover, the argument presents only two alternatives: "either" a juvenile offender is jailed, "or" the offender will repeat crimes. It is possible to imagine other outcomes from not jailing juvenile offenders: with therapy, community service, job training, or suspended sentences, some may "go straight"; others may commit different crimes instead of "repeating" their initial crimes.

   c. ***Begging the Question; Card Stacking***. The first statement in this argument is an overly general description of the programs: they "do nothing to decrease the rate of teenage pregnancy." In addition, the argument begs the question of whether the programs truly do curtail teen pregnancies. The argument also fails to address whether there are other valuable accomplishments of the programs that might make them worth keeping. (For example, such programs most likely help reduce instances of sexually transmitted diseases.) Finally, the phrase "so-called sex education programs" is also a way of card stacking; this term denigrates the programs without saying what's wrong with them.

   d. ***False Analogy; Non Sequitur***. By likening abortion to killing the homeless and pulling the plug on sick people, this argument commits a false analogy. In reality, these are all quite different situations with differing moral issues, motivations, and outcomes. Secondly, it is a *non sequitur* to assume that if abortion is permitted, people "will think it's acceptable" to commit the other actions mentioned. There's actually no demonstrated causal connection between society's permitting abortion and its accepting the murder of unfortunate people.

   e. ***False Analogy***. This argument compares two unlike things: locally imposed curfews on teenagers (often parentally supported) and curfews imposed by totalitarian governments on some or all of their population.

4. It's a good idea to set aside some time for students to see how others went about revising this paragraph. They may discover options they hadn't considered.
   Here are some of the problems with the introduction:

   — Throughout the paragraph there's a hostile, confrontational tone that undercuts the impact of the position being advanced. Sarcastic descriptions of the administrators amount to an *ad hominem* attack: "acting like fascists" and "in their supposed wisdom" (both in sentence 2) and "somehow or another they got it into their heads" (sentence 5). These accusatory descriptions of the way the administration came to impose the dress code should be replaced with a more realistic explanation of why they made the decision they did. A more objective tone is called for.
   — Inflammatory language used in the first two sentences *stacks the cards* in favor of the writer's point of view: "outrageously strong," "issued an edict," "preposterous dress code." Similar card stacking occurs in the fourth sentence when the writer refers to the administrators' "dictatorial prohibition." Such phrases need to be replaced by more neutral language.

- The writer's point that students will lose their "constitutional rights" (sentence 2) is not substantiated in any way. A brief explanation of this point would be appropriate.
- The statement (sentence 3) that "Perhaps the next thing they'll want to do is forbid students to play rock music at school dances" is a *non sequitur*; instituting a dress code has no causal relationship to restricting music at school dances. This statement might also be considered a *red herring* because it brings in an unrelated issue about which the reader might have strong feelings. In any case, this unfounded prediction should be eliminated.
- There is no sound basis for the recommendation (sentence 6) that students and parents should protest all dress codes. Any such recommendation should be reserved for the end of the essay, after a logical, well-reasoned argument has been advanced. At that point, it would be appropriate to name specific actions parents could take, such as calling the principal or speaking out at a PTA meeting.
- The final statement that if dress codes are implemented, "we might as well throw out the Constitution" embodies at least two fallacies. It is an *either/or* statement, admitting of no lesser or even other consequences. It also is a *non sequitur*, because no cause-effect relationship has been shown to exist between dress codes and the end of constitutional rights. This closing statement should be eliminated.
- Finally, the paragraph uses the cause-effect pattern but presents no evidence for the causal relationship it claims. The writer discounts the *causes* of the administrators' decision (the current dress habits of the student body) and predicts extreme and unsubstantiated *effects* of the dress code. In revising, students might choose some of the following options: dispute the administration's claims that the lack of a dress code creates problems, discuss other possible ways of handling these problems, or analyze possible negative effects of a dress code. Of course, not all of these options could be pursued in the introductory paragraph, but they point the way to possible strategies for developing the rest of the essay in a thoughtful, logical manner.

IN PRAISE OF THE "F" WORD

Mary Sherry

Questions for Close Reading (p. 514)

1. Sherry's thesis, implied, is a combination of the assertions she makes in paragraphs 2 and 4. In paragraph 2, after describing what brings students to adult literacy programs, she tells us that the real reason they wind up there is that "they have been cheated by our education system." She rounds out this point in paragraph 4 when she asserts that poor academic skills are less a result of "drugs, divorce, and other impediments" than they are a result of teachers' unwillingness to use the threat of failure as a motivating tool. Bringing these two points together, one may state Sherry's thesis as follows: "Students are cheated by an educational system that refuses to make the possibility of failure a reality."
2. Deliberately shocking, this statement gains our attention immediately. Most of us should be appalled that so many students—tens of thousands—will receive diplomas that mean nothing. We wonder how such a thing could occur. But we also wonder what Sherry means by the term "meaningless." Later in the essay, this question is

answered. Meaningless diplomas have no substance. They are useless slips of paper for those students who have been ushered through to graduation despite the fact that they have failed to achieve passing grades. Sherry concludes that passing students along in this manner cheats them in a sort of slippery-slope way. To begin, they feel increasingly inadequate as they move to higher levels without having mastered the material meant to prepare them for more advanced subject matter. Some continue on in this manner, realizing only later how little they really have learned—their lack of skill resulting, among other things, in limited job opportunities or disgruntled employers. For others, failure becomes a state of mind. Never imagining they have the power to learn and thus to move ahead, they abandon the idea of learning altogether.

3.   According to Sherry, educators don't give reasons for passing students with poor achievement records; educators make excuses instead. For instance, they say "kids can't learn if they come from terrible environments" (8) or have experienced such things as "unemployment, chemical dependency, abusive relationships" (9). In other words, neither teacher nor student is responsible for achievement, or the lack thereof; the world at large is responsible.

What excuses like this amount to is a "Why bother?" attitude, which is particularly destructive because it results in a kind of self-fulfilling prophecy: If little is expected from students, there is little incentive for either teachers or students to work hard. Such a cavalier view of students' ability to succeed falls short of addressing what Sherry sees as the real problem: the dearth of incentive in education today. She writes, "No one seems to stop to think that—no matter what environments they come from—most kids don't put school first on their list unless they perceive something is at stake. They'd rather be sailing" (8). It is not that students can't be educated, but that students are not encouraged to see education as necessary to their future success, something ultimately worth their time and energy.

4.   Regardless of distractions, be they home-life- or peer-related, in order to get students to concentrate, teachers must gain students' attention. Most educators would agree that this is often easier said than done. And Sherry doesn't provide any specifics as to how this might be accomplished other than to say that teaching style has much to do with it (4). Since most instructors would rather not resort to turning cartwheels to keep students focused, Sherry gives another option when "style alone won't do it." She writes that "there is another way to show who holds the winning hand in the classroom. That is to reveal the trump card of failure." In other words, acrobatics are not necessary to move students to concentrate. What is needed is a clarification of the road to success: stay focused on schoolwork, or fail.

Adult students, having the wisdom that comes with experience, understand the importance of education, Sherry tells us. Often their livelihood depends upon success in the classroom this time around. Thus, what lies at the heart of their motivation is "a healthy fear of failure" (9). And this—the understanding that something is at stake—can and must, Sherry believes, be instilled in all students.

5.   *validity* (1): soundness, effectiveness
semiliterate (1): partially educated
equivalency (2): equal to in value
impediments (4): hindrances, obstructions
composure (6): calmness and self-possession
radical (6): extreme, revolutionary
priority (6): something of utmost importance
resentful (7): angry or bitter about
testimony (9): public declaration
motivate (10): to stir to action

merit (11): value

conspiracy (11): a plot

illiteracy (11): the condition of having little or no formal education, especially the inability to read and write

Questions about the Writer's Craft (p. 514)

1. To convince readers that she knows of what she speaks, Sherry establishes her qualifications early on. She tells us in the first sentence of paragraph 2 that many of the students awarded meaningless diplomas eventually find their way into adult literacy programs such as the one where she teaches basic grammar and writing. In other words, as an adult-literacy teacher, she knows firsthand the type of student she refers to in the selection. Moreover, as we learn in paragraph 3, her experience as an educator has taught her "a lot about our schools." And what she has learned, as her examples make clear, directly relates to the issue of passing students through the system regardless of achievement. But Sherry doesn't stop there. To make sure her audience does not lose sight of her credibility, throughout the essay, she refers either to herself as a teacher or to her teaching experiences (paragraphs 4, 7, 9).

    Still, being a teacher is not the sum of Sherry's qualifications. Her home-life credentials her further. She is the parent of a student whose teacher used the "trump card of failure" to get him to succeed. Identifying herself at the outset and establishing her qualifications so often (and in more than one way) indicate that Sherry anticipates a possibly skeptical audience—one that requires a knowledgeable and credentialed voice if they are going to consider what she has to say, much less be led to her way of thinking.

2. The title probably makes some readers, perhaps most readers, think of a well-known obscene term. And Sherry probably hoped for this effect, for as outlandish as it seems, we might then assume she is going to argue the attributes of this term and its usage. This thought alone is likely to arouse readers' curiosity; they will want to read on to find out why Sherry applauds the "F" word. This is probably why Sherry chose this play on words for a title. Through it, she gets our attention.

3. Sherry quotes her students in paragraphs 3 and 7. By using these direct quotations, Sherry lets us experience directly how these students feel about their educational experiences and their own abilities. Through their words, Sherry demonstrates that the problem she sees is very real. She has come to understand the problem by listening to the statements she now shares with us. The students' direct testimony is her most valid proof that a problem exists. Although Sherry articulates the issue and argues the point, her students' comments illustrate that there is no one better than the students themselves to convey the reality of the problem.

4. Sherry's main proof that the threat of failure can work comes in the form of a personal example. We learn that although nothing could move Sherry's son before, he was motivated to succeed in his English class by the threat of flunking (5–6). Although Sherry concedes that one piece of proof is hardly enough—"I know one example doesn't make a case" (7)—this one example helps her support her position in a number of ways. To begin, using a personal example brings her readers closer to her and thus closer to her subject matter. In addition, this particular example has special power because it consists of a parent, a student, a teacher: There is someone in the example with whom almost any reader can identify. Parents can imagine themselves in Sherry's shoes, having to accept that the threat of failure is the best way to motivate their child. Teachers can envision themselves as Mrs. Stifter, adhering to a an unpopular policy because it brings about the hoped-for results. And

students can ally themselves with Sherry's son, a boy who chooses to succeed when the only alternative is to fail.

LET'S TELL THE STORY OF ALL AMERICA'S CULTURES

Yuh Ji-Yeon

Questions for Close Reading (p. 519)

1. Yuh states her thesis in paragraph 10, after a long and tantalizing introduction. She writes, "Educators around the country are finally realizing what I realized as teenager in the library. . . . America is a multicultural nation, composed of many people with varying histories and varying traditions who have little in common except their humanity, a belief in democracy and a desire for freedom." She restates it in paragraph 19: "The history of America is the story of how and why people from all over the world came to the United States, and how in struggling to make a better life for themselves, they changed each other, they changed the country, and they all came to call themselves Americans." The essay as a whole argues that students should receive information about the many streams of ethnicities that compose our country so that they can appreciate the contributions and struggles of all types of Americans.

2. The history books she was assigned in school portrayed America as formed by and developed through the efforts of white people such as "Lewis and Clark, Lincoln, Daniel Boone, Carnegie, presidents, explorers, and industrialists" (2). These portrayals are limited, and they place white European-descended people as the central players in our history. Her own research as a teenager determined that many other nonwhite groups had made contributions, but these were left out of the history. In the field of agriculture, she discovered that immigrants from Asia had cultivated California's deserts and worked the sugarcane fields in Hawaii; an Asian had developed the popular breed of cherry that now carries his name, Bing. Asians had also served in the U.S. armed forces in the World War I, but were denied citizenship nevertheless (4). In looking into history texts, she discovered that the only references to nonwhites were oversimplified and one-dimensional. African Americans were discussed only as slaves. Native Americans were portrayed as "scalpers" (2), as wild and violent. Her investigations thus led her to the conclusion that "the history books were wrong" (9). She has a special interest in righting the wrong because she herself is a nonwhite immigrant from Asia. Her evidence includes numerous examples of Native American (3, 15), Asian (4), African American (5, 15), and Hispanic (6) contributions to American life.

3. Yuh believes that history courses should teach about the various cultural groups that helped shape the nation (10, 14). More than this, however, students should "be taught that history is an ongoing process of discovery and interpretation of the past, and that there is more than one way of viewing the world" (14). What might look like a "heroic" achievement from one point of view, for example, could be considered barbarism from another, she notes, referring to the American domination of the Native American lands of the West (15). She believes all the various points of view about events in the American past should be presented.

4. Yuh believes that the truth about American history is multiple and that "there is more than one way of viewing the world" (14). But the most important reason for rewriting American history is that given by a New York State Department of

Education report: students should learn how to "assess critically the reasons for the inconsistencies between the ideals of the US and social realities." In addition, they should gain the knowledge and skills that can help them participate in "bringing reality closer to the ideals" (16).

5. *albeit* (1): even if; although
    tinged (1): with a slight trace of coloration
    galore (2): in plentiful amounts
    multicultural (10, 13, 18): drawing from many ethnic and cultural groups
    interdependence (12): reliance on connected groups
    indigenous (15): native or original
    dissenting (18): disagreeing with the majority
    ethnicity (18): membership in a cultural group based on ancestry
    bolster (19): to prop up or support

Questions About the Writer's Craft (p. 519)

1. Yuh waits until paragraph 18 to mention that some people have concerns about multicultural education being divisive. By this time in the essay, she has expansively rendered her own position in concrete and convincing terms. Delaying the mention of opposing views allows her to develop her rather complex reasons for advocating multicultural curricula: that exposing the ethnic forces and achievements in our history is more accurate (10), that it presents history as interpretations rather than dogma (14), that it will help students understand the discrepancies between our great American ideals and our current social realities (16), and that it will give students the skills to help them improve our nation (16). Coming so late in the essay, the dissenting view of multiculturalism seems simplistic in comparison to Yuh's argued position, and so it is easier for Yuh to dispose of it as off the mark.

2. Yuh's examples demonstrate her point that schoolbook American history has restricted students' knowledge about what really happened in our past. She offers some specifics of traditional American history in paragraph 2 ("Founding Fathers, Lewis and Clark, Lincoln, Daniel Boone, Carnegie, presidents . . .") and then contrasts this list with numerous more detailed examples of ethnic contributions to and viewpoints about America's past. Invoking images of Iroquois government, Asian agricultural talents, and Black initiatives toward freedom from slavery, the author shows concretely that there is more to the building of America than the heroic efforts of white men. Recalling the massacre of the indigenous tribes, the denial of citizenship to Asians despite their honorable World War I service, and the American overtaking of Mexican populations in California and New Mexico, Yuh dramatically pictures how our history plowed under nonwhite peoples. These specifics indicate that there are additional facts and alternative viewpoints to those traditionally taught as our history. These specifics also fill in knowledge gaps that readers may harbor and that may leave them poorly equipped to understand and appreciate her position. Placing them before the thesis renders the reader more aware of the complexity of our history and thus more open to her position. Hence, supplying these details is crucial to the success of her argument.

3. Much of the introduction consists of the author's personal recounting of what education she received (1–2) or failed to receive (3–6) regarding ethnic forces in our history. In paragraph 7, Yuh shocks us by revealing the degrading but inevitable taunts of her childhood peers ("So when other children called me a slant-eyed chink and told me to go back where I came from . . ."). This personal approach tells us what the educational and emotional consequences are of ignoring the diversity of people who have helped build America, and so sets the groundwork for Yuh's

argument in favor of multicultural curricula in history. She returns to the personal at the end of the essay. Here she affirms that focusing on ethnicity in our country's past is a way of demonstrating that "out of many" comes the "one" (20). She then underscores the link between her, a Korean immigrant, and her white childhood "tormentors": the Americanness they have in common.

4. Yuh's stylistic repetitions begin immediately in the first paragraph, where she parallels two relative clauses: "I grew up . . . almost believing that America was white . . . and that white was best." The second paragraph uses this same device, paralleling the two last sentences and repeating the phrase "the only": "The only black people were slaves. The only Indians were scalpers." These short parallel clauses and sentences are emphatic and create a sense that "that was that," a sense of finality about the impressions she gained.

   The following four paragraphs open with the same repeated phrase: "I never learned one word about. . . . " And the sentences that follow within each paragraph begin with "Or that . . ." or repeat the words, "I never learned that. . . ." By using these repetitions, Yuh creates a catalog of her enforced ignorance. Each repeated opening signals the reader that more historical omissions are coming, and more, and even more. Through the repetitions, the reader understands that what has been left out of American history is not just one or two details, but whole vistas and vantage points from which our past looks very different.

   In paragraph 15, Yuh resumes the cataloging of omissions, again using repetitions. The first sentence sets the pattern: "the westward migration . . . *is not just* an heroic settling of an untamed wild, *but also* the conquest of indigenous peoples." The following two sentences use this "not just . . . but" structure, with small variations in wording, to convey the multiplicity inherent in our history.

CAN YOU BE EDUCATED FROM A DISTANCE?

James Barszcz

Questions for Close Reading (p. 524)

1. Barszcz doesn't state his thesis explicitly. In his final two sentences he indirectly expresses the thesis by quoting Robert Frost and interpreting the quotation in this way: "a college education requires" that a student be on campus (paragraph 9). Barszcz's thesis is a negative response to his title question "Can You Be Educated From a Distance?" and can be paraphrased simply as this: "Despite the increasing popularity of distance learning in college curricula, several significant drawbacks accompany this means of education."

2. Students like the convenience of distance learning, of being able to do their work "in . . . pajamas" (3). Schools value the cost savings; while students pay tuition, they don't physically come to campus, which results in reduced physical resource demands on the school—and, presumably, greater profits (4).

3. Barszcz says that proponents usually argue that distance learning makes education more *effective*—by giving students access to a "global virtual faculty" (5)—and more *meritocratic* (or democratic)—by potentially allowing students to shop around for quality courses rather than being tied to one institution (7).

4.   Barszcz defines education as "cultivating intellectual and moral values" and as drawing out "from within a person qualities of intellect and character" (8), in contrast to merely imparting information.

Answers to the second question may vary. Some students may agree with Barszcz's noble vision of education. Others, however, may disagree, seeing education as more pragmatic. In addition, some might argue that his claim that education draws out qualities already within a person, rather than imparts qualities, is an example of the either/or fallacy. Education creates, as well as activates, intellectual and moral qualities. Otherwise, education would only draw out qualities already within us as infants.

5.   *attrition* (3): dropping out
virtual (5): created or carried on by means of a computer network
facility (6): ease
meritocracy (7): a system that rewards ability and achievement
mechanistic (8): simplistic with regard to cause and effect
etymology (8): a word's origin and history
dormant (8): not activated
fidelity (9): accuracy of reproduction

Questions About the Writer's Craft (p. 525)

1.   Barszcz seems to have written his essay for a wavering audience—an audience undecided on the topic but open to hearing arguments. The fact that he acknowledges and refutes opposing points of view demonstrates that he doesn't assume his audience is a supportive one. In addition, he doesn't rely on overly emotional appeals (*pathos*) in his essay, and he provides sound reasoning (*logos*), particularly in refuting opposing arguments. Nor is there any indication that Barszcz assumes his audience is hostile; his somewhat sentimental argument about education cultivating intellectual and moral values would probably be dismissed by a skeptical reader. Instead, Barszcz's combined use of *logos* and mild *pathos*—a middle-of-the-road approach—reveals he's probably writing for the general public, composed of individuals not necessarily decided on the topic of distance learning.

2.   Barszcz uses division-classification here to categorize the different types of communication involved in distance learning: website postings, e-mail attachments, threaded messages, chat rooms, and minimal or no face-to-face communication. Barszcz uses emphatic order. By leaving face-to-face communication for last, he emphasizes its scant presence or total absence in distance learning.

3.   Barszcz quotes literature from Fairleigh Dickinson University (FDU) in some detail (5) because FDU's statements come across as propaganda. Inflated language such as "premier learning tool," "life-long learning," "global," "world-class," and "around the world" are likely to make readers skeptical about distance learning's possible merits. In addition, the quote is an easy target for refutation in its unrealistic claims that students will have access to the caliber of experts being touted.

4.   Barszcz's definition of distance learning (2) is specific and objective, involves no "definition by negation," and has an explanatory purpose. In contrast, Barszcz's definition of education (8) is general and subjective, uses definition by negation (education is *not* simply providing information), and has a persuasive purpose.

THE DAMNED HUMAN RACE

Mark Twain

Questions for Close Reading (p. 532)

1. Twain states his thesis in the first paragraph: "For it obliges me to renounce my allegiance to the Darwinian theory of the Ascent of Man from the Lower Animals; since it now seems plain to me that that theory ought to be vacated in favor of a new and truer one, this new and truer one to be named the Descent of Man from the Higher Animals." By this, Twain is humorously suggesting that humans beings' "traits and dispositions" are lower, not higher, than those of the other creatures.

2. Twain discovers humans have a long list of negative characteristics. He finds them cruel (4, 10), avaricious and miserly (5), vengeful (7), morally loose (7, 8), and indecent and vulgar (9). Humans are also the only animals to wage war (11), invade other countries (12), take slaves (13), and show patriotism (14). They are, somewhat paradoxically, both religious—hence intolerant of others with different beliefs (15)—and reasoning, though Twain prefers to think of them as maniacs (16). The overall defect that will forever prevent humans from ever beginning "to approach even the meanest of the Higher Animals" is what Twain terms the "moral sense" (19–20), "the ability to distinguish good from evil; and with it, necessarily, the ability to do evil" (21).

3. The earl and his party of sportsmen killed seventy-two buffalo, feasted on one, and left the seventy-one others to rot. The anaconda, in a scientific test conducted by Twain, killed only what he wanted to eat, and no more, although Twain provided him with seven calves in all. This "experiment" shows that the snake is less cruel and less wasteful than an earl, and therefore a superior creature.

4. Humans have "occasion to blush" because they feel shame about their bodies and, having a "soiled mind," feel natural behavior to be indecent. Twain points out that people cover themselves, even their chests and backs, because they are horrified at the possibility of "indecent suggestion" (9). Also, humans consciously practice cruel and loose sexual behavior such as keeping harems, behavior about which they should blush. When animals are loose in their morals, Twain says, it is because they are totally innocent.

5. *confounded* (3): confused
   anaconda 4): a type of large snake
   wantonly (4): excessively, wastefully
   chicanery (5): trickery, deceit
   heretics (10): people who openly disagree with the church
   constitutionally (19): by nature, inherently
   ineradicable (19): not removable, unerasable
   smirchless (22): without a stain, without dishonor

Questions About the Writer's Craft (p. 532)

1. Twain humorously claims to have used the scientific method in order to put his credibility on a par with that of scientists. He pretends to have conducted experiments. By this device he satirizes not only human evil and cruelty but also our arrogance in presuming to be superior to all other creatures, a "superiority" we exercise by turning the other creatures into laboratory specimens. Ultimately, Twain shows that the standard the scientists, and people in general, use to decide what

constitutes a "higher" species is invalid. Using a moral yardstick, rather than an evolutionary one, Twain demonstrates that humans are really the lowest of creatures.

2. Many of Twain's examples of human inferiority are shocking, starting with his example of the hunting earl. In paragraph 10, Twain provides a list of atrocious cruelties from human history that most students will certainly find upsetting; he mentions mutilation, gouging, flaying, imprisonment, and burning as punishments for small offenses or religious disagreements, and, conversely, minor punishments, such as a ten-shilling fine, for incredible cruelties. Also, in paragraph 15, Twain uses very strong language to discuss human religious intolerance; some students will be shocked because they are used to hearing religion spoken of deferentially. For example, Twain writes that man "cuts his neighbor's throat if his theology isn't straight" and "has made a graveyard of the globe" in trying to spread his religions. Such shocking examples and language help Twain to convince us that his main point is valid—humans are cruel and inferior creatures.

3. One or two examples would be sufficient to support his idea that humans are inferior to animals, but Twain piles on examples to dramatize his point. He wants to show that such atrocities are not isolated and rare, but habitual and common among the human species. For example, he shows in paragraph 10 that all eras of history and all peoples of the world have engaged in vicious punishments and inhumane justice.

4. Absurdity appears in this essay in the form of Twain's "experiments," ridiculous studies confronting humans and animals with moral choices. It is certainly unlikely that he tested an anaconda's killer instinct with seven calves (4) or "furnished a hundred different kinds of wild and tame animals the opportunity to accumulate vast stores of food" (5). And his claim to have put a mixture of human races and religions in a cage to see if they could learn to get along is also far-fetched (18). Ironically, the morbid details of Twain's essay come from human history: they are not creations of the writer's mind, but examples of actual human violence (4, 10, 11). As Twain notes in paragraph 16, the human record "is the fantastic record of a maniac." So the essay does contain elements of black humor, and its conclusion, "And so I find we have descended and degenerated, from some far ancestor. . . . Below us—nothing," is dark indeed.

FREE-SPEECH FOLLIES

Stanley Fish

Questions for Close Reading (p. 538)

1. Fish states his thesis in the second paragraph: "In the academy, the case is even worse: Not only is the First Amendment pressed into service at the drop of a hat (especially whenever anyone is disciplined for anything), it is invoked ritually when there are no First Amendment issues in sight."

2. By "Self-censorship, in short, is not a crime or a moral failing; it is a responsibility" (8), Fish means that a publication's decision not to print something is perfectly legal and that, in fact, publications are obliged to exercise judgment, or self-censorship, in what they print. Such decisions not to publish are legal because the First Amendment does not apply to nongovernmental entities; it applies only to the government.

3. Fish refers to the Harvard English department as "serial bunglers" because they made three mistakes in a row in dealing with poet Tom Paulin's invitation to be the Morris Gray lecturer. First, they invited him without dealing with his controversial

political views on Israel. Second, once they realized what his views were, they withdrew the invitation. Third, when the cancellation of his lecture caused a controversy, they backed down and reissued the invitation, saying that the department "'stood strongly by the First Amendment.'"

4. According to Fish, student editors who publish unpopular speech are not First Amendment heroes because their publication decisions have nothing to do with the First Amendment. The First Amendment protects speech from being abridged by Congress, not by newspapers (11). The real First Amendment heroes, according to Fish, are those who protest government policies, such as the student Toni Smith, who turned her back to the flag during the playing of the U.S. national anthem at Manhattanville College (23).

5. *vilify* (1): to defame, slander, abuse
   scurrilous (1): vulgar and vile
   firestorm (4): a sudden or violent outburst
   coherent (6): sticking together; consistent
   abridgment (11): curtailment
   hapless (13): unfortunate, unlucky
   rescind (14): to revoke
   chancellor (17): the title of the head of some universities
   egregious (18): remarkable in a bad sense
   partisan (20): favoring a political party or one side in a dispute
   empirical (20): based on experiment or experience
   pilloried (20): exposed to public contempt
   countermanded (21): revoked by a contrary order

Questions About the Writer's Craft (p. 538)

1. Fish begins by stating his thesis; thereafter, he supports this thesis with examples. Each example begins with a narrative that tells the story of an instance of controversial speech and its First Amendment defense by someone on campus. This is the view that opposes his. For each example, Fish then undermines the First Amendment defense by arguing that the First Amendment does not even apply in that situation and that the people involved were simply dodging their responsibility for "self-censorship."

2. Some students may argue that the particular group targeted in each example is irrelevant to the free speech issues being discussed, since such controversies occur frequently on campuses and involve many groups besides Jews, including African Americans, Latinos, Arabs, Muslims, gays, lesbians, and so on. Whichever group is involved, the issue is usually similar—free (and offensive) speech is pitted against the group that is offended. These students may argue that the fact that Fish's examples all involve anti-Semitism just gives the essay a certain unity it would otherwise lack and that it simply reflects Fish's own interest in controversies involving Jews.

   Other students may argue that the fact that all the examples are about anti-Semitism undermines the impact of the essay because readers may get the impression that what Fish is objecting to is quite narrow—controversial campus speech about Jews. Since his argument actually applies to controversial campus speech about any targeted group, the homogeneity of the examples unnecessarily limits the apparent scope of Fish's argument.

3. The three words of paragraph 5 ("Wrong four times") give it a great deal of emphasis because paragraphs are almost never that short. Even sentences are not usually that short, so the paragraph is quite surprising. The three words bring the reader to a stop

by completely upending the previous two-paragraph narrative and argument, conceding nothing to the opposition.

4. From the perspective of the readers of *The Chronicle of Higher Education*, Fish's *ethos* is very strong. To academic readers, a writer who has had an extremely distinguished academic career has a great deal of credibility. So Fish is writing to an audience of his colleagues. Still, that credibility goes only so far, because many of his readers may disagree with his views. In fact, Fish may have something of a hostile audience because he is taking his readers to task; after all, he is criticizing members of the academic community for their misuse of the First Amendment.

Perhaps because many readers may be hostile to his argument, Fish relies heavily on *logos*—logical reasoning and facts. His argument is based almost entirely on logic, on his claim that the First Amendment applies to the government's abridgment of free speech, not to private parties' abridgment of free speech, so that the First Amendment defense is irrelevant to the cases of controversial speech that he cites.

Furthermore, since the highly educated readers of the *Chronicle* are likely to be more susceptible to arguments based on sound reasoning than on *pathos*, Fish doesn't feel the need to use much *pathos*. The only time he clearly invokes *pathos* is in the final paragraph, in which he describes a true First Amendment hero, the student who had the courage to turn her back on the flag during the national anthem. Otherwise he relies mostly on *ethos* and *logos* to craft his argument.

RAPE: A BIGGER DANGER
THAN FEMINISTS KNOW

Camille Paglia

Questions for Close Reading (p. 545)

1. Paglia states the thesis clearly in her first paragraph: "[F]eminism, which has waged a crusade for rape to be taken more seriously, has put young women in danger by hiding the truth about sex from them." In the rest of the essay, she explains what she means by the "truth" about sex and men.

2. "Once," Paglia writes in paragraph 4, "fathers and brothers protected women from rape," but today people do not live in such close-knit clans and families. Also, rape was once punishable by death, but today the penalties are lighter. The author cites as evidence what she calls typical behavior in the "fierce Italian tradition": "a rapist would end up knifed, castrated and hung out to dry."

3. According to Paglia, "feminism . . . keeps young women from seeing life as it is" (5). By this, she means that there are truths "we cannot change" (6) about the nature of men and sex, truths that should be told, not hidden. There are quite a few generalizations about sex and men in the article that appear to be the "truths" that she is describing describes. One is the commonness of "rape by an acquaintance" throughout history (3). Another is the "sexual differences that are based in biology" (6), which cause men to rape in order to create their masculine identity (7, 14). "Masculinity," she says, "is aggressive, unstable, combustible" (18). Another "truth" for Paglia is the idea that women need protection, by the "clan" (3–4), by the "double standard" (11), and by their own self-awareness (19). Later, she talks about the truth embodied in the "sexual myths of literature, art, and religion" which "show

us the turbulence, the mysteries and passions of sex. . . ." (14). She insists "there never was and never will be sexual harmony" (15).

4. Paglia believes that women must be more vigilant and guard against male aggression. In paragraph 8, Paglia writes that women going to fraternity parties are putting themselves in danger; in her view, a women who goes alone, gets drunk, or goes upstairs is asking for trouble (8). In paragraph 15, she writes that "every woman must be prudent and cautious about where she goes and with whom." In her conclusion, Paglia explicitly states that date rape can only be solved by "female self-awareness and self-control." A woman must rely on her own resources to prevent rape and should involve the police if a rape does occur.

5. *inquests* (2): judicial inquiries, often before a jury
    testosterone (8): male sex hormone
    constituted (13): set up or established
    grievance (15): a complaint against an unjust or illegal act
    judiciary (19): the system of courts in a country

Questions About the Writer's Craft (p. 545)

1. Both paragraphs begin with statements that seen incontestable; in using these ideas, Paglia is establishing common ground, an area of agreement between herself and the reader. In paragraph 6, most readers will fully accept the first statement, "we must remedy social injustice whenever we can." They would also agree with the next assertion, that "there are some things we cannot change," and with the third, "there are sexual differences that are based in biology." Many readers, however, would debate the nature of those differences; some would feel that biology ordains only the physiological distinctions, while Paglia obviously means that people's psychology and behavior are also determined by their sex (7–8, 14). Other statements in paragraph 6 are equally debatable: that feminism "believes we are totally the product of our environment" and that it is incorrect to believe that our environment can override biology. Paglia offers no proof for these assertions.

    Paragraph 8 also begins with some general assertions that most readers would accept: "College men are at their hormonal peak. They have just left their mothers. . . ." Many readers will also agree that college men "are questing for their male identity." (Of course, some readers will add that college women are likewise questing for their identities, sexual and otherwise.) After this point, however, Paglia draws some conclusions which many readers will contest and which are not proven: that "in groups [college men] are dangerous," that fraternity parties are treacherous for women, that "a girl who lets herself get dead drunk at a fraternity party is a fool" (some readers would call anyone that drunk a fool), and that "a girl who goes upstairs alone with a brother . . . is an idiot." The latter two statements are judgments; as such, they are impossible to "prove," and Paglia offers no evidence regarding them.

2. Paglia uses numerous comparisons and contrasts in the essay. First, she describes the way acquaintance rape was handled in the past, in contrast with today's means of handling it (3–4). Throughout she contrasts the "feminist view" of sex with what she considers the accurate view. In paragraph 6, for example, she contrasts the position of "academic feminism" regarding sexual differences—that all but the biological are produced by society—with the correct view, her own. She concludes the paragraph with an analogy: "Leaving sex to the feminists is like letting your dog vacation at the taxidermist's." A few paragraphs later, she contrasts the "sugar-coated Shirley Temple nonsense" of the feminists (9) with the idea that "aggression

and eroticism, in fact, are deeply intertwined" (10). Then she contrasts the "broken promises" of the 1960s view of women with the "cold reality" of rape (11).

Paglia also develops a contrast between the feminist response to date rape and her own view of how to cope with it. The feminists show outrage and shock, according to her (2, 19, 15, 19). She contrasts male and female sexual appetite in paragraph 14, concluding that "it takes many men to deal with one woman." Then she compares the "high-energy confrontation" style of dealing with male vulgarity with the "dopey, immature, self-pitying women walking around like melting sticks of butter" (16). And in her conclusion, Paglia compares two ways of coping with date rape, calling the police or "complaining to college committees" (19).

3.   This blunt style is found in paragraph 4, beginning with "Feminism has not prepared them for this." In paragraph 6, only the second sentence uses a transitional word ("but"). Paragraphs 7 and 8 also rely on a sequence of mostly short sentences without any transitional phrases. In paragraph 11, only the phrase "in short" introducing a summary statement provides any formal coherence. The first few sentences in paragraphs 15 and 16 (up to "In general") and most of paragraph 19 also lack transitions. Paglia's avoidance of transitions creates emphasis for what she has to say. She seems to pound her ideas into us, not wasting time with smoothing the way or being gradual. This style portrays the writer as extremely sure of her position, to the point of being aggressive, almost relentless.

4.   There are numerous instances of highly connotative language in the essay. Paglia tends to emphasize or exaggerate the negative elements of feminism and men's behavior. For example, in her introduction she calls rape an "outrage" and asserts that feminism has "waged a crusade." In paragraph 3, she pronounces acquaintance rape "a horrible problem," and in the next paragraph calls young women "vulnerable and defenseless." She describes a fraternity party as "Testosterone Flats, full of prickly cacti and blazing guns" and says men are "dangerous." Later in the same paragraph, she labels girls who trust fraternity men "fools" and "idiots" (8). Her descriptions of feminism are particularly negative: she says its "sugar-coated Shirley Temple nonsense" (9) has brought "disaster" on young women.

Strongly worded absolute statements also occur frequently in relation to both men and feminism. Her very first sentence is an example: "Rape is an outrage that cannot be tolerated in civilized society." Other examples of extreme negative judgments include the following: "No, they can't" (4), "He was wrong" (6), "There never was and never will be sexual harmony" (15), "Women will always be in sexual danger" (4), "The sexes are at war" (7), "When anything goes, it's women who lose" (11), "men and women misunderstand each other" (13), "feminism cut itself off from sexual history" (14), "to understand rape, you must study the past" (15), and "The only solution to date rape is female self-awareness and self-consciousness" (19). Paglia's use of *pathos* makes the essay exciting to read and adds electricity to her ideas, and some readers will find her stimulating and convincing. However, many readers will find her pitch to our emotions an offensive tactic that decreases her credibility in their eyes.

COMMON DECENCY

Susan Jacoby

Questions for Close Reading (p. 550)

1. Jacoby expresses her thesis in paragraph 3: "What seems clear to me is that those who place acquaintance rape in a different category from 'stranger rape'—those who excuse friendly social rapists on the grounds that they are too dumb to understand when 'no' means no—are being even more insulting to men than to women." In the rest of the essay, Jacoby shows the absurdity of the notions that men simply can't distinguish between "no" and "maybe" and that "mixed signals" cause date rape.

2. Gratitude is not necessary or appropriate, Jacoby feels, because her old boyfriend was acting in a normal responsible manner, as one does in "civilization" (6–7). In a parallel situation, if he had led her on and she had restrained herself from stabbing him, she would not expect him to be grateful for her restraint. She would have simply been acting in a civilized and normal way. People don't need to be "grateful" when others treat them correctly instead of immorally.

3. For Jacoby, civilization is the condition in which men and women can understand each other, even though there may be mixed signals. She explains in paragraph 7 that her old boyfriend was civilized because he accepted what she said as her true meaning, that she did not want sexual intimacy, and left her apartment. He was angry, but he did not violate her. As civilized creatures, men and women are capable of understanding and respecting each other's wishes and relating to each other on more than just a physical level.

4. Jacoby believes that "even the most callow youth is capable of understanding the difference between resistance and genuine fear; between a halfhearted 'no, we shouldn't' and tears or screams; between a woman who is physically free to leave a room and one who is being physically restrained" (14). If men couldn't tell the difference, Jacoby implies, they would have to be pretty stupid creatures, and to insist they can't make these distinctions is therefore to insult their intelligence. As she points out in paragraph 4, those who insist that date rape is understandable or natural—the "apologists for date rape" (4)—think "men are nasty and men are brutes." These are certainly insulting terms to apply to half of civilization. And if these apologists (such as Camille Paglia) were correct, women would have to "regard every man as a potential rapist" (10). As a result, a woman would have to decide very early in a relationship, perhaps before ever being alone with a man, whether to have a sexual relationship with him or not, because any slight hint of interest on her part might trigger the "rampaging male" to rape her (18). Such extreme suspicion and caution would also be insulting to a civilized person.

5. *apologists* (4): people who make a defense
   baser (4): morally lower
   deluded (10): believing something false to be true
   unsubtle (12): unintelligent; lacking in fine distinctions
   implicit (16): implied; hinted at
   benighted (18): intellectually ignorant
   erotic (18): arousing sexual desire or love
   rampaging (18): rushing furiously and violently
   ambivalent (19): of two minds; unable to make a choice

Questions About the Writer's Craft (p. 550)

1. In paragraph 4, Jacoby interprets the belief of date rape "apologists" that men can't understand "no." She says this belief implies that men have no "impulse control" and are "nasty . . . brutes" at heart. If this is true, Jacoby says, then it logically follows that a woman would have to be "constantly on her guard" to prevent men from raping her. "If this view were accurate," Jacoby continues, "few women would manage to get through life without being raped, and few men would fail to commit rape" (5). In this sentence, Jacoby draws out the extreme logical consequence of the premise that men can't understand "no." Since it is obviously not true that practically all women are rape victims and practically all men rapists, the premise appears to be untrue. In paragraph 15, Jacoby uses *reductio* again: "[T]he immorality and absurdity" of the mixed-signals excuse for date rape is apparent, she says, when the phenomenon of gang rape is examined. If a woman gives a leading sexual signal to a fraternity brother, then how is that an excuse for a whole bunch of them to gang rape her? She concludes the paragraph by asking a question pointing to the absurdity of the premise: Since the girl showed interest in one brother, "how could they have been expected to understand that she didn't wish to have sex with the whole group?"

2. Jacoby bases much of her argument on the premise that men and women are not so different (while Paglia's view is that men, with their uncontrollable passions, are very different from women). In paragraphs 5, 6, and 7, Jacoby compares the situations and behaviors of men and women and finds them similar: "all of us, men as well as women, send and receive innumerable mixed signals in the course of our sexual lives" (5); "men . . . manage to decode these signals . . . and most women manage to handle conflicting male signals" without resorting to violence (6); "I don't owe him excessive gratitude for his decent behavior—any more than he would have owed me special thanks for not stabbing him through the heart if our situations had been reversed" (7). Jacoby's thesis is, in fact, essentially a comparison-contrast statement; she believes date rape is the same as—that is, is comparable to—"stranger rape." She is critical of those who contrast them. She thus develops the contrast between the "apologists'" view of date rape and her own in the essay as a whole. Also implicit throughout the piece is the contrast between her ex-boyfriend, who left in a huff but who did not rape her even though she had led him on, and those men who do rape women they are seeing socially. In the conclusion (19), this contrast appears as that between "real men," who "want an eager sexual partner," and men who prefer a "woman who is quaking with fear." Finally, there are two contrasting views of sex discussed in paragraphs 12–13 and 19: sex as "an expression of the will to power," as involving "domination" (12), and "sex as a source of pleasure" (12).

3. The introduction consists of an anecdote, described in the third person and presented very objectively and dramatically. The opening line could be that of a romantic short story: "She was deeply in love with a man who was treating her badly." Only after she explains the plot of this little story does she admit it is autobiographical: "I was the embarrassed female participant" (3). This anecdote vividly portrays the reality that is one of Jacoby's main points: that "mixed signals" between males and females are common, and that if such confusions were the natural cause of rape, rape would be much more common than it is. That Jacoby herself has an example of a potential "date-rape" situation from her own life makes her credible on the subject of the usual course of male-female relations and also reveals her as an honest, thoughtful writer; that is, it contributes to a positive *ethos.*

4. For the most part, Jacoby's tone is even and balanced, and this makes her a very credible commentator on her subject. Even her sentence style demonstrates a balance of phrasing in which sequential statements are expressed using similar sentence structure. For example, she writes that "those who place acquaintance rape in a different category from 'stranger rape'—those who excuse friendly social rapists . . . are being even more insulting to men than to women" (3); "men are nasty and men are brutes . . ." (4). Other parallel statements occur in paragraphs 5, 6, 7, 12, 13, 16, 18, and 19: "all of us, men as well as women, send and receive . . . and that is as true in marital beds at age 50 as in the back seats of cars at age 15" (5); "Most men somehow manage to decode these signals without using. . . . And most women manage to handle conflicting male signals without . . ." (6); "I don't owe him excessive gratitude for his decent behavior—any more than he would have owed me special thanks for not stabbing him . . ."; "Most date rapes do not happen because a man honestly mistakes a woman's 'no' for a 'yes' or a 'maybe.' They occur because a minority of men . . . can't stand to take 'no' for an answer" (7); "no distinction between sex as an expression of the will to power and sex as a source of pleasure" (12); "the act of rape is defined not by a man's actions but by a woman's signals" (12); "It is true, of course, that some women (especially the young) . . . And it is true that many men (again, especially the young) . . ." (13); "the difference between resistance and genuine fear; between a halfhearted 'no, we shouldn't' and tears or screams; between a woman who is physically free to leave a room and one who is being physically restrained" (14); "a woman has the right to say no at any point in the process leading to sexual intercourse—and that a man who fails to respect her wishes should incur serious legal and social consequences" (16); "it would be impossible for a woman (and, let us not forget, for a man) . . ." (18); "neither the character of men nor the general quality of relations between the sexes is that crude" (19); "feminists insist on sex as a source of pure pleasure rather than as a means of social control" (19); "Real men want an eager sexual partner—not a woman who is quaking with fear or even one who is ambivalent. Real men don't rape" (19). These numerous balanced statements convey an impression of writing that is carefully crafted and of ideas that are well thought out.

There are, however, a few places where Jacoby's word choice seems judgmental and almost mocking; this style predominates when she is discussing the position of the antifeminists. She speaks derogatorily of their views: "This is the line adopted by antifeminists like Camille Paglia" (10)—even her invented term, "antifeminists," is derogatory to her opposition. "According to this 'logic,'" she sneers in paragraph 11, calling Paglia's analysis "unsubtle" (12). In her view, "using mixed signals as an excuse for rape" is immoral and absurd (15). In addition, Jacoby's portrayal of the thought process of gang rapists is very satirical: "Why she [the victim] may have even displayed sexual interest in *one* of them. How could they have been expected to understand that she didn't wish to have sex with the whole group?" (15). Finally, she burlesques Paglia's point of view with a description of a "rampaging male misreading" a woman's intentions (18).

TIME TO THINK ABOUT TORTURE

Jonathan Alter

Questions for Close Reading (p. 554)

1. Alter essentially states the essay's thesis in paragraph 1: "In this autumn of anger, even a liberal can find his thoughts turning to . . . torture . . . to jump-start the stalled investigations of the greatest crime in American history." He more succinctly restates his main idea in the final paragraph, where he asserts, "[W]e need to keep an open mind about certain measures to fight terrorism, like court-sanctioned psychological interrogation" (10).

2. The main form of torture that Alter champions is psychological torture, and he provides examples of what forms this kind of torture might take: "tapes of dying rabbits or high-decibel rap" (2), truth serum (2, 8), the threat of deportation to nations like Saudi Arabia that punish convicts violently (2, 9–10), and, most importantly, court-sanctioned interrogations (6–7, 10). In paragraph 5, he describes some of the tortures that Israel has inflicted on terror suspects. Oddly, it's not fully clear whether he supports these measures; he seems to, but he doesn't explicitly state as much. But in paragraph 9, he applauds a variety of psychological torture tactics that historically worked in various nations.

    What Alter appears to oppose clearly, on the other hand, is the legalization of physical torture, but even here his position is a bit murky. He never fully explains or exemplifies what he means by "physical torture" (apart from his flippant reference to "cattle prods or rubber hoses" in paragraph 1) but declares, "We can't legalize" it because "it's contrary to American values" (10). It's important also to note that Alter emphasizes that physical torture cannot be *legalized*, but he never says it shouldn't be *used*. In addition, he argues in favor of administering truth serum to terror suspects, but even this practice could be considered by some to have an inhumane physical element.

3. He implies that people are foolish if they don't realize that pre-9/11 methods of dealing with terrorism are now, since the tragedy, obsolete. Before the events of September 11, 2001, he implies, we all were naïve and complacent to a degree, but to maintain such a frame of mind since then is foolish or, worse, dangerous.

4. The "strange moral position" that Alter identifies is how the legal communities in Israel and the United States allow torture to occur but would never legalize it for fear of casting an ethical blemish on their legal systems. This is what he means when he says, "They prefer looking the other way to giving even mild torture techniques the patina of legality" (7). What he implies is that there is a degree of hypocrisy among these parties in their "don't ask, don't tell" policy regarding torture.

5. *stalled* (1): delayed
    decibel (2): a unit used to measure intensity of sound
    serum (2): fluid, usually from blood or animal tissue
    deportation (2): the expulsion of an undesirable alien from a country
    quibble (3): to find fault or criticize for petty reasons
    provision (3): a stipulation or qualification, especially in an official document
    tepid (3): lacking enthusiasm; lukewarm
    staunch (3): firm and steadfast; faithful
    anachronism (4): something out of its proper time period
    laundering (4): disguising the nature of funds by channeling them through an
        intermediate agent

extracting (5): obtaining despite resistance
detainee (6): a person held in custody or confinement
patina (7): a change in appearance, usually due to corrosion
sanctioned (10): given official authorization or approval
squeamish (10): easily shocked or sickened

Questions About the Writer's Craft (p. 554)

1. The first instance in which Alter employs Rogerian strategy appears in paragraph 2, when he dismisses those who argue in favor of the old status quo and against the need for drastic new tactics: "Some people still argue that we needn't rethink any of our old assumptions about law enforcement, but they're hopelessly 'Sept. 10'. . . .'" In paragraph 3, he posits that the Senate's antiterrorism bill has provoked only "tepid" opposition even from those who would normally decry such legislation—evidence, he implies, that dramatic measures being taken against terrorism are appropriate. Alter similarly uses to his advantage the seeming lack of outrage on the part of opponents when he discusses Alan Dershowitz's opinion in paragraph 6. Typically a vehement proponent of civil rights, even Dershowitz, observes Alter, allows room in his reasoning for a "torture warrant" whereby judges decide whether torture tactics are warranted on a case-by-case basis. In addition, after he has advocated Dershowitz's model for court-sanctioned torture, Alter essentially accuses of hypocrisy those in Israel and the United States who oppose such a notion while allowing torture to happen nonetheless (7). Alter's final use of Rogerian strategy appears in paragraph 8, when he acknowledges the drawbacks of sodium pentothal and of harsh torture but says that the former "deserves a chance" nevertheless.

    Regarding the second question, students' reactions may vary. Some students may find Alter's citation and refutation of the opposition satisfactory, while others might deem it inadequate.

2. In the first five sentences of paragraph 2, he alternates between using questions and parenthetical statements. The function of the questions is to catch readers' attention and almost to beg for agreement. The parenthetical remarks, on the other hand, are a means for Alter to present information that reinforces the legitimacy of the questions he asks. Overall, this departure from normal sentence writing allows Alter to catch his reader's eye and to appeal to him or her on a more informal level.

3. Alter contrasts the views of Alan Dershowitz with the mindset of the legal communities in Israel and the United States. Dershowitz says that torture should be court sanctioned, like search warrants, for individual cases. But, according to Alter, judges and lawyers in Israel and the United States would never agree to such a practice, as the court's tolerance of any type of torture would result in an ethical blemish on the legal system. Alter goes a step further, however, to suggest that these same legal communities would have no problem instead looking the other way when torture is, in fact, employed.

    This contrast functions to support Alter's argument in favor of reasonable and limited use of torture to fight terrorism. In fact, his entire concept seems to be based on Dershowitz's model. By contrasting Dershowitz's reasonability on the issue with the hypocrisy of the legal systems that refuse to adopt Dershowitz's model, Alter reinforces his own position.

4. Although he divides torture into psychological and physical categories, saying the former is acceptable while the latter is not, nowhere does he set forth a clear definition of what constitutes each. Of the two, the category of psychological torture is developed more fully. Alter provides numerous examples of actions that would fit in this category in paragraphs 2, 5, 8, and 9, yet nowhere does he set forth a concrete

definition of it. Worse still is his characterization of physical torture, which is neither defined nor exemplified except for his passing reference to "cattle prods or rubber hoses" (1). Rather, Alter leaves it to the assumptions and imagination of readers as to what constitutes this variety of torture.

While some readers might be satisfied with Alter's distinctions, others might find his lack of clarity to represent a general murkiness of logic that detracts from his argument. If the most basic terms of what is and is not acceptable in his ideology are not clearly set forth, then how can readers accept his logic? Therefore, it would be reasonable to argue that Alter should have more systematically defined and explained his ideas rather than leaving important aspects of them to the realm of readers' assumptions.

NOW THE TALK IS ABOUT BRINGING BACK TORTURE

Henry Porter

Questions for Close Reading (p. 559)

1. Porter implies his thesis throughout but states it explicitly toward the end of the essay, in paragraph 12: "Torture is an absolute evil and there can be no allowances, especially in a country which stands for liberty and spends a good deal of time distinguishing itself . . . on those grounds."
2. Porter is referring to what he perceives as the American populace's unified, unquestioning support of its government's policies and actions—a condition he finds dangerous because it opens the door to injustices such as torture of terrorist suspects. He implies that the devastation inflicted during the 9/11 attacks has rendered the public fearful and overly willing to allow its government to do as it pleases in the name of national security. Answers to the second question will vary.
3. The topic he discusses is capital punishment. The way he connects the issue of capital punishment to that of torture is as follows: American commentators think torture is unthinkable in the United States, but if Americans can tolerate "inflicting great pain and fear in the execution of convicted murderers," then why stop there? After all, he argues with irony, torture is less permanent and less barbaric than execution. As a result, Americans need to be vigilant to ensure that torture does not become acceptable.

    Regarding the final question, answers will vary. Some students may agree with Porter's logic, while others may dismiss it as containing logical fallacies.
4. Answers will vary, but may include the following. Both authors are satisfied that readers have an appropriate idea of what *torture* means—the deliberate infliction of physical pain upon a prisoner. Or perhaps the authors didn't want to get bogged down in definitions but instead are seeking to make a larger point about whether the practice known as torture is legitimate in a post-9/11 world.
5. *cohesion* (1): the act of forming a united and consistent whole
    overhaul (1): the act of dismantling in order to make repairs
    vigorously (2): done with force and energy
    suppressed (2): curtailed or prohibited
    rhetorical (2): relating to the use of language
    modulation (2): the ability to vary pitch, tone, or intensity
    assets (3): useful or valuable possessions

steel (5): to make firm or strong

avert (5): to prevent

speculations (6): inferences based on inconclusive evidence

gurney (6): a metal stretcher with wheeled legs used for transporting patients

reprieves (6): postponements or cancellations of punishment

inadvertent (7): marked by unintentional lack of care

routinely (8): done as a common or customary practice

insurgents (8): people rising in revolt against established authority

barbarity (9): savage cruelty in actions or conduct

clandestine (10): done in secret in order to conceal an illicit purpose

derogate (11): to deviate from

consigned (12): set apart

concession (12): something that is yielded or granted

Questions About the Writer's Craft (p. 560)

1. A general thread throughout Porter's essay is that he expects more from a country as great as the United States; this sentiment works to soften the blow of the criticism he goes on to deliver. The first instance in which Porter employs Rogerian strategy is in the opening words of the essay, "For America's supporters"; he implicitly includes himself in that sympathetic group. This friendly gesture establishes common ground between Porter and those he's about to criticize. Porter concludes the essay in similar fashion; he compliments the United States in that it "stands for liberty and spends a good deal of time distinguishing itself . . . on those grounds" (12), and he refers to Americans' "very understandable fears" (13). This is to reiterate his general sympathy for the United States despite his having some serious criticisms of it.

   Another aspect of Rogerian strategy Porter employs is his citation of "pro-torture" American commentators, such as Jonathan Alter and Jay Winick (3, 4). In acknowledging these opposing points of view, Porter helps his readers understand the larger context of the debate into which he's entering, while also using some points of view as a springboard for his own. He takes Winick's example of Abdul Hakim Murad and spins off a couple of ironic rhetorical questions about anything being justified in order to avert American deaths. Porter then cites a commentary in *The New York Times* positing that "the U.S. is still a long way off using torture" (6), only to then refute that claim by arguing that given the American tolerance of the death penalty, torture is not far off. Similarly, he plays devil's advocate in paragraph 10 in saying that if the U.S. government authorizes political assassinations, then torture, which can "perversely" be argued as less cruel, is not far behind. In ironically adopting this alternate point of view, Porter ultimately undermines it. Finally, Porter optimistically observes that some good that comes out of the "pro-torture" proposals is that at least this grave issue is being discussed in a public forum (12). After allowing for this benefit, however, he asserts his strong belief that more commentators need to declare the injustice of torture in this same public forum.

2. Porter's tone fluctuates throughout the selection. For much of the essay, he presents objective- and neutral-sounding logic regarding the precedents for torture being used by the U.S. government. In some places, however, he comes across as impassioned and subjective, such as in the phrases "blind cohesion" (1), "the institutions . . . which failed the people so drastically" (1), "fiercely uncritical mood" (3), and, most dramatically, in the final sentence of paragraph 12: "Torture is an absolute evil and there can be no allowances, especially in a country which stands for liberty and spends a good deal of time distinguishing itself . . . on those grounds." Apart from his overall objectiveness and occasional subjective outbursts, Porter adopts still

another tone in a few instances: a condescending, patronizing manner, particularly when discussing the U.S. government and populace. In paragraph 2, he begins, "If these things were discussed as vigorously [in the United States] as they are here [in England] . . ." (2) with at least a hint of superiority in his tone. And later in the same paragraph, he becomes clearly insulting when he asserts that the U.S. president "does seem to betray a pretty basic intellect—even to Americans" (2).

3. Porter implies differences in the intellect and demand for public discussion of government policies that characterize each nation. In paragraph 2, he begins, "If these things were discussed as vigorously [in the United States] as they are here [in England] . . ." (2), suggesting that there is a lack of serious discussion of important policies in the United States when compared with the norm in England. Later in the same paragraph, he pulls no punches when he asserts that the U.S. president "does seem to betray a pretty basic intellect—even to Americans" (2), attacking the intellect not only of the president, but of the general populace as well. Though he doesn't explicitly mention England here, one might infer he does not regard his native country with the same condescension. And in paragraph 6, Porter subtly contrasts the two nations—again, to England's benefit, but students may not necessarily be aware of this: He decries the barbarity of the death penalty, which is legal in the United States but *not* in England.

   These contrasts Porter draws between England and the United States support his thesis: that Americans and their government need to forthrightly address the fearsome potential of using torture in the name of national security. Porter's implicit claim that such a state of affairs would be unacceptable in England enhances the persuasive force of his argument.

4. Porter first makes use of examples in paragraphs 3 and 4, when he cites commentators who have been arguing that torture may be warranted. These examples serve to establish context for Porter's opposing argument. The example of Abdul Hakim Murad in paragraphs 4 and 5 serves a different function; it is part of Porter's use of Rogerian strategy to understand the rationale of the opposition. He even poses some compelling rhetorical questions based on this example. Interestingly, Porter never fully refutes the power of this example, but rather switches gears to make an analogy between capital punishment and torture. In paragraph 6, he cites statistics to illustrate the frequency of executions in the United States and discusses the fact that only the United States and Somalia refused to sign a particular UN anti-execution convention. These facts work to illustrate Porter's idea that execution is a barbarous practice that makes the United States more likely to indulge in torture. In paragraphs 8 and 9, Porter discusses how the United States already is guilty of supporting regimes that "routinely practice torture" elsewhere in the world. The appalling examples he cites further illustrate his point that the United States is on the verge of using torture on its own soil, a possibility that the public needs to vehemently oppose.

THE BORDER ON OUR BACKS

Roberto Rodriguez

Questions for Close Reading (p. 564)

1. Rodriguez's thesis is dispersed throughout the essay. It could be stated as follows: "American sentiment against illegal immigrants from Mexico and Central America

has deep racist roots, and these immigrants have a legitimate claim to be anywhere on the continent of North America, since their ancestors lived there."

2. The title, "The Border on Our Backs," means that immigrants set the borders in North America, not white politicians who draw arbitrary national boundaries on a map. In paragraph 10, Rodriguez describes the migrations of the ancestors of present-day immigrants as covering the whole continent. Therefore, according to Rodriguez, Mexican and Central American immigrants are at home wherever they are: "If anything, we are back."

   Another interpretation of the title is that immigrants are constantly burdened by questions of immigration and border integrity—in a sense, this is a cross they must constantly bear.

3. According to Rodriguez, American policies on immigration set up a "two-tiered society" of legal and illegal human beings. This is similar to apartheid, a policy of legalized segregation and political and economic discrimination against peoples of non-European ancestry that used to be the law in South Africa.

4. Rodriguez thinks that African Americans, Indian Americans, and other disadvantaged American subgroups should be the inspiration for illegal Mexican and Central American immigrants. That's because these groups provide a model for how to fight for and attain civil rights in U.S. society.

5. *scapegoats* (1): those who take the blame for the sins of others
   draconian (3): cruel, severe
   repatriations (3): sending people back to their country of origin
   apartheid (3): a system of legalized racial segregation in South Africa
   bigotry (6): intolerance for the beliefs and practices of others
   dragnet (6): a network of measures
   vilification (6): defamation, slander
   delude (7): to deceive
   indigenous (9): native
   obliterated (9): wiped out
   traversed (10): went from one end to another; crossed
   amnesty (10): a general pardon
   remanded (10): sent back
   complicit (10): associated in wrong-doing

Questions About the Writer's Craft (p. 565)

1. The so-called U.S. political dictionary is of course nonexistent; these definitions are Rodriguez's way of provocatively stating the opposition's perspective and establishing his point of view. The idea that these definitions are from a U.S. political dictionary suggests that all Americans hold these views of Mexicans and Central Americans, a suggestion that many Americans would find offensive. The definitions themselves are exaggerated and ironic, which sets the tone for the remainder of the essay. This use of hyperbole is double-edged. On the one hand, it can engage readers who are already likely to sympathize with Rodriguez's point of view, but on the other hand, it can alienate readers who may find themselves unfairly rendered here.

2. In paragraph 6, Rodriguez supports his claim that American attitudes toward Mexican and Central American immigrants are fundamentally racist by citing racial profiling of individuals at borders, immigrant raids that target "brown peoples," and the focus on the southern border with Mexico rather than the northern border with Canada. He presents each of these as a rhetorical question, the answer to which he

considers self-evident. The evidence, as such, is not concrete. He is appealing more to *pathos* than to *logos* here.

3. The Mexican and Nahuatl expressions serve several purposes. First, they help to establish Rodriguez's credibility as a spokesman for illegal immigrants from Mexico and Central America; clearly, he has an intimate knowledge of their world, down to idiomatic and indigenous expressions. Second, some of them, like *migra* and *nopal*, are vivid expressions that give color and interest to the writing. Third, they serve to include some readers and exclude others since they are used mostly without translation. This actually suggests that Rodriguez is not targeting a general American audience but instead is expecting that his essay will be read mostly by people with a Hispanic background.

4. The main fallacy in this argument is a "begging the question" fallacy. Rodriguez fails to support his claim that Mexican and Central American immigrants have a right to be anywhere in North America. The fact that their ancestors may have moved freely around the continent in the past (if indeed that is true) doesn't mean that present-day immigrants have the same right. Political systems of organization are different today, and national borders are significant barriers to migration throughout the world.

SE HABLA ENTITLEMENT

Star Parker

Questions for Close Reading (p. 569)

1. Parker states her thesis in the fourth paragraph: "I don't buy that, along with life, liberty and the pursuit of happiness, our Creator endowed anyone with the right to sneak into the United States, bypass our laws and set up shop."

2. Parker objects to immigration advocates adopting the strategies of the civil rights movement because the civil rights movement was about "enforcing the law, not breaking it" (7). According to Parker, the movement focused on getting enforcement of existing laws (the post–Civil War constitutional amendments that granted rights to freed slaves). In addition, she points out that Mexicans do not seem to find it necessary to demonstrate and demand the benefits of a free society in Mexico, where they do have rights, but do become politically active in the United States, where they don't have rights.

3. Parker attributes the increase in the size of the federal government to the large immigrant population of the United States. According to Parker, these immigrants make demands on taxpayers' money by needing schools, health care, law enforcement, and other government services, thereby perpetuating the welfare state.

4. Parker objects to the feeling of entitlement that she claims immigrants have because in fact illegal immigrants have no legal standing here and thus no rights, especially not the rights of citizens. According to Parker, illegal immigrants are entitled to nothing in the United States.

5. *entitlement* (title): a right to benefits, especially those specified by law
   libertarian (1): a person who believes in the principle of liberty
   conundrum (1): a kind of riddle
   inalienable (3): not to be removed or transferred
   provoke (4): to make angry, to irritate

bogus (6): false
garb (6): clothing
paragon (14): a model of perfection

Questions About the Writer's Craft (p. 569)

1. Parker uses the second strategy for refuting opposing points. She starts with her proposition (paragraphs 1–4), cites an opposing view in paragraphs 5, 10, 13, and refutes these points in paragraphs 7-9, 11-12, and 14. She then concludes with additional evidence supporting her argument (the burden immigrants place on government resources) in paragraphs 15 and 16.

    The first opposing view is that immigrants have a right to be here; she refutes this by saying that immigrants snuck into the country, breaking laws, and have no rights as a consequence. The second opposing view is that almost half of all Mexicans would prefer to live in the United States, presumably because of the economic opportunities here. She casts doubt on this by indicating that Mexicans support leftist political candidates whose policies do not favor economic expansion. The third opposing view is that the Latino immigrant community simply wants to be free to work and maintain traditional families. Parker refutes this by citing crime, high drop-out rates, and out-of-wedlock births in the Latino community in southern California. Finally, she claims that immigrants tax the resources of the United States by demanding services.

    Students might argue that each of Parker's refutations is effective, in part because she keeps the discussion narrowly focused. She does not raise issues that might undermine her argument. For example, she doesn't discuss the huge economic contribution of immigrant labor to the U.S. economy, or social justice issues such as children's right to an education, or immigration policies that break up families when some members are deported.

    Students might also argue that Parker's refutations are ineffective because she glosses over important counterarguments—that a major reason illegal immigrants sneak over the border is that American businesses are eager to hire them, that Mexican and American cultures are very different when it comes to economic issues so it's not surprising so many Mexicans would rather emigrate than reform their own economy, and that most members of the Latino community are law abiding.

2. Parker compares and contrasts the Latino and black communities of southern California in order to show that the Latino community has as many problems of poverty as the black community. The problems she cites undermine the traditional family values that immigrants supposedly espouse. According to Parker, they serve to show that the immigrant community is not a desirable addition to the United States.

3. Parker's use of words and phrases from the Declaration of Independence serves to establish her *ethos* as a patriot whose principles are derived from one of the United States's most important and revered documents. These inalienable human rights do not include illegal immigration, which is lawbreaking, according to Parker. By using these words, Parker sets herself up alongside the Founding Fathers and in opposition to those who are not U.S. citizens.

4. The language indicating Parker's emotions and reactions helps establish her as an ordinary person having deep-seated responses to the immigration issue. These words and phrases create a link to the reader, who can recognize her humanity in her reactions. This appeal to *pathos* makes Parker's argument stronger than if she had merely relied on logic to refute the positions of pro-immigrant groups.

COMBINING
THE PATTERNS

The brief discussions which follow provide insight into the dominant or organizing patterns of development and the blend of patterns in the essays in this section.

PROFESSIONS FOR WOMEN (p. 588)

Virginia Woolf

Woolf's speech to the Women's Service League relies primarily upon narrative to convey that a woman must overcome two obstacles before she can devote herself to her profession, whether it be writing or some other work. Woolf launches her narrative with little hint of where she is leading; her thesis is revealed only gradually as she recounts the narrative of her beginnings as a writer and the two inner struggles she endured in order to be a success. One struggle is narrated as a battle against "the Angel in the House," the tendency to fulfill the traditional role of woman as supporter, flatterer, and caretaker of men. The second is recounted as the woman writer's discovery of an explosive and hidden subject: the passions and truth of the body. The narrative format allows Woolf to deliver her experiences in a dramatic, even electrifying way, rather than discursively or analytically. Within the narrative, Woolf makes use of description in paragraph 3, where she helps us to understand what the "Angel in the House" represents by describing her demeanor and behavior, and in paragraph 5, where she describes the writer as a fisherman. Also within the narrative, Woolf conveys the process by which a person might begin as a writer (paragraph 2) and succeed in writing novels (paragraph 5: "He [the novelist] has to induce in himself a state of perpetual lethargy . . .").

Near the end of the essay, Woolf compares her professional experiences to those of the women in the audience, suggesting that although the listeners are not writers, their way is obstructed by inner "phantoms and obstacles" like her own (7). If women writers, she notes, occupied in "the freest of professions for women," must tussle with "ghosts," "prejudices," and "rocks," then "how is it in the new professions which you [the listeners] are now for the first time entering?"

WHERE DO WE GO FROM HERE: COMMUNITY OR CHAOS? (p. 593)

Martin Luther King, Jr.

King argues eloquently for a change in the mindset of world leaders and citizens, a change away from militarism as the major means of problem solving to the use of peaceful methods of conflict resolution. He supports his argument largely with reasoning, but also relies upon cause-effect, exemplification, definition, and comparison to examine and validate his viewpoint. The thesis is introduced in the first sentence of the essay and supported by a reference to the increasing military technology that dominates the international scene. In paragraph 2, King shows that there is no valid cause for international squabbling over resources, since modern science assures enough resources and transportation of them to support all nations.

King then compares the words and deeds of "large power blocs," finding that they often promote peace verbally but indulge in arms stockpiling and development all the while (4). He cites historical examples of conquerors who killed in the name of peace (5), and then uses a contemporary war—Vietnam—to deplore the same tendencies in our nations today (6), before restating the need to reconcile the gap between our words and deeds. In cautioning that we "read the warning on history's signposts," he again implies that the effect of our military buildup will be disastrous. In paragraph 8, King asserts that not only is peace the desired effect or result of international dealings, but it is the "means," or cause, of that achievement. "We must pursue peaceful ends through peaceful means." Paragraph 9 continues the argument that the effects of war, particularly of modern war, are too calamitous to entertain. Paragraph 10 begins with a plea for the study of peace, implying the positive effects this will have on our world community, and paragraph 11 discusses the negative "ancient habits" that have caused violence in the past. Paragraph 12 provides a definition of nonviolence, differentiating it from the mere absence of violence. In moving toward a conclusion, King argues in paragraph 13 that only "a mental and spiritual re-evaluation" will bring about the effects he seeks, "a new world" where peace reigns. He uses the example of Ulysses and the Sirens to explain further what he means by affirming peace (14), and in the final paragraph, he closes his argument with the contrast of "world power struggle" with what he terms "a peace race." Throughout the essay, King uses many persuasive tactics, ranging from eloquently balanced phrasing and repeated phrases (2, 3, 4, 6, 14, and others), to the use of descriptive detail, metaphor, and highly connotative words (5, 6, 14).

THE WORLD HOUSE (p. 597)

Martin Luther King, Jr.

In "The World House," Martin Luther King, Jr., argues that the people of the world must learn to live together and ensure justice and freedom for all people everywhere. In support of this position, strands from numerous patterns of development interlock, creating a complex texture of imagery, logical reasoning, and eloquence. In supporting his assertion that humans now live in "a world house," he contrasts the modern world of speed and technology with the recent past (paragraphs 3–4). Within this contrast, he uses several examples (3) and much descriptive detail (4). The technology he invokes is identified as the cause of the interrelatedness that underlies the "world house" (4). He compares our present to the future effects likely to result from continued scientific research (5), again using descriptive details. In paragraph 6, he points out that the revolution in technology parallels, that is, is similar to the revolution of the spirit that is also occurring throughout the world; and in 7, he uses descriptive imagery to present the process of liberation he sees spreading worldwide. The cause of this clamor for freedom is identified in paragraph 8: the inevitable yearning of the downtrodden for release. He uses the metaphor of "chapters" in the "continuing story" of humans' struggle to be free, citing the Moses story in the Bible and the civil rights struggle in the United States as only two examples of the impulse toward liberation. He argues then that some people always ignore or deny liberation, using as an example Rip Van Winkle, who slept through the American Revolution (9–10). He returns to comparison-contrast in paragraphs 11–15, indicating through analysis, imagery, and quotation that our technological progress has not been matched by spiritual progress, that our external and internal realms are out of sync. At the end of 15 through 16, he returns to cause-effect, predicting that if we "minimize the internal of our lives and maximize the external, we sign the warrant for our own day of doom."

THE SANTA ANA (p. 601)

Joan Didion

In this essay, Didion blends several patterns to achieve two distinct ends: a definition of the Santa Ana phenomenon and a causal analysis of its impact on the people and things that lie in its path. The thesis, that "the violence and the unpredictability of the Santa Ana affect the quality of life in Los Angeles" (6), is not stated until the final paragraph, but Didion develops this idea over the course of the essay as she explains what the Santa Ana is and how it influences atmosphere and behavior. In the opening paragraph, she describes the "unnatural stillness" of her surroundings as a Santa Ana approaches, saying that the Los Angeles air is charged with tension and unease (1). At this point, she provides an initial definition of the Santa Ana as "a hot wind from the northeast . . . drying the hills and the nerves to a flash point" and begins to demonstrate some of its effects. She provides a string of brief examples illustrating that everyone feels its onset without explicitly knowing of its arrival: the baby frets, the maid sulks, Didion, herself, has a worthless argument, then lies down, "given over to whatever is in the air." A personal anecdote structures the second paragraph, as Didion recalls Santa Ana lore and her first encounters with Santa Ana–related behaviors. Having observed and felt the effects of the hot wind, Didion says she can empathize with those Indians who, as folklore had it, "would throw themselves into the sea when the bad wind blew" (2).

She goes on to describe in vivid detail the ominous tranquility of her Pacific coastal surroundings during a Santa Ana, which results in bizarre, off-kilter human behavior, such as that of her neighbors who would either remain indoors with the lights out or roam the place with a machete, claiming to have heard a trespasser or a rattlesnake. Didion continues exemplifying the Santa Ana's impact in the third paragraph, where she quotes Raymond Chandler's observations about the hot wind's idiosyncratic effects on people. For the remainder of the paragraph, Didion provides scientific evidence to bear out the folk wisdom about the Santa Ana. Using definition and division-classification strategies, Didion identifies the Santa Ana in meteorological terms as being of the *foehn* category of winds, which are known to have unpleasant and inevitable consequences wherever they occur. She goes on to provide examples of the scientifically observed effects around the world of these "persistent malevolent winds" (3). Paragraph 3 ends with further scientific definition of the Santa Ana and its electromagnetic characteristics, which Didion suggests explain this wind's "mechanistic," negative impact on human beings.

In paragraph 4, Didion draws a brief contrast between the misconception about California weather as "numbingly bland" and the reality of its "violent extremes" caused in part by the Santa Ana. Here Didion goes on to offer data demonstrating the harrowing, fiery aftermath of four different Santa Ana periods. This presentation of factual evidence continues through paragraph 5, where she chronicles in numeric detail the havoc wreaked in 1957 by the longest-running Santa Ana in recent history. And in paragraph 6, Didion piles on further examples of the destructive toll (human and environmental) taken by this ostensibly harmless, but ultimately malignant, phenomenon. In a final attempt to convey the Santa Ana's overwhelming influence on the psyche of Southern Californians, Didion employs a comparison: just as the permanence of New England life is tied to winter's reliability, the impermanence of Los Angeles life results from the Santa Ana's unpredictability. Didion forcefully concludes her analysis by saying that the Santa Ana's effects demonstrate "how close to the edge we are" (6).

MARRYING ABSURD (p. 604)

Joan Didion

The title of "Marrying Absurd" conveys its thesis, which is stated at the beginning of paragraph 2: "What people who get married in Las Vegas actually do expect . . . strikes one as a curious and self-contradictory business." In other words, rapid Las Vegas weddings are absurd. They're incongruous, too quick—both comical and grotesque, idealistic and clichéd. Blending different patterns of development, Joan Didion shows the absurdity and sadness of these makeshift marriages. While pink champagne bubbles float at their surface; an undercurrent of urgency and desperation flows below.

In paragraph 1, Didion immediately launches into the process by which couples marry in Las Vegas. The bride and groom attest either that they have parental permission to marry or that they're old enough to marry without it. Someone pays $5 or $15 for a marriage license. That's it. Absurdly brief. Hardly a process at all.

Didion then moves into contrast for the rest of paragraph 1. Unlike marriages in all other states, Nevada marriages require no blood test or waiting period. Primarily through description, Didion juxtaposes the natural and artificial, traditional and offbeat, bringing out the incongruities that make Las Vegas marriages fragile and absurd. Across the silent desert, electric signs shout advertisements for wedding services. From a flat highway, people view signs eighty feet tall. Las Vegas is a city of contradictions: call girls and brides. Words signify their opposite: a crassly mercenary chapel advertises "sincere and dignified" weddings; a wedding organist plays "When I Fall in Love, It Will Be Forever" in a state as well-known for quickie divorces as quickie weddings. Paper windows mimic stained glass. A bride wears an orange mini-dress rather than a white, floor-length gown. The father of a bride jokes about wedding-night loss of virginity, but his daughter is visibly pregnant. Already a mother, another bride drunkenly attempts to carry out motherly duties: "I gotta get the kids. I gotta pick up the sitter."

Didion also uses examples to convey the absurdity of Las Vegas weddings, especially their ludicrous rapidity. She includes a couple of brief narrative anecdotes in paragraphs 4 and 5 to illustrate the "curious, self-contradictory business" (2) of Vegas weddings. A battery of other examples serves the same purpose. On August 26, 1965, she tells us, 171 couples married in Las Vegas. A justice of the peace who performed 67 of the ceremonies reached a speed of three minutes per wedding (1). Advertisements, too, illustrate speed. Their wording is abbreviated: "Witnesses Available," "Ample Parking" (3). Couples quickly move from motel, to courthouse, to chapel, and back: "Free Transportation from Your Motel to Courthouse to Chapel and Return to Motel." The honeymoon occurs in the same place as the wedding ("Honeymoon Accommodations" a sign advertises). Wedding organists play "only a few bars" of the traditional wedding march (4). The sign indicating a wedding in progress states, "One moment please."

"One moment" in which to declare a potentially lifelong commitment? Not good enough, Didion indicates. And herein lies Didion's implied causal analysis: Giving heavy commitments lightweight treatment—the hallmark of Vegas-style weddings— leaves them vulnerable to breakage.

.